British Town Maps

A History

Roger J. P. Kain
& Richard R. Oliver

British Town Maps
A History

Roger J. P. Kain
& Richard R. Oliver

An online Catalogue of British Town Maps relates to this book hosted
by IHR Digital, School of Advanced Study, University of London:

http://townmaps.data.history.ac.uk

A British Academy Research Project

[opposite] Map of Berwick-upon-Tweed
attributed variously to Matthias Merian c.1650
or Johann Christoph Beer c.1690.

BRITISH LIBRARY

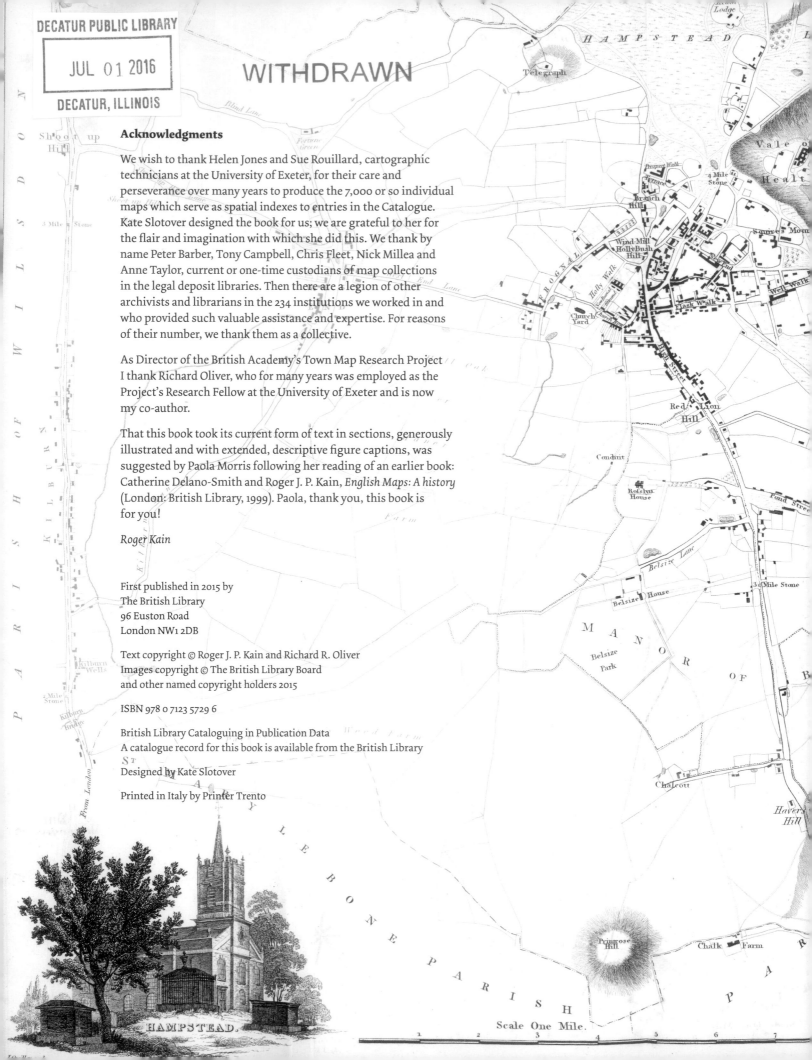

Acknowledgments

We wish to thank Helen Jones and Sue Rouillard, cartographic technicians at the University of Exeter, for their care and perseverance over many years to produce the 7,000 or so individual maps which serve as spatial indexes to entries in the Catalogue. Kate Slotover designed the book for us; we are grateful to her for the flair and imagination with which she did this. We thank by name Peter Barber, Tony Campbell, Chris Fleet, Nick Millea and Anne Taylor, current or one-time custodians of map collections in the legal deposit libraries. Then there are a legion of other archivists and librarians in the 234 institutions we worked in and who provided such valuable assistance and expertise. For reasons of their number, we thank them as a collective.

As Director of the British Academy's Town Map Research Project I thank Richard Oliver, who for many years was employed as the Project's Research Fellow at the University of Exeter and is now my co-author.

That this book took its current form of text in sections, generously illustrated and with extended, descriptive figure captions, was suggested by Paola Morris following her reading of an earlier book: Catherine Delano-Smith and Roger J. P. Kain, *English Maps: A history* (London: British Library, 1999). Paola, thank you, this book is for you!

Roger Kain

First published in 2015 by
The British Library
96 Euston Road
London NW1 2DB

Text copyright © Roger J. P. Kain and Richard R. Oliver
Images copyright © The British Library Board
and other named copyright holders 2015

ISBN 978 0 7123 5729 6

British Library Cataloguing in Publication Data
A catalogue record for this book is available from the British Library

Designed by Kate Slotover

Printed in Italy by Printer Trento

HAMPSTEAD.

Scale One Mile.

Contents

Introduction 6

1. Defining a town 16

2. Defining a town map 28

3. Town maps for general and specific purposes 34

4. Making and printing town maps: engraving,
   lithography and zincography, printing in colour,
   photography in map reproduction 44

5. Maps that survive, maps that are lost 56

6. Earliest town maps 62

7. The 'remapping' of British towns 78

8. Towns as property: estate maps, enclosure
   maps, rating maps and tithe maps 104

9. Maps of towns in works of reference 116

10. Maps of towns in directories 130

11. Street maps 136

12. Street atlases 156

13. Maps of towns in tourist guidebooks 168

14. Mapping towns for military purposes 180

15. The Board of Ordnance and the origins
    of the Ordnance Survey 196

16. Mapping town boundaries 204

17. Sanitation maps and Ordnance Survey town plans 210

18. The apogee of Ordnance Survey town mapping 216

19. Fire insurance maps 226

20. Maps for town planning 230

Notes and references 238

Index to Online Catalogue of British Town Maps 243

    CBTM Online Catalogue 245

    List of towns in the Online Catalogue, the number
    of maps catalogued for each town, and the range
    of dates covered by the maps of each town 246

List of figures 253

Index 255

Introduction

Note: When we refer to particular maps which are described in the Catalogue of British Town Maps we identify them by citing their five-digit catalogue identification numbers in parenthesis within the text.

THE RESEARCH UNDERPINNING this book comprises the final part of a long-term (1985–2014) series of research projects at the University of Exeter and now the School of Advanced Study, London. These projects have built up our understanding of the large-scale mapping of Britain (England, Wales and Scotland). Work on nineteenth-century parish tithe maps is published, as is our analysis of enclosure maps.[1] The third part of this overall suite of projects – to research large-scale town maps of Britain – was awarded British Academy Research Project status in 1998 and funding by the Arts and Humanities Research Council. The support of the British Academy and the AHRC is gratefully acknowledged.

From the outset of the project, dissemination was envisaged through both electronic and printed

media. This printed book component provides, in addition to a narrative history of urban maps and mapping arranged in twenty primarily thematic sections, an index of the primary contents of the electronic Catalogue of British Town Maps (CBTM). This catalogue contains cartobibliographic data and descriptions of the topographic and other contents of each of some 7,163 maps, together with index maps for each indicating the area depicted on a map. The Catalogue is mounted on a fully searchable website, hosted by the Institute of Historical Research, School of Advanced Study, University of London, from which components can be downloaded. The maps are also searchable via the simple Google Maps search function. After selecting a county, users can open the Google Maps feature which indicates hyperlinks to all the available map entries for that particular county. The URL is http://townmaps.data.history.ac.uk

Town maps are preserved in a wide variety and number of archives and libraries – national, regional and local. Notwithstanding the number of town maps that are extant, their wide dispersal and their utility to historians, there are few descriptive and analytical finding aids to identify and locate maps of a particular place. It is hoped that our Catalogue helps fill this lacuna by locating, cataloguing and providing information on cartographic characteristics, topographic content and bibliographical data for each map as a publicly and permanently available research tool of all extant town maps in public archives and libraries from the earliest to 1900. By 1900, Ordnance Survey large-scale plans were effectively the universal base for urban mapping by both private companies and public bodies. A unique feature of the resource is the inclusion of PDF images clearly outlining the area of an urban settlement depicted on a particular map (many maps portray a part only of a town).

Town maps are of relevance as sources to a wide variety of historians and others whose research touches on the urban past. There can be few urban historians, or indeed private/public sector users concerned with urban issues, who do not need to use town maps as an index to the location of things and events at some time in the past. For some investigations, such as town planning history, this kind of map-derived topographical information is at the very heart of the research process. Town maps are, though, much more than mere mirrors in which the physical reality of the past is reflected – they can be read as 'texts' in the same sense that paintings, film and theatre can be 'read' as texts, and so are of relevance to a broad spectrum of cultural-historical research. Outside academia, environmental conservation officers use maps to date buildings, and the legal profession consults them for property boundaries or rights of way that are in dispute. Town maps are an important educational resource for project work in UK secondary schools at Key Stage

4, for students aged 16–19, and in Higher Education. Many town maps are objets d'art in their own right, and are subjects for connoisseurship and collecting.

The overarching intention of the Catalogue is to guide historians interested in a particular place to those maps extant and available to researchers in archives and libraries to which the public have access. Thus it is aimed at users of maps as sources of data rather than map historians concerned, for example, with unravelling the printing history of a particular map through a series of states or editions. It can provide a starting point for those studies, as evidenced recently by Brian Robson's magnificent 2014 study of the town maps of John Wood (see Section 7 below), but it will not obviate inspecting maps for that kind of study. However, it does provide urban historians and others with sufficient information to be able to decide whether travelling to an archive and inspecting a particular map is likely to help them with their enquiries. The library and archive searches which underpin this book and the Catalogue were conducted over a period of some twenty years, as specified in the opening of the Index to the Catalogue on page 243 below. As time passes, and as more records with maps are deposited and other maps are revealed by revised archive cataloguing, this Catalogue of British Town Maps will become increasingly a partial record of what is available. It is also likely that many maps in books have escaped our notice.

Towns present map-makers with the most complex and challenging of all landscapes to depict. Buildings within a town tend to be of different ages, styles (vernacular or designed) and functions. They are arranged on their plots along streets in different ways; streets may be broad and ruler-straight, or narrow and irregular, or may be formally created terraces, crescents, circles or squares. Towns also contain a range of land uses – residential, commercial, industrial, administrative, ecclesiastical, recreational – which contribute to spatial differentiation. They might be sited on hilly or on relatively level terrain. And underlying everything, invisible in the landscape but a key to the urban texture, is the pattern of property ownership.

Concomitant with the heterogeneity of townscapes is a variety of cartographic types or genres subsumed within the general designation of 'town map'. Two maps drawn from this variety illustrate this fact. The first is a late-sixteenth-century manuscript bird's-eye view map of the city of Exeter – not drawn to a strict scale, highly decorated, topographically generalised yet rich in transient detail (fishing and ships are shown sailing on the River Exe, woollen cloths are hung out to dry on tenter racks) [**Fig. 1,** *overleaf*]. As well as being a representation of topography, this map is also in many ways a celebration of the wealth and power of this town in early modern times. John Hooker's portrayal of the

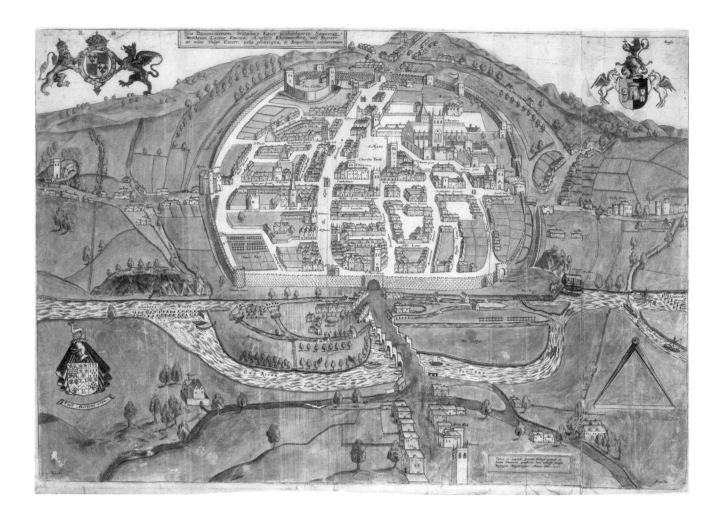

[**Fig. 1**] John Hooker's *Map of Exeter*, engraved by Remigius Hogenberg c. 1587, 370 by 545 mm. It is not surprising that Exeter finds itself in the company of London, Cambridge, Oxford and Norwich as one of the earliest British towns to be surveyed and mapped; it ranked high on the hierarchy of English towns in late Elizabethan England. Hooker's map is a bird's-eye view of the city taken from an imaginary viewpoint from the west, with the River Exe running across the map from left to right. Suburbs outside the walls are shown, buildings are portrayed with details of their elevations, the principal buildings and streets are named, and there is much detail on the life of the City. Hooker's map was much reproduced, adapted and copied by contemporaries and near contemporaries (for example, by John Speed in 1611 and in Braun and Hogenberg's *Civitates orbis terrarum*) and even as decoration on a leather screen. (CBTM 20603) [British Library, Maps C.5.a.3.]

city in which he was Chamberlain from 1555 has been studied from many angles and analysed for what it can tell us about Exeter's architecture and townscape, but important questions remain.[2] Why was this map made at all? Why was a considerable sum of money expended on it? What was its intended purpose? There are no straightforward answers to these questions, but we can be certain that Hooker's map is more than a factual, topographical description of the walls, streets and buildings of a cathedral city. It tells us something of the economic importance of the place, and its iconography conveys much deeper messages. The coats of arms of the City of Exeter and the Bishop of Exeter pictured in the upper corners of the map doubtless acknowledge Queen Elizabeth I's patronage. In this sense the map is a celebration of the wealth and power of this important town under her government. Reflecting as they do the political significance of a community, their activities and their wealth, town maps such as John Hooker's map of Exeter serve many interests beyond the strictly practical.

The second example is of a small part of Manchester as depicted by the Ordnance Survey on its very large-scale, highly detailed, printed, late nineteenth-century town map series, maps which mark the high point of detailed urban topographic mapping in Britain [Fig. 2, *overleaf*]. Almost every town of more than 4,000 population was surveyed and mapped at this scale. These maps meant the effective eclipse of

privately sponsored original mapping of towns, other than for very specific engineering purposes and the like. They can trace their inception to the growth of interest in public health reform following the issue of Edwin Chadwick's report on the sanitary condition of the labouring population of Great Britain in 1842. After 1894 the 'town scales' were largely superseded by the smaller 1:2500; the 'occasion' of sanitary reform and the backlog of infrastructure improvement was passing.

[Fig.2] Ordnance Survey 1:500 (126 inches to a mile) Lancashire sheet 104.6.19, surveyed in 1888. This extract is of part of Manchester and represents the most sophisticated development of urban topographical mapping in Britain. Some 400 towns were mapped at this or the 1:1056 (60 inches to 1 mile) scale between 1842 and 1895, with the remainder of towns represented on Ordnance Survey 1:2500 (25 inches to a mile) mapping. At the exceptionally large scale of 1:500, urban topography can be mapped in great detail. Streets and important buildings are named, the internal layout of public buildings is depicted, features as small as street lamps are located accurately, and much other highly detailed information is represented, for example the position of water taps (W.T.) and stopcocks (S.C.). On the other hand, the map is devoid of people (cf. Hooker's map on page 12), and the third dimension of the townscape – building elevations – is absent entirely. [British Library Maps OST 215 – Manchester sheet CIV.6.19]

BRITISH TOWN MAPS

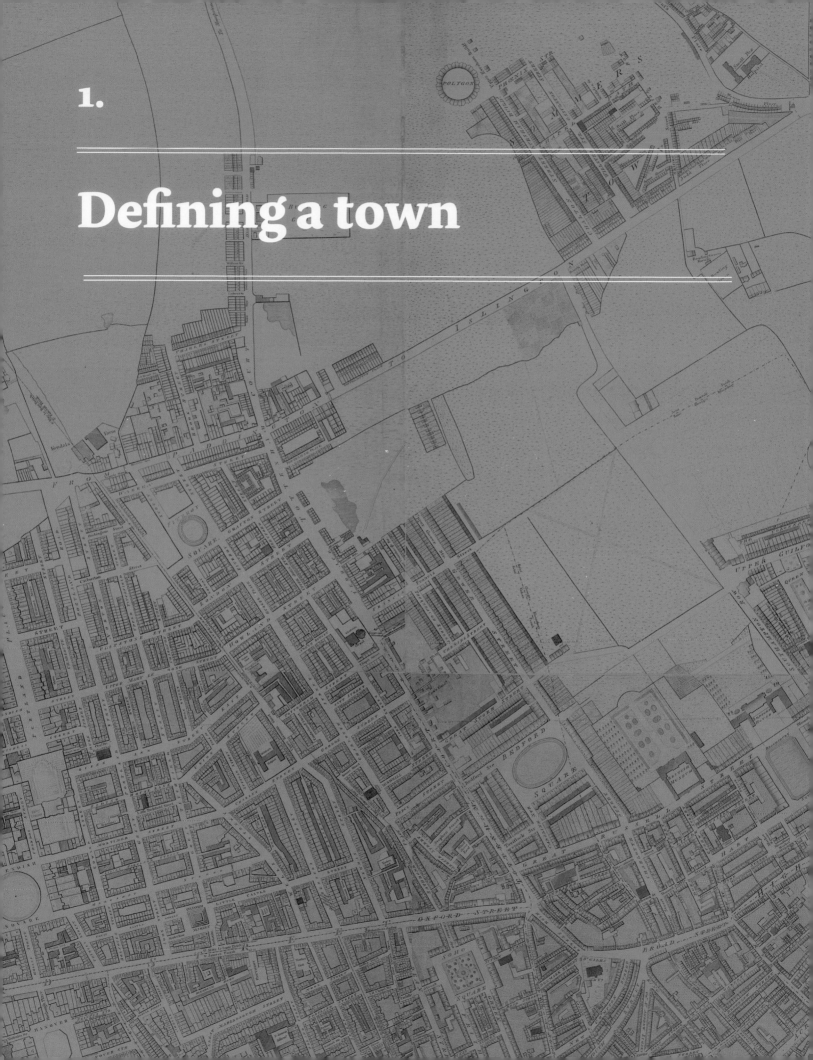

1.

Defining a town

'WHAT IS A TOWN?' is not a question answered easily or unequivocally. One distinguishing, but not essential, feature is the presence of a market providing a service function extending beyond the immediate needs of a settlement itself. It is generally accepted that at the Norman conquest in 1066 there were very few settlements in Britain that would qualify as towns on this 'service' definition, but over the next 250 years or so a large number of places gained charters, either for holding markets or for more extensive trading privileges. Some charters were granted to well-established settlements that had developed a trading function; others were granted to landowners who had founded new settlements, hoping to attract incomers and trade. This process of town foundation was already faltering by the early fourteenth century, and it came very much to a stop after the Black Death of 1348–9.[3] It is a matter for debate how far the British economy continued to stagnate in the fifteenth century, but it seems clear that population only started to grow again significantly in the sixteenth century. However, this growth was not accompanied by a burst of town foundation similar to that which had characterised the later twelfth and thirteenth centuries. Indeed, John Speed's maps of towns in England and Wales, made between about 1606 and 1609 [Fig. 3, *overleaf*], suggest that many walled towns contained considerable amounts of undeveloped land.

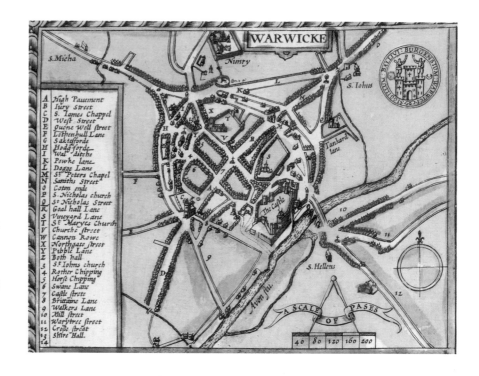

[**Fig. 3**] Like the Ordnance Survey some 200 years later, John Speed was more of an improver than an innovator. He admitted to 'dipping my sickle into other men's corn', and his *Theatre of the Empire of Great Britain* of 1611 was largely based on the work of others, notably Christopher Saxton. Speed's great contribution was to survey over fifty towns, which were included as insets on his county maps: here is **Warwick**. (CBTM 18437) [Inset on 'The counti of Warwick the shire towne and citie of Coventre described': British Library Maps C.7.c.20]

In the seventeenth century a few market charters were granted to established settlements, and a handful of new towns appeared, mostly ports such as Devonport, Falmouth and Sheerness. In the eighteenth century increasing population and industrialisation led to many settlements expanding into towns and further new towns were developed, especially in Scotland. More common, however, were planned extensions to existing settlements: the New Town at Edinburgh is an outstanding example [Fig. 4, Fig. 5, *overleaf*, **Fig 6**, *p.* 22, **Figs 7 and 8**, *p.* 23], and similar development accounts for much of the 'eighteenth-century' character of Bath . 'Industrial' new towns continued to appear in the nineteenth century: a quintessential example is Middlesbrough. Associated nineteenth-century developments were the 'railway towns', of which Crewe, Eastleigh, Horwich and Swindon are

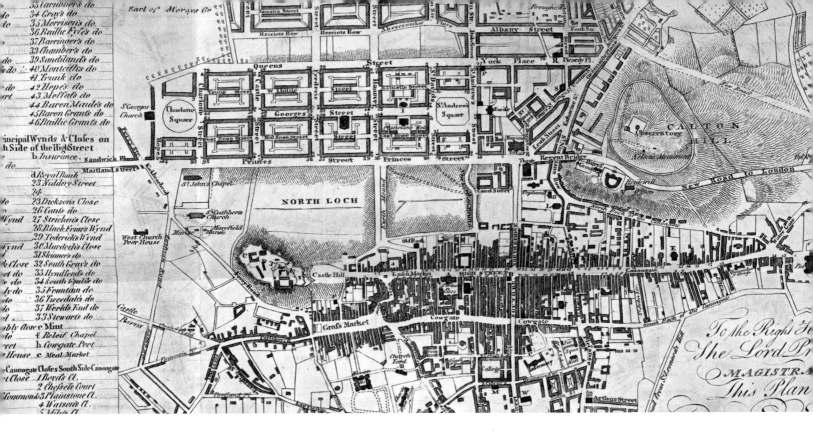

familiar examples, though only the first two were completely new foundations. Railway companies were characterised by a high degree of vertical integration and all four towns developed around locomotive and carriage-building works.

A different sort of 'railway town', largely confined to the periphery of London, was that which developed in association with what the Victorians termed 'residential traffic' – the commuters of today. Some of these were old-established towns with a developed service function, such as Croydon and Bromley; others were on 'greenfield' sites, as at Surbiton and Woking. These places were towns in terms of size and with populations not dependent, directly or indirectly, on agriculture for a living, rather than because they possessed market or other higher-level service functions. Developments in public health in

[**Fig. 4**] Additions to towns might simply be extensions of existing streets, or they might be complete new suburbs whose plan bore no resemblance to the original settlement. Perhaps the most striking example of this was Edinburgh: here an extract from a plan published in *The New Picture of Edinburgh* of *c.* 1820 shows in its lower part the old town, characterised by a single long main street – now the Royal Mile – with numerous short ways leading off. The upper part of the map includes the New Town, laid out from the 1760s along formal, classical lines. (CBTM 22022) BL 010370.p.25]

[Fig. 5] The Steyne at Brighton, 1778. This is almost exactly contemporary with the first published map of the town. Both map and view were produced when Brighton was enjoying its first fame, and before patronage by the Prince Regent.

[From British Library, Maps K. Top. 42.17b]

[Fig. 6] The High Street, Oxford, in 1803, by William Delamotte. In contrast to Brighton, Oxford's renown was long-established, and since 1588 there had been a long series of maps of the city. Both places attracted visitors; as a centre of learning, Oxford could also expect to attract curiosity from overseas scholars and others. [From British Library, Maps K. Top. 34.23a]

[**Fig. 7,** *left*] Cambridge marketplace by Thomas Rowlandson, 1803. This is a reminder that university towns had originated, like all other towns in the Middle Ages, as trading centres. Cambridge marketplace is irregular, and reflects the organic growth of the town. [From British Library, Maps K. Top. K. 8.47a]

[**Fig. 8,** *above*] Tuesday Market Place, Kings Lynn, by Butcher, 1797. Kings Lynn was founded as a town in the late eleventh century, and quickly developed as one of the most important ports in England, so that within fifty years a second 'newe towne' was founded, to the north of the first. This status was reflected in the spacious marketplace, which is that of a 'planned' rather than an 'organic' town. Unlike some other east coast ports, Kings Lynn continued to be prosperous in the early modern period, and this was reflected both in the surviving exchange of 1681 (later used as a custom house), and the exuberant market cross of 1710, demolished in 1831 because of structural problems. [From British Library, Maps K. Top. 31.29c]

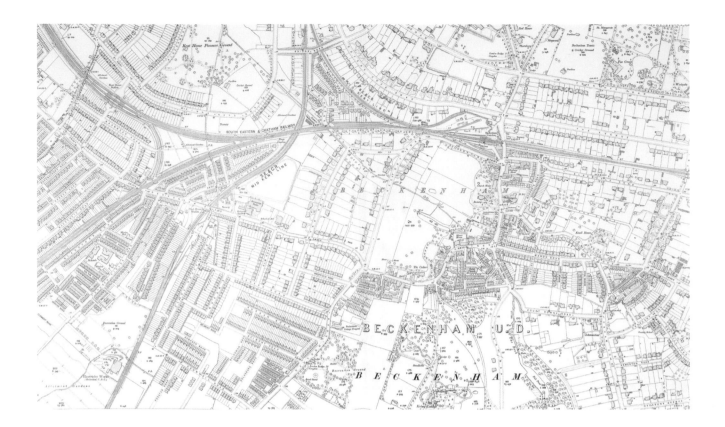

[Fig. 9] In 1908 Beckenham still had something of the air of a village, even though it was officially an 'urban district': as yet the railway, which had served the town since 1856, had only had a modest effect. [British Library, Maps OS, 1:2500 Third Edition Kent sheet VII.15]

the second half of the nineteenth century resulted in many of these places being designated successively urban sanitary districts or, from 1894, urban districts. Further development in the earlier twentieth century saw a number of these places flowering into fully fledged chartered boroughs in the 1930s [Figs 9, 10].

Recreational resorts which depended on the supposed health-giving properties of either mineral springs or seawater had begun to develop in a modest way in the seventeenth century, usually on the strength of patronage by gentry or the developing commerce-based middle classes. But it took the coming of the railways, from about 1840 onwards, for both inland resorts such as Buxton and Harrogate and seaside places such as Blackpool, Bournemouth,

[Fig. 10] By 1930 Beckenham had been joined to London by building; in 1935 it became a municipal borough. [British Library, Maps OS, 1:2500 second revised edition (1929–33) Kent sheet VII.15]

Clacton and Skegness to develop significantly. Urban district or borough status by the late nineteenth century was sufficient to define such recreational or residential places as 'towns' [Fig. 11, *overleaf*].

We decided at the outset of the research project on which this book is based to be inclusive, and thus to record maps for all places that at some time merited the tag 'urban'. To this end we identified places with early market functions by reference to Alan Everitt's list of markets active in the sixteenth and earlier seventeenth centuries, a list based largely on Christopher Saxton's survey of England and Wales in the 1570s and John Adams' *Index villaris* of a century later.[4] Both of these sources exclude Scotland. A useful supplement is the series of 'topographical dictionaries'

published by Samuel Lewis in the 1830s, which cover the whole of Britain. Otherwise, the most useful source to identify British towns is Ordnance Survey maps published up to 1914. The Ordnance Survey identifies places considered to be towns by giving their names in upper-case lettering, though the official printed instructions to surveyors do not contain wholly objective criteria on the distinction between a town and a village. In 1906, for example, towns were to be defined on the basis of 'local knowledge', which amounts to reputation.[5] Nor were judgements consistent through time, as there are examples of Ordnance Survey maps depicting a place in capitals, that is as a 'town', whereas a near-contemporary map does not.[6]

[**Fig. 11**] Clacton is typical of many seaside resorts that developed during the nineteenth century following the coming of the railway. The Ordnance Survey 1:2500 mapping, revised in 1896, shows that at that time the town still extended over only a modest **area.** [British Library, Maps OS, 1:2500 second edition Essex sheet 48.7]

BRITISH TOWN MAPS

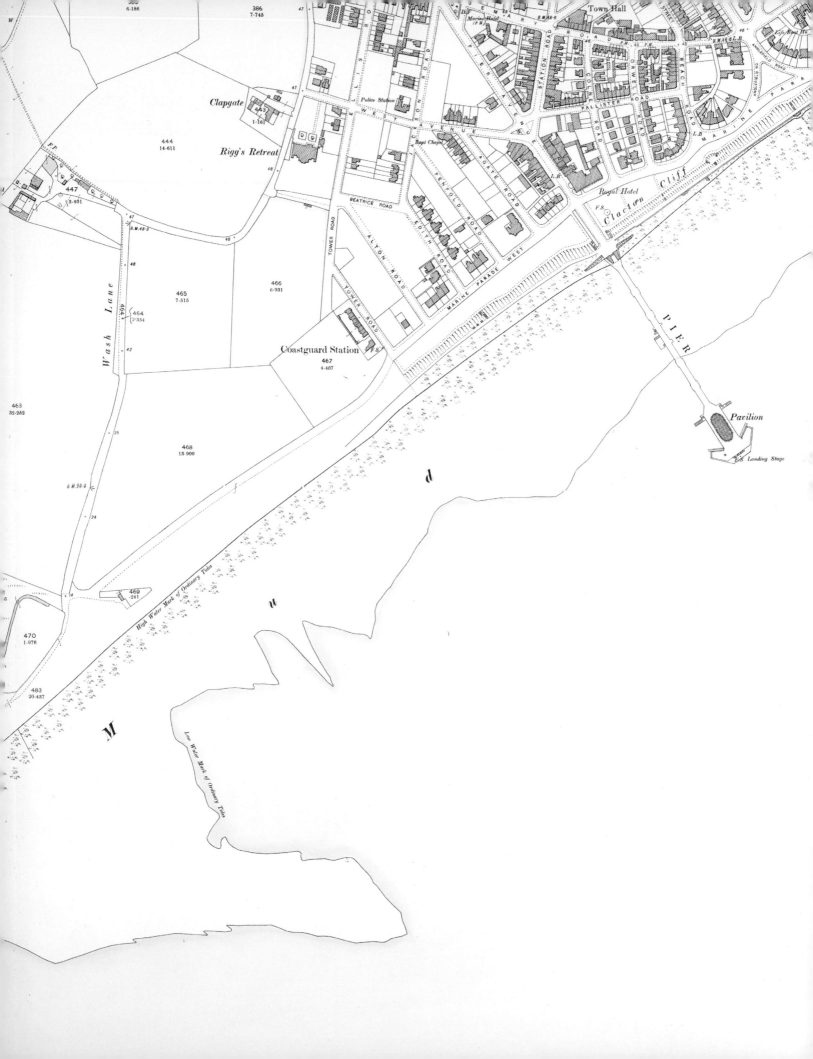

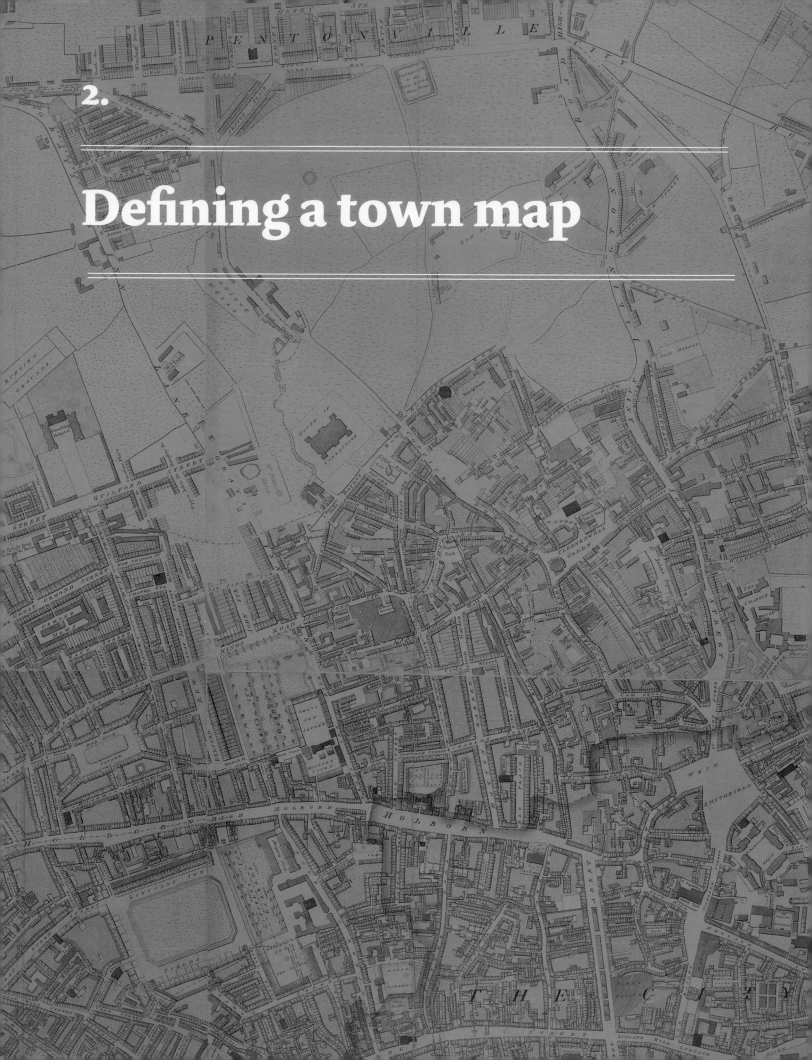

2.

Defining a town map

MAP SCALE IS FUNDAMENTAL to our working definition of a town map for the *Catalogue of British Town Maps* that underpins this book. The minimum map scale for inclusion in our study is 2.5 inches to 1 mile (1:25,344). We have chosen this scale because it is about the smallest at which it is practicable to name streets and otherwise relate map and ground, and to record particular urban features and characteristics in a thematic manner.[7] We have endeavoured to include all maps at this scale or larger that cover the whole of the built-up area of a town at the time that the map was made and also those that cover an identifiable district within a town – for example, maps of individual townships in the suburbs of Manchester and Leeds and of parishes and wards in the City of London.[8] We have excluded deposited plans for canals, railways and other schemes that sought Parliamentary authorisation, and plans of projected engineering works and urban redevelopment that provide only a narrow transect of a town, rather than a comprehensive view of either the town itself or of a recognised district within it [**Figs. 12 and 13**, *overleaf*].

Maps of towns so defined vary considerably. At one extreme there is London, with more than 400 separate maps (not counting editions or 'states') created between the 1550s and 1900, many of which went into numerous editions or were copied by other publishers. At the other end of the spectrum, a considerable number of towns have no known extant

[**Figs. 12,** *right,* **and 13,** *below*]
These are town maps stripped
to the bare minimum to serve
the dual purpose of indicating
routes through a town and
principal buildings of interest
to visitors. Figure 12 is Lichfield
in Staffordshire; Figure 13 shows
Northampton. [From the *AA Road
Book of England and Wales,* London: The
Automobile Association, n.d. [1925],
pp 356, 407: private collection.]

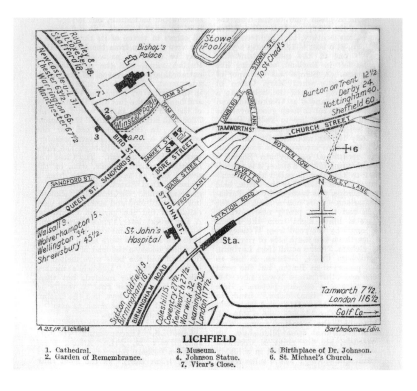

LICHFIELD

1. Cathedral.
2. Garden of Remembrance.
3. Museum.
4. Johnson Statue.
7. Vicar's Close.
5. Birthplace of Dr. Johnson.
6. St. Michael's Church.

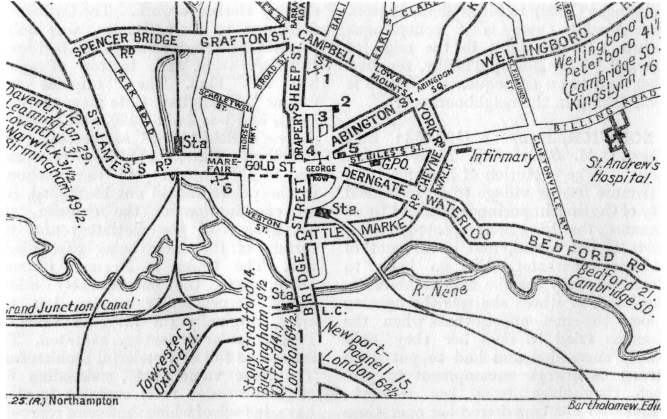

NORTHAMPTON

1. St. Sepulchre's Church.
2. The Welsh House.
3. Market Square.
4. All Saints' Church.
5. Town Hall.
6. St. Peter's Church.

mapping at 1:25,344 or larger before the advent of 1:10,560 Ordnance Survey maps produced from 1840 onwards. We lay emphasis on 'known extant', partly because once a manuscript map which was never copied has been lost, then its data are irretrievably lost, and partly because a number of printed town maps are only known from single, seemingly chance survivals. This underscores the fact that even printing a map may not ensure its survival. Several town maps produced by the prolific map-maker John Wood in the 1820s and 1830s are known only from an apparent single survivor. Many maps are only available publicly as photographic copies or transcripts of varying quality and usefulness. Early maps – say before 1800 – survive of some apparently very small places; conversely, they do not survive for some very substantial ones. For example, the first extant map for Glasgow that accords with our criterion is an estate map of 1765 depicting part of the emerging city (21857); the first printed map of what was already well on its way to becoming the largest city in Scotland only appeared in 1773 (21977). In contrast, St Andrews – a university town, with all the status that implied – had been mapped as early as *c.* 1580 (23510) [**Fig. 14,** *overleaf*]. For other places, pre-Ordnance Survey mapping of a town might be incidental to the main function of the map, as with an estate map which portrays all land and properties owned by a particular individual or institution.

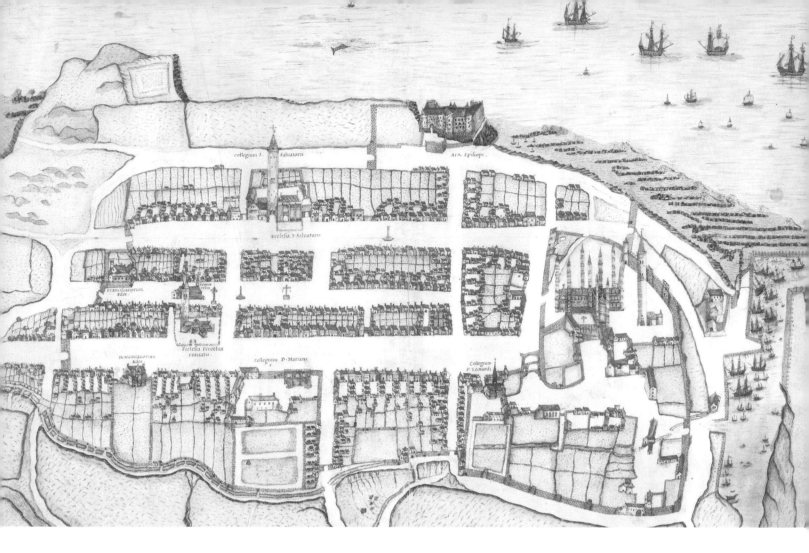

[Fig. 14] John Geddy, *S. Andre. sive Andreapolis Scotiae Universitas Metropolitana*, c. 1580. This is the earliest detailed map of a Scottish town. The scale is about 1:2000, but in practice the plan of the town narrows more to the east than is shown here. A comparison of the buildings shown on the map with those that survive indicates that depiction of structures on the map was quite realistic. (CBTM 23510) [National Library of Scotland, MS 20996]

This study covers the whole of Britain: Wales and Scotland as well as England. Although distinct as nations, both Wales and Scotland had been subject to strong English influence before incorporation into the United Kingdom. No known Welsh town maps had been produced when Wales was joined to England in 1535. The development of Welsh town mapping was modest until the early nineteenth century. Scotland differed from Wales as it retained distinctive legal, land tenure, ecclesiastical and administrative systems after union, and these affected the nature of some later cartography. Tithes are an example: they were abolished in Scotland in 1633 without any

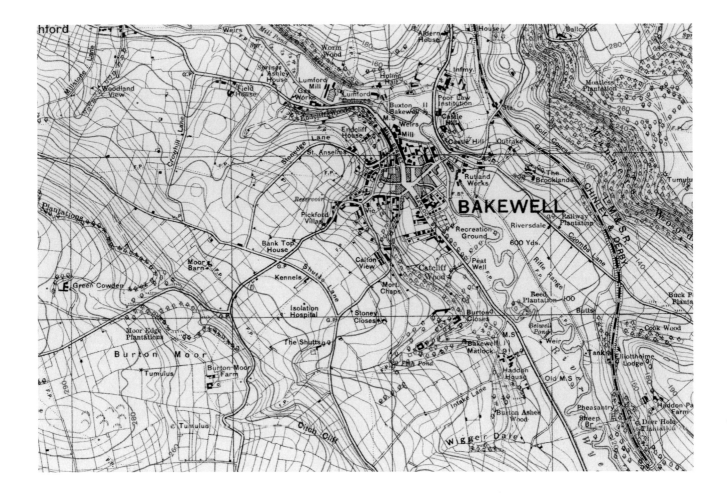

[Fig. 15] Towns might be mapped as part of larger entities. Bakewell in Derbyshire, illustrated here, was mapped by the Ordnance Survey for the War Office as part of a military training series at 1:25,000. Detail in the centre of the town is sparse; the church is only shown (as a circle surmounted by a cross) because it is a 'referring object' for directing artillery fire. The close-interval contouring gives an excellent impression of the physical setting of the town. [GSGS series 3906, sheet 44/38 SE: Ordnance Survey, 1934: private collection].

use of mapping. In England and Wales, by contrast, a tithe commutation process dates to around 1840 and critically was accompanied by large-scale maps which for many small towns are key cartographic representations of the urban area. By contrast, there are types of map and map-making well represented in England and Scotland, but far less so in Wales: the large-scale urban surveys of the 1820s and 1830s are examples [Fig. 15].

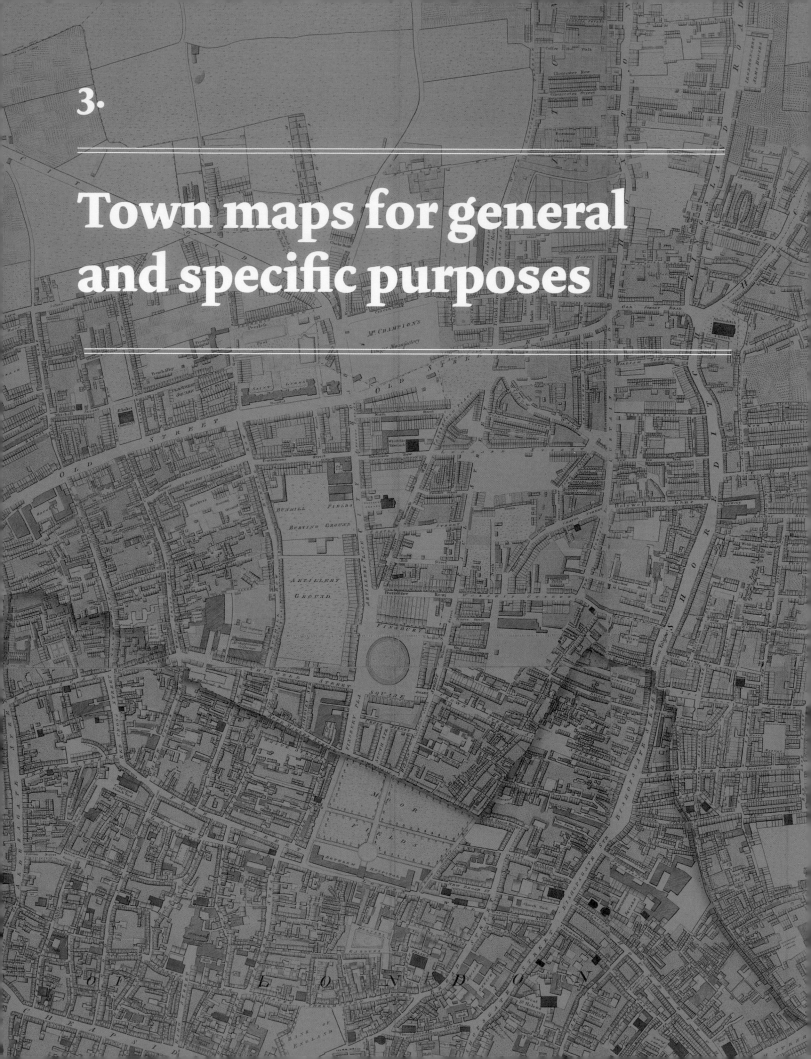

3.

Town maps for general and specific purposes

TOWN MAPS CAN BE divided into two broad categories or genres: first, those that are intended to appeal to a general audience, notably for wayfinding or as a location reference to places, and second, those which are made for specific purposes.

The prime exemplar of general-purpose mapping is that of the Ordnance Survey; examples of specific-use maps include those made for sanitary planning, estate management, as records of administrative boundaries, or for portraying the distribution of various urban activities or characteristics, for example schools and other educational establishments. A variation is mapping that is prepared for a specific purpose, but includes urban areas as an incidental part of the territory mapped: notable examples are tithe maps and military maps, discussed in Sections 8 and 14 respectively. A further dichotomy is between maps that record towns as they actually are – an essential for general reference or wayfinding maps – and those that are effectively a plan for presumed further physical works. It is axiomatic that general maps are printed and published. Specific-purpose mapping includes both maps whose purpose is so specialised that a single manuscript is sufficient, and those where there is a need beyond a single agency to justify the cost of printing.

General-use reference maps can be divided into two further categories: maps as guides to be used when out and about in a town, and those that are

[Fig. 16] The so-called 'Copperplate Map'. It is unusual for a map or survey to survive as printing plates rather than in printed form, but such is the fate of the first large-scale survey of London, executed in the later 1550s. As with the near-contemporary map of Norwich by William Cuningham, it is unclear why it was made, or who made it. No copy of the map is known, which may indicate that very few examples were printed, but three of the fifteen copperplates have come to light. The detail here depicts Moorfields, and shows both the pictorial treatment of buildings and the use of figures to give realism to 'public spaces'. (CBTM 18537) [Detail: British Library, Maps 188.q.1(4) Moorfields sheet]

paper surrogates for the townscape. The first need to be portable; the second need not. The distinction is not hard and fast, as the same map can serve both to be carried folded in the pocket and to be displayed on a wall. Maps that are suitable for carrying about need to be at scales where the ground can easily be related to the map, but not so cumbersome that an inconveniently large amount of paper is needed to represent the area of interest. For this reason the lower and upper limits for street maps for wayfinding are about 2.5 inches to 1 mile (1:25,344) and about 12 inches to 1 mile (1:5280); the average is around 5 to 8 inches to 1 mile (1:12,672–1:7920). Map scales smaller than about 1:25,000 render it impossible to name other than the most important streets, but may be useful for both general reference, to give the wider context of an urban area, or for synoptic views of large areas such as London and the West Midlands conurbation, with the whole built-up area depicted on a single sheet of paper. Smaller scales do work for some specialised purposes, as for depicting administrative divisions, the general pattern of transport infrastructure, or other thematic uses where an overview is important. Examples of maps that would be far too cumbersome to use on the ground include all the basic surveys of London from the 'Copperplate Map' (late 1550s: 18537) [Fig. 16], through Ogilby & Morgan (1675–82: 21332) [Fig. 17, *overleaf*], Rocque (1737–46: 18545) [Fig. 18, *p. 39*] and Horwood (1792–9: 18655) [Fig. 19, *pp. 40–41*] to the Ordnance Survey of 1862 onwards [Fig. 20, *p. 42*]: all these are at scales varying from about 1:1200 to 1:2500. Horwood's map, in forty sheets, measures about 5 m across by 2.5 m high. These are maps for displaying on a wall, or for use as sheets atlas-style, but not for carrying about.

The distinction between general- and specific-purpose mapping is not a rigid one. For example, from their first use for geological mapping in the 1830s, Ordnance Survey maps have been used as base maps for such special purposes; the development of the Ordnance Survey's own 'town scales' in Britain in the 1840s and 1850s was to provide base maps for planning and recording sanitary works in towns. Similarly, later in the century commercial mapping was overprinted for various purposes, for example to show electoral districts or to plot the distribution of infectious diseases. The Rounthwaite map of

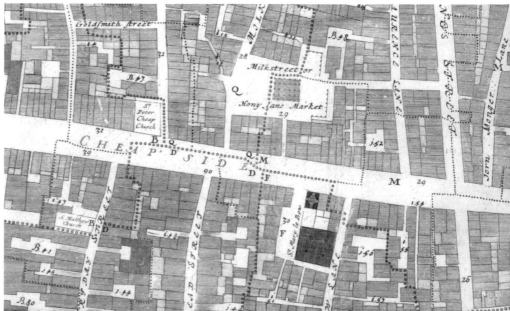

[Fig. 17] John Ogilby aspired to map the whole of Britain in unprecedented detail: in the event, this septuagenarian only managed to publish a map of the roads, the town of Ipswich, and London, illustrated here (CBTM 18542). The lavish scale – 1:1200; 100 feet to 1 mile – was complemented by a high level of detail, including internal divisions of tenements. This was the first new survey of London after the Great Fire of 1666, and was itself not replaced until some sixty years later, by the work of John Rocque. This extract includes Cheapside in the City of London. [A large and accurate map of the City of London ichnographically describing all the streets, lanes, alleys, courts, churches, halls and houses, &c. Actually surveyed and delineated, by John Ogilby Esq; His Majesties Cosmographer, 'actually survey'd and delineated by John Ogilby Esq and William Morgan Gent. His Majesty's Cosmographers', c. 1676. Detail: British Library, Maps Crace Port.2.61]

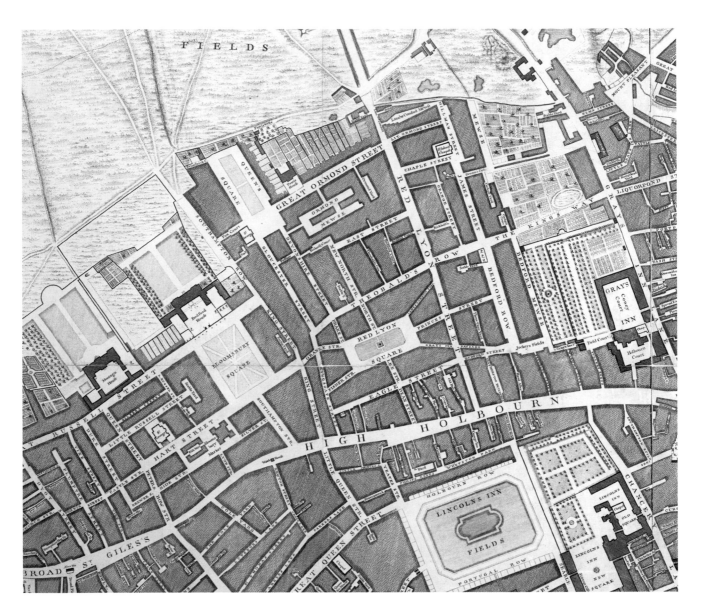

[Fig. 18] John Rocque made a substantial contribution to the mapping of England in the middle decades of the eighteenth century. His most ambitious project was a remapping of London, the first since Ogilby's in the 1670s. It was published in 1746. The built-up area had expanded greatly in the intervening seventy years, and so Rocque had to cover a much larger area. His scale at 1:2400 was half that used by Ogilby, and he did not map detail behind frontages. Nonetheless his survey provided the basis for numerous derivatives, including many maps designed for visitors to the capital. This extract includes High Holborn, Lincoln Inn Fields and, left, the building of the British Museum, which stood on the edge of the then built-up area.

(CBTM 18545) [Detail: British Library, Maps 3480 (293)]

[Fig. 19] The most elaborate survey of London before the coming of the Ordnance Survey was carried out by Richard Horwood between 1792 and 1799. He used a scale similar to Rocque's – 1:2376 – but supplied far more detail, including divisions behind frontages. As there were 1,116 subscribers to the map, its large scale was evidently no deterrent to its sales. The enlargement depicts some of the residential squares of the West End. (CBTM 18655) [Detail: British Library, Maps Crace Port. s.173]

Sunderland of 1883 was used for both these purposes (19977).

The range of special-use maps was extended considerably in the nineteenth century, and some specific types, notably School Board maps, appeared only in the last third of the century [Figs 21, 22, p.43]. Others appeared earlier, and usually remained in manuscript even after the advent of cheaper printing technology as there was simply not enough interest, or were not enough users, to justify reproduction of copies. Examples are the parish and ward maps of London (e.g. 13799–13824 inclusive). More specialised examples include electoral maps (Northallerton [1793]: 20108), and varieties of religious maps, for example, the 'sanctuary maps' of c. 1540–1 (18709, 20194, 20196).

[Fig. 20] The most detailed map of London is the Ordnance Survey's at 5 feet to 1 mile (1:1056), surveyed between 1862 and 1872. It took 326 sheets to cover the whole of the capital. When the mapping was revised between 1891 and 1895, building growth had been such that 775 sheets were required. It was this sort of expansion, with its implications for fieldwork, that brought about the demise of the so-called 'town scales', such as the 1:1056. This is an extract from sheet 7.74, completed in 1872 and published in 1875. As compared with Horwood (Figure 19), there is an enormous increase in the amount of detail shown – not least in the treatment of the numerous Thames-side industrial premises.

[British Library, Maps OS London (edition of 1862–72) sheet 7.74.]

[Fig 21] Stanford's Library Map of London, first published in 1862, is at a scale standardised by the Ordnance Survey, which at this time had only mapped London in 'skeleton' form. The Stanford map was produced initially for the Metropolitan Board of Works, which needed a general base-map, but soon proved capable of being adapted for many other purposes, including as the basis for a geological version and for Charles Booth's celebrated map of London poverty of 1889. Another use was as the basis for a series of maps of London School Board areas. The extract depicts part of Finsbury, as published in 1862. (CBTM 18546) [British Library, Maps 11.c.5;]

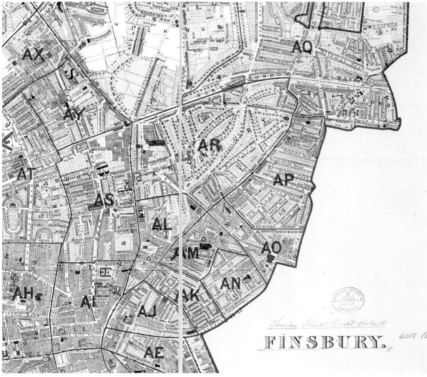

[Fig 22] Figure 22 shows the same basic mapping as figure 21 but revised and then overprinted for School Board purposes in 1879. Although the Ordnance Survey completed publication of London at the 1:10,560 scale in 1884, the Stanford map was less cluttered with detail, and was a serious competitor. (CBTM 18546) [from British Library, Maps 4018.(2).]

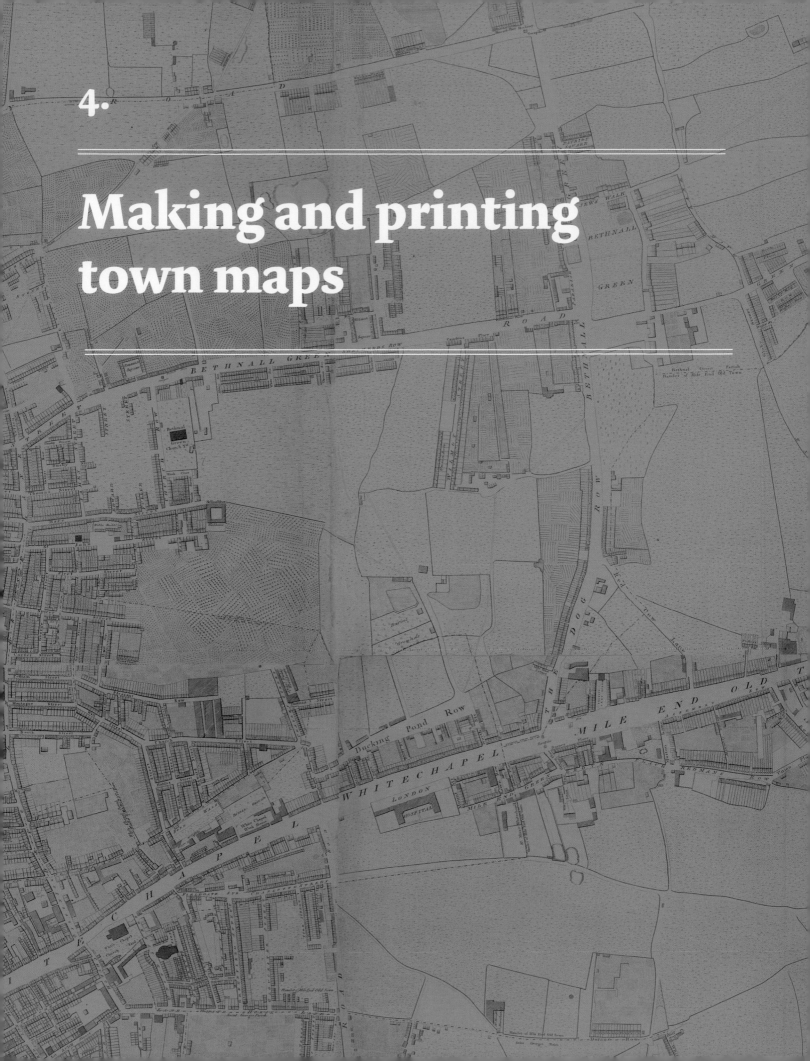

4.

Making and printing town maps

AN UNKNOWN NUMBER of manuscript maps of towns was doubtless made in the medieval period before the first printed town maps appear from the mid-sixteenth century onwards. The relatively few such manuscript maps that survive may argue that they were never very numerous in the first place or that subsequent loss has been significant. After about 1560 the proportion of manuscript maps as a total of all surviving urban maps gradually falls, until by the late nineteenth century they are unusual, and invariably associated with some special purpose.

Engraving

The first printed town map known to us dates from 1472, and for the next 330 years the only viable method for map printing was by incising a plane surface. Maps were engraved on wood by cutting away material so that the lines and text were raised. The disadvantages of such an image are that, once engraved, it could not easily be altered for updating and revision, and the amount of material to be cut away might well exceed that which remained – a not unusual situation with maps. For this reason few wood-engraved town maps are encountered. Much more favoured for map-making was engraving on metal. Copper is the usual medium, though a few instances of pewter are known, while engraving on steel was in vogue in the second quarter of the nineteenth century. Common to all

these so-called 'intaglio' engravings is that the image is incised into the metal, and prints taken by covering the plate with ink, wiping away surplus ink outside the incisions, and then passing the plate and paper through a roller-press. In the words of a later writer, 'When the paper was pressed down on the copper the ink transferred its affection to it and the map was printed'.[9] Copper was the favoured medium because it is relatively soft and easy to cut into; thus it is possible to revise the plate by hammering the back, burnishing the front surface and re-engraving new data. An engraved plate could be very long-lasting: some of Saxton's county maps of the 1570s were reprinted throughout close on 200 years.

Lithography and zincography[10]

The lithographic process was discovered in 1798 by Alois Senefelder, and was second only to the introduction of print more than 300 years earlier in its significance for reproducing maps. Lithography depended on the physical properties of a particular type of limestone found only in one locality in Bavaria. An image drawn on this stone in greasy ink could be repeatedly inked-up and prints taken from it. As the image was drawn on to the surface, rather than incised as on an engraved plate, it could be produced much more quickly. Printing from the stone was also much faster. Once an image had been printed, the stone could be cleaned and a new image drawn, or the

lithographic stone with its image might be stored for reprinting at a later date.

The earliest lithographic maps could not compete in subtlety of image with either finely penned manuscript drawing or with an average standard of copper engraving, but the speed of preparation meant that the technique was well suited to maps that needed to be reproduced quickly. It is, therefore, unsurprising that some of the earliest surviving lithographed maps are small-scale ones prepared for the War Office from 1808 onwards. As preparation costs were much less than for engraving, the method was soon adopted by commercial users, but at first maps printed lithographically tended to be those where only one printing was likely to be needed, enabling stones to be wiped straightaway. Maps to illustrate property sale prospectuses are one such type. Representative of another are the maps accompanying Parliamentary Boundary Commissioners' reports in 1831–2. In the late 1830s and early 1840s a number of tithe maps were lithographed.

Lithographic stones are cumbersome. In his English patent of 1801 Senefelder suggested that zinc might be a substitute, and a zincographic process was patented by Federico Lacelli in 1834. Zinc plates were artificially grained to simulate a lithographic surface and were of a similar weight to copper plates. The image quality tended to be inferior to that of stone, and so the older but more cumbersome method

continued to be used for some maps until well into the twentieth century. The Ordnance Survey started to use lithography for printing large-scale maps in about 1854, but quickly changed to zincography. However, when the Ordnance Survey began printing its small-scale maps in colour from the mid-1890s onwards, printing was from stone as zinc did not yield a clear enough image. Zinc printing was much improved in the first decades of the twentieth century, but stones were still in use for some small-scale Ordnance Survey maps in the early 1940s.[11]

After about 1860, few commercial map-makers printed directly from copper. Two exceptions are the Salmon map of Nottingham at 1:2400 of 1862 (19829), engraved by Wyld and perhaps intended as a prestigious wall map [Fig. 23], and the Roper map of Widnes, Lancashire, at 1:2160 of 1879 (15326), produced for the Widnes Local Board.

Printing in colour

Because it was necessary to damp the paper to enable the ink to 'take' properly, copperplate printing was unsuited for colour printing; the paper medium was distorted by moistening and drying. This is especially significant where close register is important, as on maps. The only really practicable way of colouring engraved mapping was by hand: the technique was widely used, though usually for enhancing information

on the engraving rather than for additional information.[12]

Colour printing for maps became practicable with the introduction of lithography, which does not need paper to be moistened and thus obviates distortion. Even so, colour lithographic printing was only adopted gradually in Britain.[13] The Edinburgh firm of John Bartholomew was producing good colour work by the late 1870s, and the mass-produced 'District Railway' Map of London of the 1880s (18283) was multi-coloured [Fig. 24, overleaf]. Even so, in the 1890s there were still publishers who printed their maps lithographically in one or two colours, and then added further colours by hand: G. W. Bacon and Gall & Inglis are notable companies which employed this practice for urban mapping.

[Fig. 24] The street map could present itself either as wholly objective, with an apparently neutral vocabulary of significant buildings, open spaces and railway stations, or it could be consciously customised for publicity purposes. A notable example of this was *The 'District Railway' Map of London*: a clear, basic street map of London turned into a publicity vehicle by showing the District Railway and its affiliated lines in red, together with connecting horse-bus services. The map may have been designed as much for display as a poster at railway stations as for guiding the traveller, but as reputedly over half a million copies were sold, it evidently had wide appeal. This extract includes Hyde Park and Kensington. (CBTM 18283) [Detail: British Library Maps 3485. (105).]

The most numerous hand-coloured maps are Ordnance Survey 1:2500 sheets. Up to 1893 they were usually printed in black from zinc, and then colour was added by hand for buildings (two shades), roads and water. A few revised sheets with hand-coloured water were still produced as late as 1915 [Fig. 25].[14] The Ordnance Survey was not unaware of colour printing: in 1856–61 a few 1:2500 maps of built-up areas were experimentally colour-printed, but the very limited numbers required made colour printing uneconomic [Fig. 26]. It was quite otherwise with relatively mass-market street maps.[15]

Photography in map reproduction

Photographic techniques were adopted quite slowly in map reproduction processes.[16] Photographic reduction to re-scale images was used by the Ordnance Survey from 1855, and facilitated the production of smaller-

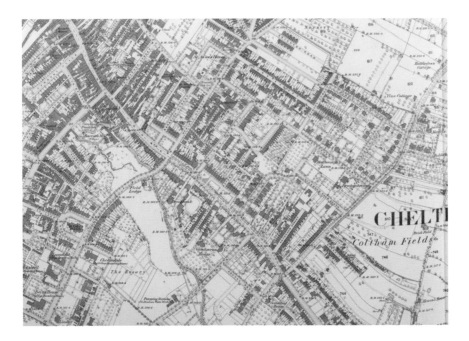

[**Fig. 25**, *left*] The colourful style of the Ordnance Survey 1:2500 first edition mapping is exemplified by this extract, covering part of Cheltenham. The colour was applied by hand, using stencils, and the sheet cost 11s 6d (£0.58) coloured – or 2s 6d (£0.13) uncoloured when published in 1884. Not many coloured versions were sold. [Detail: British Library, Maps OS 1:2500 first edition Gloucestershire sheet XXVI.8.]

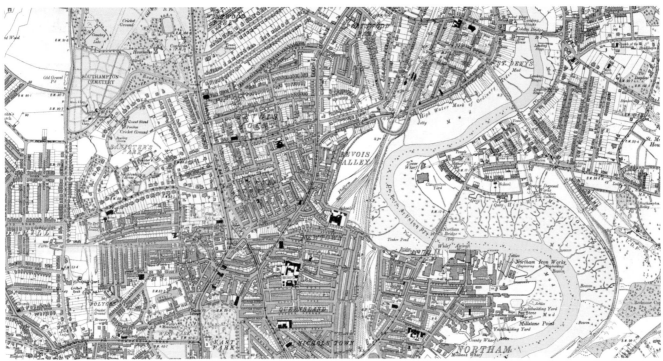

[**Fig. 26**, *above*] The apogee of coloured Ordnance Survey large-scale maps is the 'Town Maps' series, published between 1920 and 1924. The colour scheme is in essence an elaboration of that used on the 1:2500 first edition, with the addition of green for parks and woodland, and purple for tram routes. The relatively high price – 5s (£0.25) for a sheet mounted on 'cloth' – probably militated against the commercial success of these most attractive maps. The Ordnance Survey's headquarters was in Southampton at this time, and it is identified on this extract covering the north part of the town centre, but no special attention is drawn to it – in contrast to the practice of some commercial publishers. [Detail: British Library, Maps 2605. (4).]

[Fig. 27] Among the more remarkable town maps of the nineteenth century is the modestly titled *Cambridge, 1859* by 'E. Monson, Land Surveyor, Draughtsman, and Photographist'. In some 'Notes and observations' Monson explains building conventions and 'Map – How obtained': 'The outline of Streets was obtained from the large Skeleton Map of 1856 in the Town-chest, reduced to a scale of 6 chains to the inch, by Photography. Details were filled in from the old published maps. The town was then gone over Map in hand (railway fashion of revision) and all observed differences of importance corrected; it was then redrawn and Photographed. The map is printed with silver, the Notes are letterpress. The time occupied in the Drawing, Photographing, and revision was about three months.' The map itself is in four pieces. The letterpress includes population of parishes, numbers in schools and number of members of societies. (CBTM 20691) [Cambridge University Library, Maps.aa.18.Q.1]

scale maps from large-scale basic surveys. In 1859 E. Monson produced a map of Cambridge (20691) which used direct photographic prints: the limited practicable size of photographic plates meant that the map area of 49 by 63 cm had to be made up from four prints. It seems to be unique [Fig. 27].

In 1859 the process of photo-zincography was developed simultaneously, by John Osbourne in South Australia and by the Ordnance Survey at Southampton. In essence, this enables a photographic print to be transferred to zinc for volume printing. When in 1882 the Ordnance Survey began producing six-inch maps by direct photo-reduction from 1:2500 sheets, available negative sizes forced the introduction of 'quarter sheets' of 460 by 310 cm [Fig. 28]. Later developments enabled larger sheets to be produced,

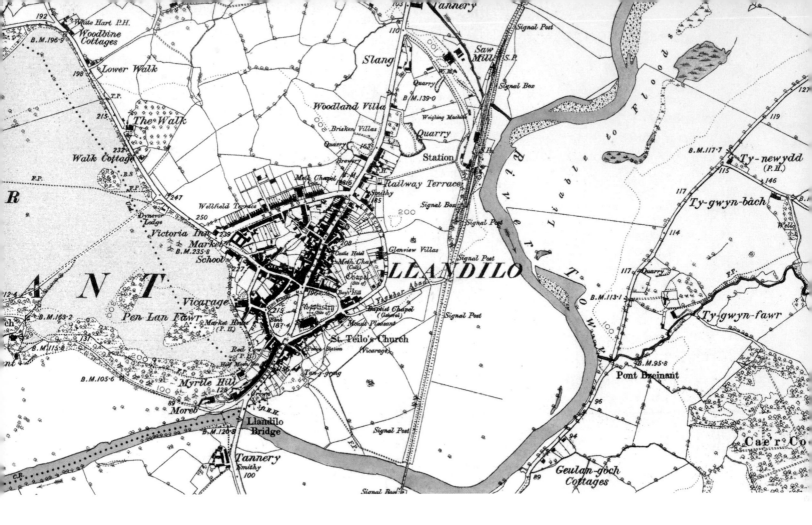

but the glass negatives used were as bulky to store and much more fragile than copper or zinc plates. From 1900 lighter zinc plates were available and as they used less metal it became economic to retain plates for future reprinting. For same-scale reproduction, negatives were rendered unnecessary by the 'Vandyke process', by which it was possible to photographically develop a sensitised zinc plate by placing a manuscript drawing on top and exposing it to strong light.

Commercial publishers were less enthusiastic users of photography than was the Ordnance Survey. Older-established firms such as Bartholomew, Johnston, and Philip continued to rely heavily on

[Fig. 28] Although the Ordnance Survey developed a photo-zincographic process in 1859, it was only from 1881 onwards that it was applied to domestic map production. The six-inch maps were slow to appear, as they had to be reduced from the parent survey at 1:2500 and engraved. To speed up the process, direct photo-reduction from 1:2500 drawings was adopted. The result is a rather crowded-looking map, but one which could be published very quickly. This illustration is of the market town of Llandeilo in Carmarthenshire. [Detail: British Library, Maps OS 1:10,560 first edition Carmarthenshire sheet XXXIII SE.]

[Fig. 29] An advertising map worked two ways: for a stranger to a town it offered a street-guide; for advertisers it offered a shop-window for their services. This illustration is of the 'Business Street Map of Croydon', published by the Borough & County Advertising Company of Leicester, *c.* 1895. Perhaps surprisingly for a town that by this time had a population of 100,000 or so, Croydon seems not to have had an entire street map devoted to it. Although there are thirty-eight advertising panels round the sides, some advertisers took more than one panel. Similarly to maps issued by estate agents, these may have been designed to appeal as much to prospective residents as to visitors: the former would be interested in removal firms, whereas the latter would be unlikely to be customers of coal-merchants. As with *The 'District Railway' Map of London* (see Figure 24), such maps could function both for display on a wall, or folded for the pocket for wayfinding. The map is oriented to east rather than north, probably for reasons of accommodating the shape of the built-up area to a standard landscape format. (CBTM 20788) [British Library, Maps 5345. (4)]

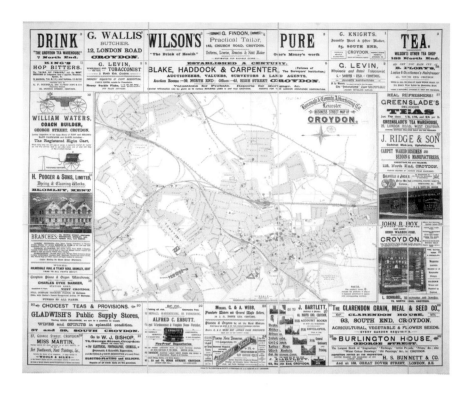

engraving and lithographic transfer, although they did sometimes use photography as a short-cut in scale transformation, for example to reduce a map to fit the particular page size of a guidebook. George Bacon and Company and a number of local publishers copied Ordnance Survey maps using photographic processes when making maps for street and business directories (Ashton-under-Lyne, 19393).[17] Apart from considerations of image quality, a practical discouragement to using photo-lithographic methods more extensively was the heavy historic investment that these companies had made in engraved plates. Bartholomew were still using their copper plates into the 1960s. Photographic processes were adopted more readily by those with less of a stake in the past. In 1887 a group of three maps of districts around Manchester

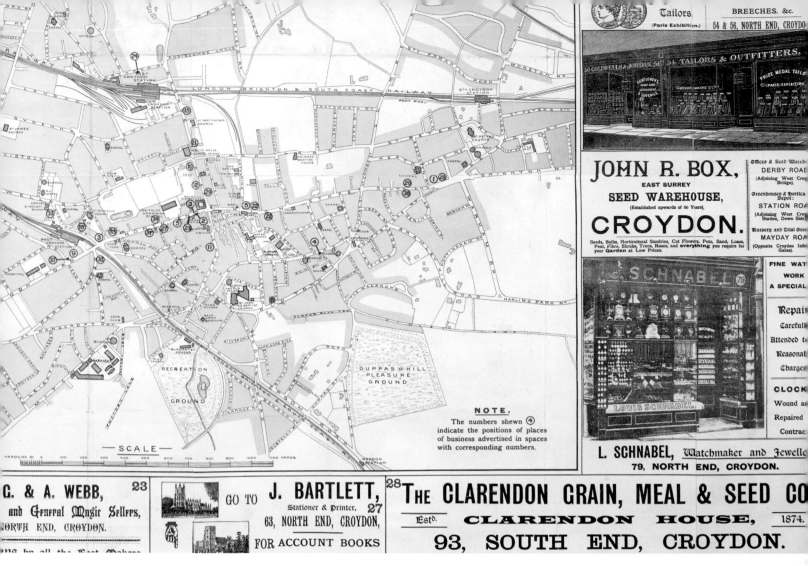

were produced for Richard Collinson, 'Estate and Insurance Agent', from pen-and-ink transcripts of Ordnance Survey maps, suitably revised for new streets (19638–19640). The same basic process was used by various publishers of what were often referred to at the time as 'business street maps' – essentially advertising maps [Figs 29, 30]. These were marketed for wayfinding, but revenue from advertisements in the map margins was commercially critical.

[Fig. 30] Detail of the 'Business Street Map of Croydon' as in Figure 29.

5.

Maps that survive,
maps that are lost

[Fig. 31] One of the more remarkable maps of the later nineteenth century was the survey of Widnes and its surroundings, at a scale of 1 inch to 180 feet (1:2160). It was made under the Local Government Act of 1858 for Widnes Local Board, whose device appears at the head of each sheet. It is apparent from marginal notes that there was also a seventy-two-sheet map at 1:360 that is now lost. This was surveyed in 1875 under the direction of Henry C. Roper, C.E., of Dudley, and the reduced map was engraved in 1879, in Ordnance Survey style, by Isaac W. Petty & Son of Manchester. The engraving of the rural part outdoes the Ordnance Survey in quality of finish, although the content is more in line with traditional rural mapping. Broken names follow Ordnance Survey style, in that completion in a sheet margin is in italic, regardless of the style used on the map proper. (CBTM 15326) [The National Archives, RAIL 1033/376–377]

IN 1879 HENRY ROPER had a map of Widnes engraved (15326) [Fig. 31]. The reason for its making seems obvious enough: it depicts the whole area of the Widnes Local Board's area of responsibility at a scale substantially larger – 1:2160 – than the largest-scale map available at that time from the Ordnance Survey, which was at the much smaller 1:10,560 scale and also some thirty years out of date. But what has happened to the even larger scale 1:360 maps of Widnes town in seventy-two sheets, referred to in the marginalia of the surviving 1879 map? It may be hazarded that the large-scale mapping has been lost as it remained in a single manuscript copy while the 1:2160 map survives in multiple copies by virtue of being engraved and printed.

Once a manuscript map is lost, so are the data unique to it [Fig. 32, *overleaf*]. Sometimes manuscript maps were produced in multiple copies so that they

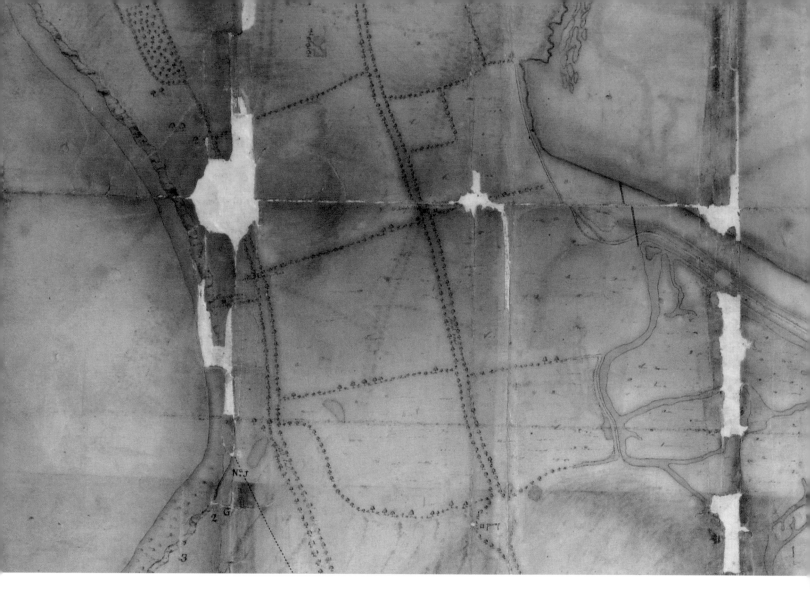

[Fig. 32] This manuscript map of 1729 shows both the defences of Harwich and the erosion of soft cliffs nearby. As a manuscript map it is a unique document and it is clear that it has been heavily used. Folding of the map has caused some of the drawing to wear away, such that it is now 'lost' and the whole map is badly discoloured. (CBTM 18587) ['Plan of the town of Harwich', 1729, original scale 1:2400: The National Archives, MPD 1/169.]

could be deposited at various locations. For example, all tithe maps produced from 1837 onwards were produced in three copies: one each to be retained by the Tithe Commission in London, the diocese and the parish. Almost all the copies in the first two categories survive, but possibly no more than a quarter or a fifth of the parish copies.[18] The maps produced for Local Boards of Health from 1850 onwards were notionally only produced in manuscript, and there is no reliable list of how many were made, other than of those made by the Ordnance Survey. Of the thirty-one maps

produced by the Ordnance Survey, five were engraved or lithographed as regular Ordnance Survey products and thirteen survive in manuscript. Nine are lost completely; of the others, two survive in contemporary manuscript transcripts, Derby is represented by a lithograph of the 1:2640 general map (17001), but a detailed map of the town at 1:528 known to once have existed has not been located. Three others survive in contemporary lithographed copies, although for Worthing (14307) the sheet covering the town centre is missing. Thus printing does not of itself guarantee the survival of a map [Fig. 33, p. 61].

Even when maps survive, possibly in multiple copies and printings in different collections, it can still be difficult to determine the context of their making. We make frequent reference in this book to Ordnance Survey practice; this is not because we see the Ordnance Survey as more important or the custodian of the proper way to do things, but simply because, although its records fall far short of completeness, it is relatively well documented and well studied compared with most commercial cartographic organisations.[19] The notable exception to this is the Edinburgh firm of John Bartholomew, whose voluminous records are now deposited in the National Library of Scotland. However, urban mapping in Britain was a relatively small part of Bartholomew's business: the successive editions of *The Times Atlas* are far more representative of the

firm than are their street maps. Much the same could be said of companies such as Johnston, Philip and Bacon. The one apparent exception is the Geographers A–Z Map Company, which is mostly concerned with production of street maps.[20] Paradoxically, our source of knowledge for some aspects of later nineteenth- and earlier twentieth-century commercial mapping practices is Ordnance Survey records.[21]

The electronic *Catalogue of British Town Maps* which accompanies this printed book provides researchers with a starting point to find out what maps exist for a particular place. It is a long-standing popular myth that the British Library has 'a copy of every book published', and by implication of every map. It does not, and the other legal deposit libraries by no means fill all the gaps, though they all have their individual strengths. Sometimes maps are indeed in the legal deposit libraries, but they are in books, and not separately catalogued. Other printed maps are to be found only in local libraries or record offices: some may only survive in private collections, and knowledge of their existence and sight of their contents depends on the public-spiritedness of their owners.[22] As a result certain types of map are knowingly under-represented in our *Catalogue*. This applies especially to advertising maps. The *New Business Map of Cardiganshire*, of which 1,309 copies were printed on 23 February 1909, advertises 'Maps of over 1,000 Cities & Towns' in Britain, yet we have found very few of

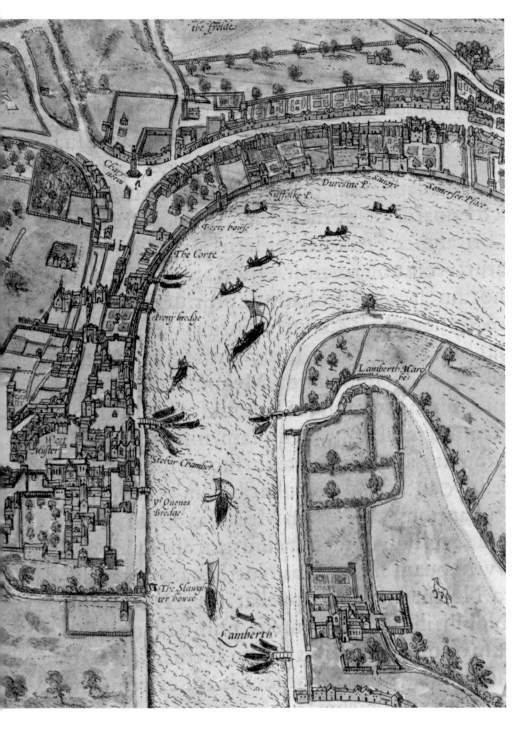

[Fig. 33] The map of London included in Georg Braun's and Remigius Hogenberg's *Civitates orbis terrarum* of 1572 was based on the survey of the 1550s for the so-called 'Copperplate Map' (see Fig. 16, p. 36). This extract depicts the area of Westminster, and includes part of the 'copperplate survey' of which the original is now lost. (See Fig. 39, p. 71, for the complete map.) (CBTM 18462) [From Georg Braun and Remigius Hogenberg, *Civitates orbis terrarum*, Vol. I (1572): British Library, Maps c.29.e.1]

these surviving.[23] No doubt this reflects contemporary attitudes: the maps were printed on relatively friable paper, and were seen as ephemeral. The object was to make money, not to provide national geographical infrastructure.

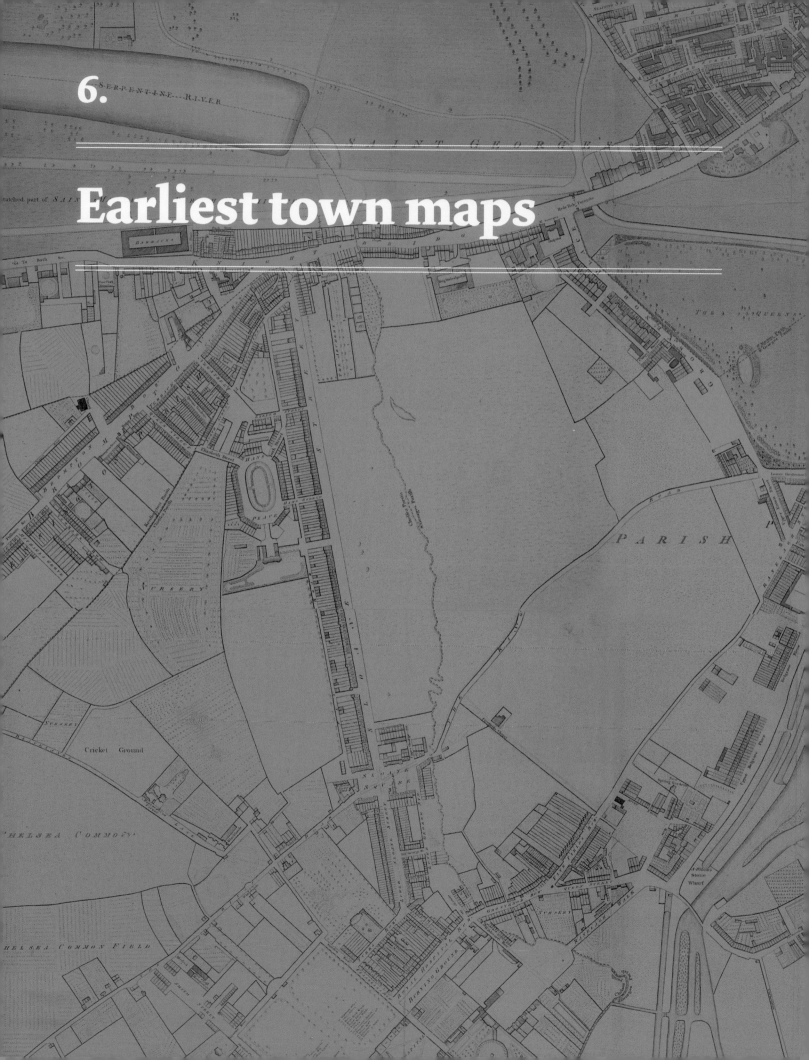

6.

Earliest town maps

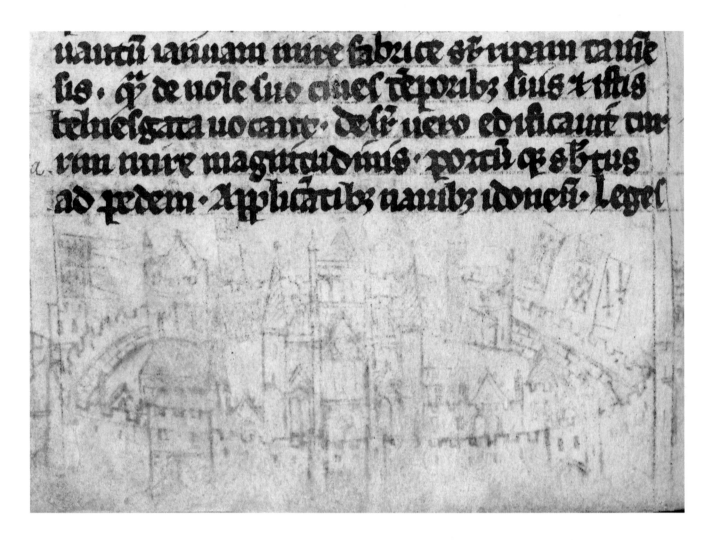

ONE OF THE EARLIEST graphic images of a British town, 'London from the North' by Matthew Paris *c.* 1250, depicts fairly accurately the view from Highgate.[24] The two earliest maps in our *Catalogue* appear to derive by visualisation from a distant point rather than by measured survey. The provenance of both is as illustrations in books. The earliest is a schematic map of London drawn on a leaf of a copy of the *Chronicles* of Geoffrey of Monmouth, dated to *c.* 1300 (19876) [Fig. 34]. It can be interpreted as the city seen from the north: perhaps from Hampstead Heath.[25] The second is a manuscript map of Bristol,

[Fig. 34] What may be the earliest recognisable map of a town in Britain is this example in a copy of the *Chronicles* of Geoffrey of Monmouth, dating from *c.* 1300. This depiction of London is symbolic: to the left is the Tower of London, to the right is St Paul's Cathedral, and round them runs the wall. The image measures 10 by 4 cm. (CBTM 19876) [British Library, Royal MS 13.A.iii, [p. 28v].]

1479, by Robert Ricart, included in another historical work: *The Maire of Bristowe is Kalendar* (23271). This may have been sketched from a vantage-point to the south-west of the city, perhaps from the steeple of St Mary Redcliffe [Fig. 35].[26]

Although these two maps are unquestionably depictions of towns, from the point of view of the student of townscapes their importance is as symbolic, rather than literal, representations. By 1550 in England, the map as a plan true to the actual ground had been established. Drawing to scale was something that was particularly applicable to engineering, and engineering at this time essentially meant military works. It is, therefore, unsurprising that the earliest scale maps or near-scale maps of towns were made for military purposes. Portsmouth was mapped by 1545 and 1552 (23505) [Fig. 36, *overleaf*].[27] There are two military-oriented maps of Dover, of *c.* 1530 (23155) and 1532 (21469), which are discussed further in Section 14.

Around 1540–1 three maps were made to show areas where criminals could claim sanctuary: Norwich (20196), Southwark (20194) and York (18709). These plans were probably produced in response to an official order to all towns, *c.* 1541, to produce plans showing places of sanctuary so as to inform the forthcoming legislation for the abolition of places of sanctuary. This request for maps seems to have been the urban equivalent of Thomas Cromwell's order of 1538 for the coasts of England to be surveyed.[28] The

[Fig. 35] Robert Ricart, who compiled *The Maire of Bristowe is Kalendar* in the late 1470s, evidently felt that study of the history of the city of Bristol would be helped by illustration. Buildings are to be interpreted symbolically rather than literally. The image measures 12 by 18 cm. (CBTM 23271) [Bristol Record Office, 04720 [fo.5b].]

Sent Johnes yate Sent leonardes yate And the newe
yate. And nomore was bilde not many yeres after
And thenne Brynne repaired home obw see in to his
owne lordeshipp of Burgoyne and there abode al his
lyf. And kyng Bellyne abode at Newe troy And
bilde there a noble yate fast by the Water of Tamys
and called it. Bellynges yate after his owne Name and
Reyned nobly all his lyf and lieth at newe Troye.

Bristollia.

Porta S.

Bristoll

Porta Nova

alta Crux

Porta S. leonardi

Porta S. Nichi

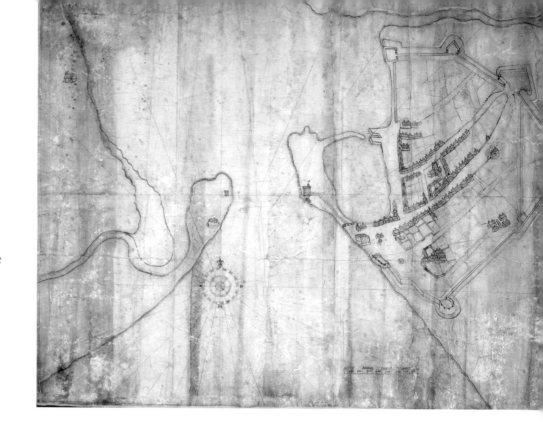

first map of a Scottish town has a similar political dimension: it depicts a siege of Edinburgh in 1544 from an English perspective (23403).[29] A map of Ashbourne in Derbyshire of 1547 (18586) was one of another well-developed genre of early maps – those which illustrate properties involved in a legal dispute [Fig. 37]. All these maps were a response to immediate and particular needs. None is known to have provided a basis for successors.

The first two printed maps of British towns appeared in the late 1550s, and though they contrast in many ways – not least by representing extremes of map size – they have in common a purpose of reference rather than wayfinding. One is a map of Norwich, attributed to William Cuningham and published as an illustration in *The Cosmographical Glasse*, a book on surveying, map-making and

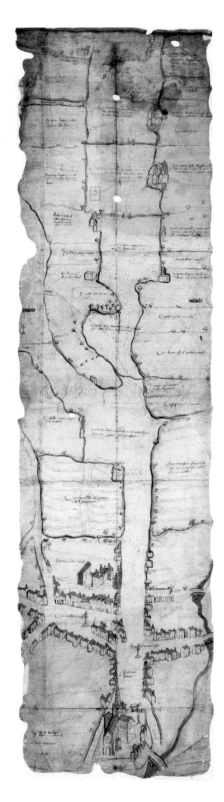

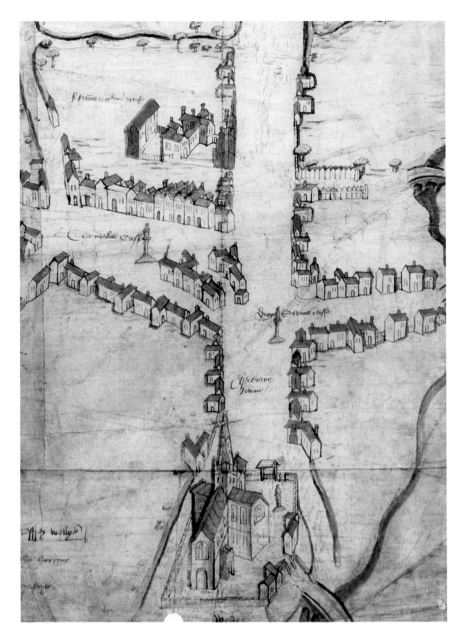

[Fig. 37] The illustration of lawsuits was an important motive for making some of the comparatively few detailed maps that survive from before the later sixteenth century. One such is a map of Ashbourne, 1547. The general effect is more of a bird's-eye view than of a plan map, and the comparatively large size relative to the detail shown – 36 by 132 cm – suggests something designed for laying out before an audience. It is incidental to the purpose of the map that it depicts a town. The enlargement includes the market place and the parish church.

(CBTM 18586) [The National Archives, MPC 1/35]

cosmology, of 1559 (20770) [Fig. 38]. Cuningham was not a surveyor: the book is a compilation and the map of Norwich may have been included simply because a manuscript version was to hand. It may be derived from some local mapping of the type created in the context of the Sanctuaries' Bill of 1541 but its overall structure and appearance is clearly derived from Jörg Seld and Hans Weiditz's woodcut map of Augsburg of 1521.[30] Nor, as it depicts some buildings before they were modified or demolished in the later 1540s, was it in any sense up to date.[31] It is more in the nature of a bird's-eye view rather than a plan map. Its scale varies from approximately 1:5000 north–south to 1:10,000 west–east. Its size – about 41 by 30 cm – seems not unduly modest until it is compared with its near-contemporary, the so-called Copperplate Map of London (18537).

The Copperplate Map is so called because it survives only fragmentarily, as three out of a conjectured original total of fifteen engraved copper printing plates. No contemporary prints made from the plates are known. When complete it would have measured at least 225 by 110 cm. It has been suggested that the map, unprecedented in Britain but with European predecessors, was commissioned by Hanseatic merchants to be used in the course of diplomatic dealings with the English: the intention might have been that copies would be presented to influential persons rather than sold.[32] Churches,

NORDOVICVM ANGLIÆ CIVITAS ANNO 1558

palaces and other significant buildings are shown pictorially on this map with a degree of realism. Other buildings seem to be depicted conventionally [**see Fig. 16,** *p. 36*].

A few years later a somewhat smaller – about 180 by 70 cm – woodcut version of this map of London was prepared, which is now known as the 'Agas' map.[33] Here, too, size worked against preservation: the three surviving copies are of a state dateable to *c.* 1633. The Agas map preserves the substance, if not the scale or the style, of the Copperplate Map. Common to both is size: these are maps to be displayed – probably by persons of influence and wealth – rather than carried about. The Copperplate Map provided the basis for Georg Braun and Remigius Hogenberg's map of London of 1572 (18462), 48 by 33 cm, demonstrating how an unwieldy map could provide the data for a more manageable derivative for inclusion in their monumental collection of town plans, *Civitates orbis terrarum* [**Fig. 39**]. The wayfinding street map was still some distance over the horizon.

Over the next forty years a handful of towns in England were mapped and published. These repeated the pattern exemplified by Norwich and London: there are compact maps created as book illustrations, but others are much larger-format display maps. The first printed maps of Cambridge and Oxford are exemplars. Richard Lyne's map of Cambridge, 1574 (20684), resembles that of Norwich in that it is relatively small

[Fig. 39] Georg Braun and Remigius Hogenberg's *Civitates orbis terrarum* sought, as the title suggested, to map all the cities of the world, and they invited readers to contribute depictions of towns. The publication of the eventual six volumes was spread between 1572 and 1618. London is included in the first volume. Braun and Hogenberg's is not the first map of the city, but it was probably the first to achieve a wide circulation, particularly in Europe. It is based on the survey of the 1550s for the so-called 'Copperplate Map' (see Fig. 16, p. 36): it is unknown whether it was a direct copy, or whether it was derived from a now unknown intermediate map. In keeping with the international audience and contemporary scholarly conventions, the marginal text is in Latin, although on the map proper it is in English and includes 'Charyncros', 'Towre', and 'Ye Gounefownders', north-east of Aldgate. Close inspection shows evidence of bull- and bear-baiting on the south bank of the Thames. The figures in the foreground are a standard feature of maps in *Civitates orbis terrarum*.

(CBTM 18462) [From Georg Braun and Remigius Hogenberg, Civitates orbis terrarum, Vol. I (1572): British Library Maps c.29.e.1]

[Fig. 40] Like many other early printed maps of towns, Richard Lyne's depiction of Cambridge of 1574 was produced as an illustration to a book, rather than as an independent document in its own right. It illustrates John Caio, *Historia Cantebrigiensis academiae*. Caio, otherwise Caius, had recently founded Gonville and Caius College, and wished to promote Cambridge as an historic seat of learning, in opposition to Oxford. There are three coats of arms: of Queen Elizabeth I, of Cambridge and of Matthew Parker, Archbishop of Canterbury. In keeping with its status as a book illustration, the map is page-sized (30 by 43 cm).

(CBTM 20684) [British Library, Maps 2.e.131]

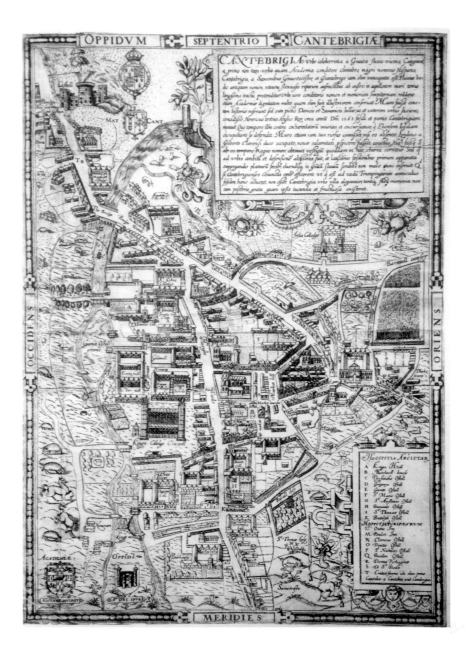

– about 30 by 43 cm – and appeared as an illustration in a book, John Caio's *Historia Cantebrigensis academiae* [Fig. 40].[34] Ralph Agas's map of Oxford, 1588 (19365) more nearly resembles the Copperplate Map, in that it is very large – about 115 by 85 cm – and evidently intended for display [Fig. 41]. Lyne intended to illustrate, Agas to celebrate; but both maps provided a basis for later derivatives, in a similar way to the Copperplate Map

BRITISH TOWN MAPS

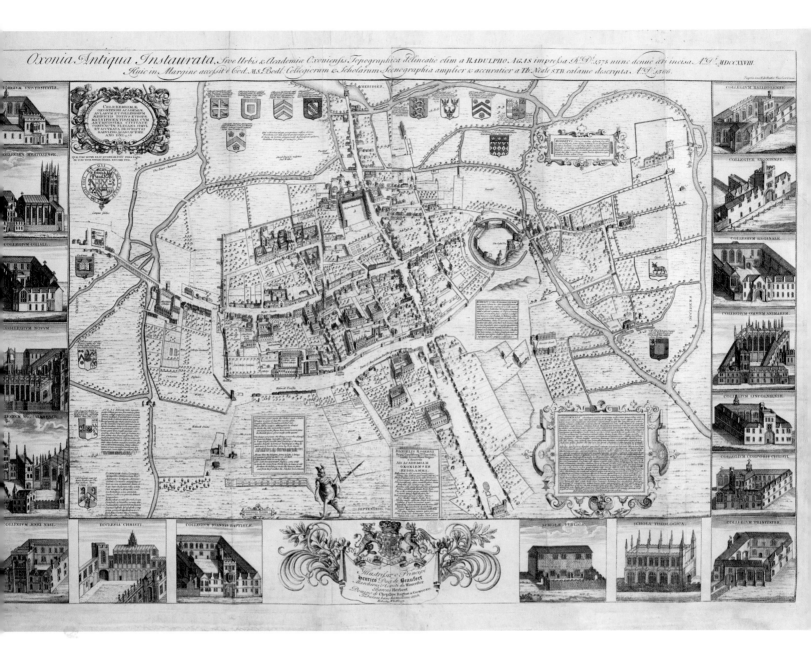

[Fig. 41] Though there is no evidence that Ralph Agas had anything to do with the large woodcut map of London that is known by his name, he did map Oxford, in 1588 (CBTM 19365). Unlike Richard Lyne's map of Cambridge of 1574, added to a book, Agas's Oxford was intended as a map for display, measuring as it did 115 by 85 cm.

However, the detail of Agas's map is not commensurate with the large scale – about 1 inch to 150 feet (1:1800). As with Lyne's Cambridge and Braun & Hogenberg's London maps, the use of Latin perhaps denotes scholarly aspirations. The text includes a note on the foundation of Osney Abbey. (CBTM 19365) [British Library, Maps K.Top.34.9.]

[Fig. 42] Ralph Agas's 'Bedforde shire. A surveigh there of the Maner of Toddington...' made in 1581 is one of the best-known early estate maps. It was made for Lord Cheney and illustrates perfectly how the mapping of smaller towns was often a by-product of a survey of a landowner's properties. This extract covers most of the town, which occupies a very small part of the total map area. (CBTM 20665) [British Library, Add. MS. 38065]

of London and the Norwich map. These are all maps which provided the desk-bound scholar with a virtual townscape.

Town maps for a general range of uses emerged in the late sixteenth century. By this time the military map was well established as a genre, though, as is recounted in Section 14, its spread is geographically limited. Estate maps – maps of properties – constitute a second manuscript genre and are discussed further in Section 8. Estate maps appear in the archival record in the later sixteenth century and examples continued to be produced for the next 300 years. One of the best-known early examples is Agas's map of Toddington in Bedfordshire, 1581 (20665). At this time Toddington had a market, and so qualifies as a 'town', but Agas mapped the whole manor. This example demonstrates how a map can include an 'urban area' but not really be a 'town map' [Fig. 42].

It is characteristic of early town mapping that much was undertaken by map-makers whose main activities lay in other fields of map-making. A first exception is John Speed, who in 1611 published his *The Theatre of the Empire of Great Britain*. The main substance of this atlas is a series of maps of counties, mostly derived from the maps Christopher Saxton produced in the 1570s. An innovative feature is Speed's mapping of cathedral, county and some other significant towns as insets on the county maps. Of the total of sixty-seven towns so mapped, twelve are based on existing maps, including those of Cambridge, Exeter, Norwich and Oxford, while the remainder were surveyed by Speed himself [**Figs. 43, 44, 45, 46,** *overleaf*].[35] Whereas the maps of Cuningham, Hooker and Lyne are confined to books, and the Agas map of London is substantial in size, Speed's maps are compact. They are not, however, maps to be used on the ground for wayfinding, as they do not show even main routes. What Speed supplied, in both his maps of counties and in the inset town plans, is a substitute for landscape and townscape, not an aid for those out and about on the ground. His maps also provided survey data for a number of later imitators.

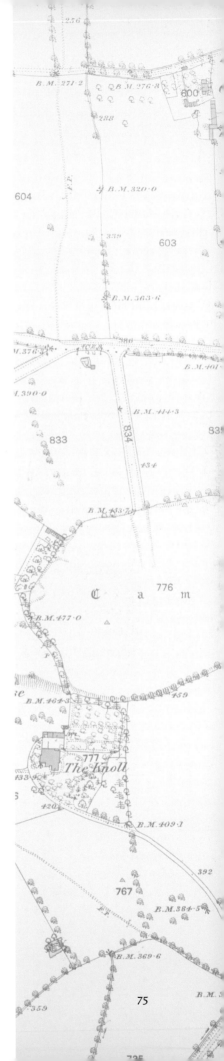

Figures 43, 44, 45, 46
It was much easier to copy an existing map than to survey anew, and all the maps of Oxford illustrated in 43, 44, 45 and 46 are derivatives from Ralph Agas's map of Oxford of 1588.

[**Fig. 43**] is by John Speed, and was published in the *Theatre of the Empire of Great Britain* in 1611. (CBTM 18432) [From British Library Maps C.7.c.20] c.f. Figure 3.

[**Fig. 44**] is by Rutger Hermannides, and was published in his *Britannia Magna*, in Amsterdam in 1661. *Britannia Magna* is a compilation and simplification: thus, though Oxford's colleges are shown, they are not named. Similarly, it is unclear from the vegetation ornament whether orchards or gardens are intended. (CBTM 21374) [British Library, 796.a.5]

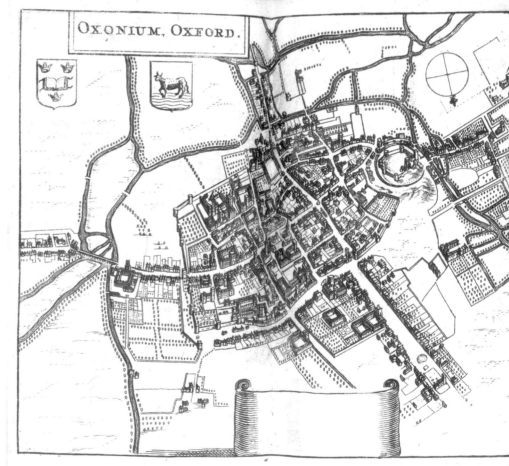

BRITISH TOWN MAPS

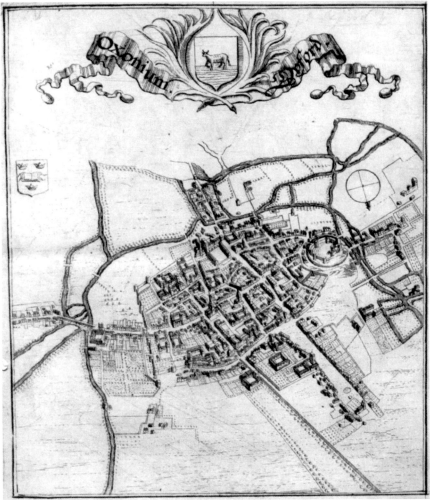

[**Fig. 45**] is from Philip Lea, *Oxford Buckingham & Bark-shire. By C:S: corrected and amended with many additions by P: Lea*, in *All the shires of England and Wales described by Christopher Saxton being the best and original maps with many additions and corrections by Philip Lea*, c. 1689. Speed's derivative of Agas, which had appeared on a copy of Saxton's survey, is here copied onto Saxton's original plate, which by 1689 was in the hands of Philip Lea. The inclusion of Speed-derived plans was perhaps a mixture of 'added value' and seeking a competitive edge over other county maps. (CBTM 21156) [British Library, Maps C.21.e.10: inset on Oxford Buckingham & Bark-shire.]

[**Fig. 46**] This copy of Agas (via Speed) has been variously attributed to Matthias Merian, c. 1650, and to Johann Christoph Beer, c. 1690. The title, 'Oxonium. Oxford.' is another example of the continuing use of Latin as the international language of scholarship – although maps of this sort no doubt aspired to reach a much wider audience than had Agas's original. (CBTM 19732) [British Library, Maps c.27.e.3.(1).

7.

The 'remapping' of British towns

JOHN SPEED'S MAPS MARK the end of a first phase of published town mapping in Britain, in the way that some county maps, by people such as William Smith and John Norden, marked the end of a first phase of English county survey.[36] A new map of London by Faithorne and Newcourt was published in 1658 (18539), though it is likely to have been started in 1643. Civic pride is suggested as the motive for publication [Fig. 47, *overleaf*].[37] Like the Copperplate Map it was large – 162 by 85 cm – and comparatively few copies seem to have been produced: only two survive. It was rendered obsolete rather precipitately by the Great Fire of London in 1666, though it did provide a framework for broadsheet, relatively mass-market, post-Great Fire depictions of London.

The effective start of the 'remapping' of British towns was marked by two near-simultaneous developments: the publication of James Millerd's map of Bristol in 1670 (20407), and John Ogilby's elaborate scheme for a combination of national topographic and urban survey. Millerd's initiative was an essentially local affair – his only other published map seems to be that of Chepstow, 1686 (22476) – but Ogilby's was quite otherwise. He enjoyed the support of King Charles II, anxious to emulate Louis XIV of France and appear as a patron of geography. Vision there may have been, but resources were meagre. Ogilby completed a survey of main roads, published as the first and only volume of *Britannia* in 1675, and surveys of two towns:

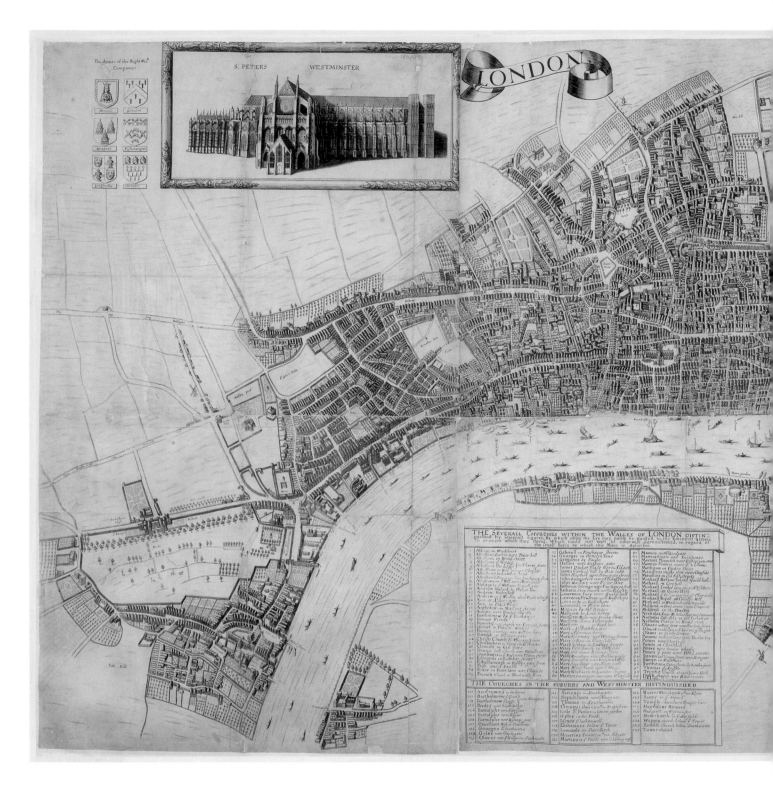

[Fig. 47] *An exact delineation of the cities of London and Westminster and the suburbs thereof, together wth ye burrough of Southwark and all ye thorough-fares highwaies streetes lanes & common allies wthin ye same Composed by a scale,* and ichnographically described by Richard Newcourt of Somerton in the Countie of Somersett Gentleman, engraved by William Faithorne. Although it was only published in 1658, internal evidence indicates that the Faithorne and Newcourt map was actually surveyed between 1643 and 1647. It was published during the Commonwealth, and it has been interpreted as a subtly subversive document intended to assert royalty as the natural state of

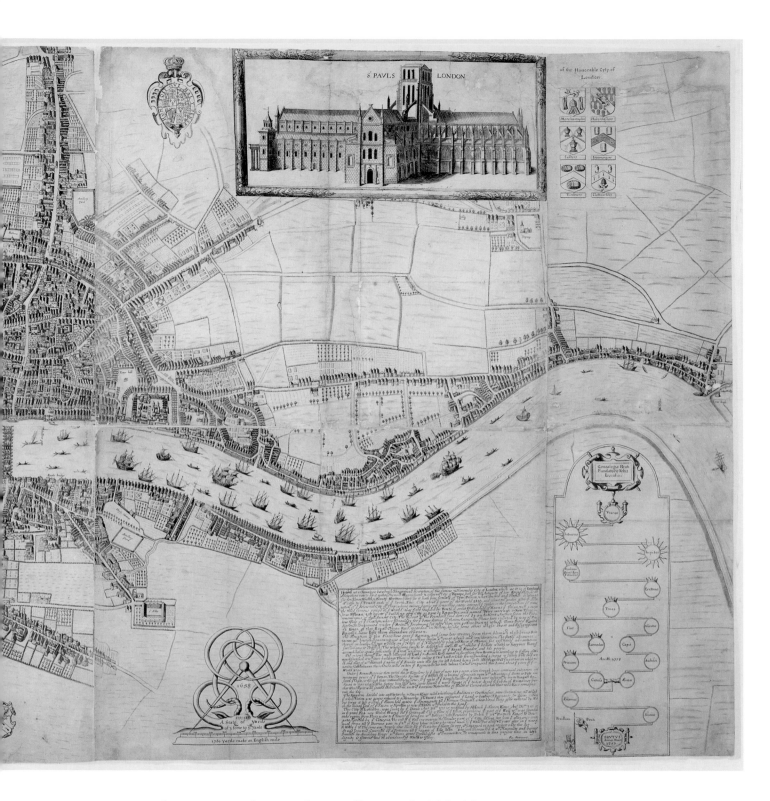

government. The survey was the first of London since that for the 'Copperplate Map' some ninety years earlier, but was abruptly rendered obsolete over four days in September 1666 by the Great Fire of London. As with other large wall maps of British cities, few copies survive. (CBTM 18539)

[British Library, Maps Roll 17.a.3]

Figs. 48 and 49, *opposite.* *In common with every other large-scale survey of London, Ogilby and Morgan's was a rich source for later mapmakers. Most derivatives are at much smaller scales, designed to provide compact reference or wayfinding maps, but the maps of wards in the City of London which accompanied John Strype's edition of John Stow's Survey of London retained much of the detail of the original. Strype's edition of Stow was first issued in 1720; the plates of the maps were reused for the 1754–5 edition of the Survey, although by then London had been resurveyed by John Roque.*

Ipswich (22174) and London (18542) with his son-in-law William Morgan.[38] Once again, these were intended for reference rather than use in the street. *Britannia* is a bulky volume, too large for the saddlebags of a horse. Ogilby's maps of Ipswich and London are wall maps at 1:1200: London measures about 225 by 150 cm, not much smaller than the Copperplate Map. As well as streets, it also depicts what can be interpreted as individual tenements in the town [Fig. 48].

Subsequent remapping of British towns proceeded at a modest pace. Although the population of London offered a large potential market, the extent of the built-up area made detailed mapping to the standard exemplified by Ogilby an expensive proposition. Ogilby and Morgan provided the basis for maps of London for the next sixty years, though often by indirect copying, with various additions and alterations accumulated along the way [Fig. 49]. London was remapped properly between 1737 and 1745 by John Rocque. In terms of scale and content Rocque was less ambitious than Ogilby: his scale is half Ogilby's at 1:2400, and details behind street frontages are omitted [see Fig. 18, *p. 39*]. On the other hand the geographical area covered by his map is much greater. Rocque went on to map several counties and towns: the latter are often insets on the former, emulating Speed. This depiction of towns within larger, relatively bulky entities underscores that these maps were intended for reference rather than for use by persons out and

[Fig. 48] Ogilby and Morgan's mapping of the area of Queenhithe and Vintry wards. (CBTM 18542) [British Library, Maps Crace Port.2.61]

[Fig. 49] *Queen Hith Ward and Vintry Ward, with their division into parishes, taken from the last survey*: a description that was more accurate when this plate was first published in 1720 than it was when it was reused in the 1750s. The derivation from Ogilby and Morgan's work is clearly apparent in the divisions behind buildings, which are schematic rather than strictly accurate.

(CBTM 18384) [From John Stow, revised John Strype, *A survey of the cities of London and Westminster, and the borough of Southwark*: British Library 1791.d.5]

about in the townscape. Omitting detail behind the frontages saved cost and meant that the horrors of places like Gin Lane, depicted so vividly by Hogarth, could be neatly sidestepped by a cartographic 'silence'.

Rocque died in 1761, apparently solvent; Thomas Jeffreys, another leading London map publisher of the time, was not so fortunate. He too commissioned county surveys that included insets of towns, but this very ambition contributed to his bankruptcy in 1766.[39] Jeffreys' greatest venture was his map of Yorkshire, published in 1771, which includes six urban insets: Kingston upon Hull (18556), Leeds (18558), Ripon

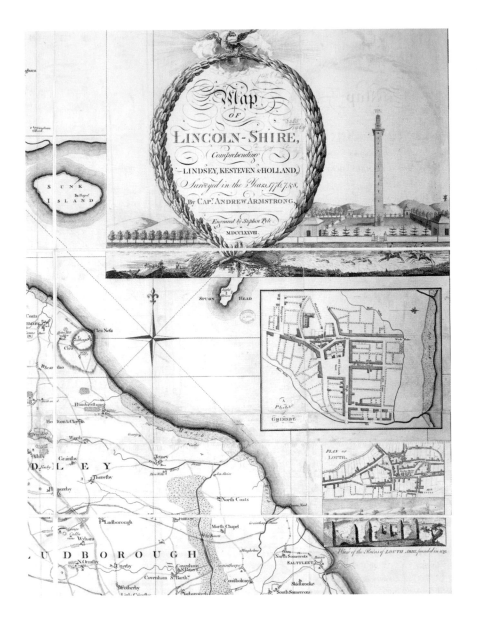

[Fig. 51] Later eighteenth-century town mapping is of variable quality. The Armstrong survey of Lincolnshire, published in 1779, is one of the less distinguished county surveys, and this is reflected in the mapping of Grimsby and Louth, which were fitted in an area of sea below the title of the map. The depiction of the abbey ruins occupies almost as much space on the map as does the depiction of the town; it may be suspected that drawing the abbey was much quicker than surveying the town. The depiction of Dunston Pillar, close to the town centre, occupies a much larger area than do the plans of either Grimsby or Louth. (CBTM 18600) ['Plan of Louth', from Map of Lincoln-Shire, comprehending Lindsey, Kesteven & Holland, surveyed in the years 1776, 7, & 8, by Capt. Andrew Armstrong. Engraved by Stephen Pyle. MD CCLXXVIII: British Library, Maps *3355. (16.)]

(18555), Scarborough (18560), Sheffield (18557) and York (18559). While some of the details of Jeffreys' enterprise are uncertain, it is known that he used local surveyors: one such was the Fairbanks family, who depicted their home town of Sheffield [Fig. 50]. Other county map-makers used insets similarly: the Armstrongs offered four such on their large map of Lincolnshire of 1779, but inexplicably omitted the county town itself [Fig. 51]. William Faden, who by 1800

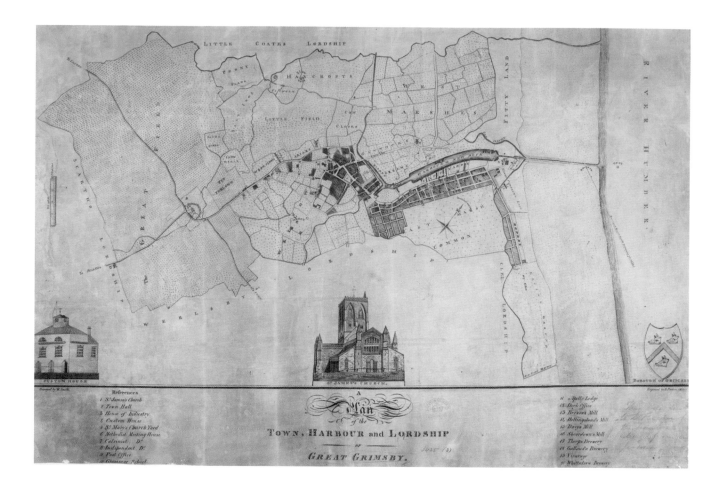

[Fig. 52] In 1801, with a population of 1524, the decayed port of Grimsby in Lincolnshire was perhaps not the most obvious candidate for a map – except that a new dock had just been completed. This perhaps explains the map by W. Smith and G. Parker of *c.* 1812, with the custom house depicted as prominently as the parish church. (CBTM 18227) [British Library, Maps 3425. (3).]

had claims to be the leading British map publisher, also published county maps with insets of towns; by 1820 he had acquired many of the plates of county maps created by other publishers.[40]

Other town map-makers had lower profiles. Some made only a single map, such as William Raistrick, who mapped Kings Lynn in 1725 (21067), or Robert Hall, who mapped Boston in Lincolnshire in 1742 (19346). In view of Boston's then decayed state, such a map may perhaps be explained as a publicity device, designed to attract commerce. Several other ports did commission charts of their approaches in order to encourage trade.[41] Advertising

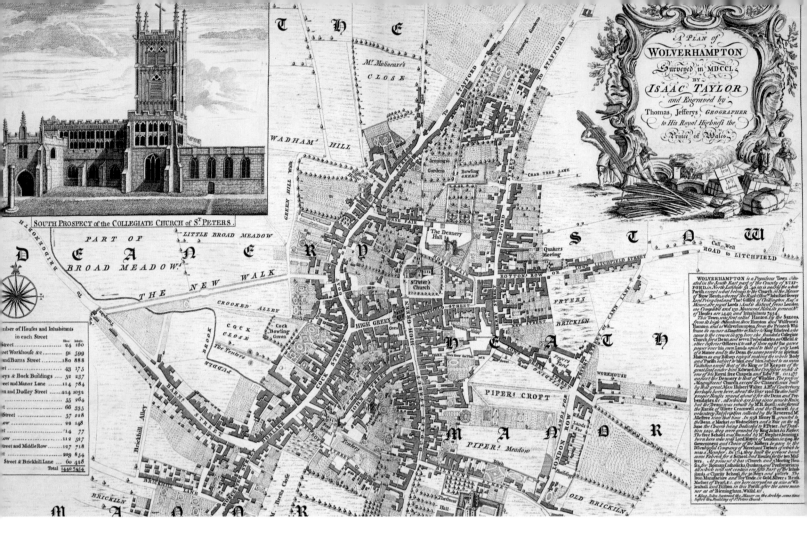

the new dock may likewise explain the rather later map of Grimsby, further north along the coast [Fig. 52]. Some cartographers made two or three maps of nearby places. For example, Samuel Bradford mapped Coventry in 1750 (18323) and Birmingham in 1751 (20181); Isaac Taylor, better known for county and estate surveys, mapped Oxford in 1750 (20405), Wolverhampton in 1751 (19801) [Fig. 53] and Hereford in 1754 (21044). At first Scotland rather lagged behind in both county and urban mapping but, starting with William Edgar's map of Edinburgh of 1753 (21986), the general pattern that developed was similar to that in England, with a mixture of independent town maps

[Fig. 53] Between 1750 and 1754 Isaac Taylor surveyed Oxford, Wolverhampton and Hereford. This illustration is his *A plan of Wolverhampton surveyed in MDCCL by Isaac Taylor and engraved by Thomas Jeffreys Geographer to His Royal Highness the Prince of Wales*, published in 1751. Many churches and other public buildings are shown pictorially rather than in plan, and below the title are scenes of industry befitting a town where metal-working was of ever-growing importance.
(CBTM 19801) [British Library, Maps K.Top.38.48.]

and insets on county maps. In Wales, by contrast, very little was done – the map of Brecon by Meredith Jones, 1744 (22484), is an exception, which moreover did not appear until as late as 1809 as an illustration in a county history [Fig. 54].

London was surveyed again between 1792 and 1799, at 1:2376, by Richard Horwood (18655) [see Fig. 19, pp. 40–41]. His task was more onerous than Rocque's, both because London had expanded considerably and because he mapped detail behind frontages. His map was funded by subscription, with 1,116 subscribers. In his publicity, Horwood suggested that it would be useful to lawyers interested in parish boundaries, tradesmen arranging deliveries to customers, and those wishing to calculate the exact distances between places in order to check hackney carriage fares. Possibly more significant was the contribution of the Phoenix Insurance Company, which might have thought the map useful for settling insurance claims.[42] Map scale and city size means it is a large map – it would total some 5 by 2.5 m, if the forty sheets were mounted as one. Having completed London, Horwood went on to map Liverpool (19265), where he died in 1803. As with Ogilby and Rocque, Horwood's posthumous cartographic reward was that his maps served as a basis for numerous smaller-scale derivatives [Figs 55, 56, *overleaf*].

By 1815 a further remapping of Britain was under way. Changing landscapes and refined survey

ICHNOGRAPHY
of the Town of
BRECKNOCK,
From a Plan by Meredith Jones,
Surveyor,
in 1744.

REFERENCE.

1 St John the Evangelist's
2 The Priory House Cloisters &c
3 The Castle
4 Castle Bridge
5 Upper Bridge on D°
6 Lower D°
7 Struet Gate
8 High Street superior
9 Town-Wall
10 St Mary's Chapel
11 The Bulwark
12 High Street inferior
13 Ship Street
14 Wheat Street
15 St Mary's Street
16 Glamorganshire Street
17 Captain's Walk
18 Watton Gate
19 Watton
20 Old Bowling Green
21 Water Gate
22 Bridge Gate
23 Usk Bridge
24 Usk Mill
25 Struet
26 Lion Lane
27 Church Street
28 Heol rhydd
29 The Postern
30 Pen y dref

[Fig. 54] Few Welsh towns seem to have been mapped in the eighteenth century. A qualified exception was Brecon, mapped by Meredith Jones in 1744, but not printed until 1809 in Theophilus Jones, *A history of the county of Brecknock*. By the time it reached print, the map was distinctly old-fashioned-looking. (CBTM 22484) [British Library, 188.c.10]

techniques made new county and urban maps possible and marketable. A common strand to this new generation of town surveys was that the scale of the maps, both in relation to the ground and in the quantity of paper covered, was such as to imply indoor display or reference rather than use out in the streets. As well as reference tools, such maps might function as advertisements of both a map-maker's skill, and a town's claims to attention. Monumental wall maps were no longer the preserve of London: such 'prodigy

[Fig. 55] As with later surveys, Richard Horwood's map of London provided the basis for numerous derivatives aimed at a wider market. One such was Darton & Harvey's *London Westminster and Southwark shewing the various alterations 1804.* This extract includes the north part of Lambeth. (CBTM 19523). [Detail: British Library, Maps 3480. (78)]

[Fig. 56] The derivation from Horwood is evident by comparison with Figure 55 although the 'Sand Bank' conspicuous on the later map is absent here on this extract from Horwood (see Fig. 19, *pp. 40–41*). [Detail: British Library, Crace Port.5.173]

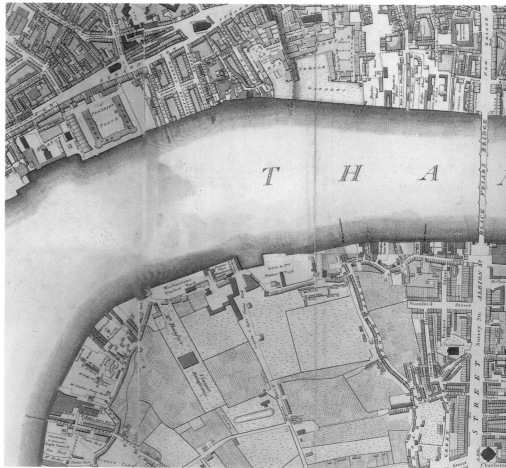

maps' were produced for, amongst other places, Edinburgh (1817: 21679), Birmingham (1828: 20210) [Fig. 57, *overleaf*], Bristol (1829: 21550), Manchester (1831: 19290), Newcastle upon Tyne (1831: 18640) and two for Liverpool, one at 1:7920 including Birkenhead (1835; 19270) and one at 1:3168 (1836: 19065) covering Liverpool alone. At Newcastle, Thomas Oliver's map was published with municipal support, and administrative as well as commercial marketing considerations perhaps came into play [Figs 58, *p. 93*; 59, *p. 94*].[43] A few lesser centres also had their display maps, including Lincoln (1842: 18221) and Grimsby (1848; 19508), both at 1:3168. The Lincoln map was produced by James Sandby Padley and, as at Newcastle, seems to have had a utilitarian municipal function as well as a less specific commercial one; the map was kept under revision, and a final edition was issued as late as 1883.[44] The Grimsby map may owe its inception to a desire to publicise the extensive docks being built at this time. Richard Baker's Cambridge of 1830 (18896), by a surveyor who had mapped the whole county a decade earlier, depicts the town at 1:7128 and includes much rural property because it lay within the borough boundary. Possibly the last in this line of large wall maps is that of Nottingham, *c.* 1862 (19829) [Fig. 60, *p. 95*], based on an earlier sanitary map of the city (20563). It is usual for these display maps to have a decorative outer border which fitted together as a complete frame when mounted as a wall map [Fig. 61, *p. 96*].

[Fig. 57] The two decades after the Battle of Waterloo in 1815 were marked by both the last attempt to map the whole country commercially, and by a series of elaborately finished maps of towns. Such a map was Beilby, Knott & Beilby's *Map of Birmingham engraved from a minute trigonometrical survey made in the years 1824 and 1825*, and published in 1828. It both celebrated the modern commercial world, and acknowledged patronage by being dedicated to Rt Hon. William, Earl of Dartmouth, Viscount Lewisham, etc, 'The zealous promoter of the interests of the town and liberal patron of its public institutions'. The scale of the map was relatively small for such an urban survey – 16 inches to 1 mile (1:3960) – which can perhaps be accounted for by trading off the size of the town against the likely market. The annotations in two empty areas, 'Elliott Refusd. Admittance', and 'Refused Admittance', suggest the inclusive ambitions of the map. The enlargement shows the centre of the town. (CBTM 20210) [British Library, Maps 197.d.2]

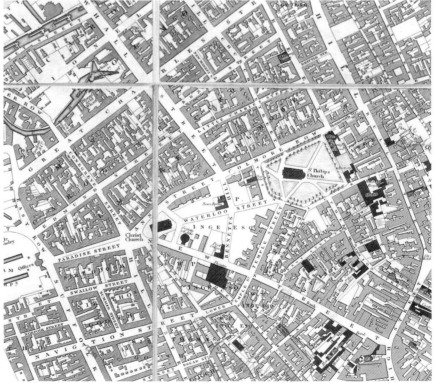

[Fig. 58] As far as is known the *Plan of the town and county of Newcastle upon Tyne and the borough of Gateshead with their respective suburbs; shewing the buildings and different properties contained therein from an actual survey by T. Oliver, Architect and Surveyor* is unusual in that it enjoyed the active support of the municipal authorities, which explains why it is dedicated to the Right Worshipful Benjamin Sorbie, Esq., mayor, and the recorder, aldermen, sheriff and council of the town and county. Thomas Oliver was the borough's architect and engineer, which may explain why there is a concentration on the details of streets and buildings, at the expense of building names. This detailed map was at 1 inch to 3 chains (1:2376), measured 99 by 130 cm, and made full use of the largest size plates then available; it was better suited to wall display or indoor reference than to outdoor use. (CBTM 18640) [British Library, Maps 10.c.43]

A map-maker who stands out in this context of a second remapping of British towns is John Wood (?1780–1847). By the second decade of the nineteenth century he had moved from Yorkshire to Scotland and specialised in urban mapping.[45] Between 1818 and 1846 he mapped at least 148 towns in Britain. Many of his maps of England and Wales survive only as single copies, so it is conceivable that other places were mapped but no map survives. He produced

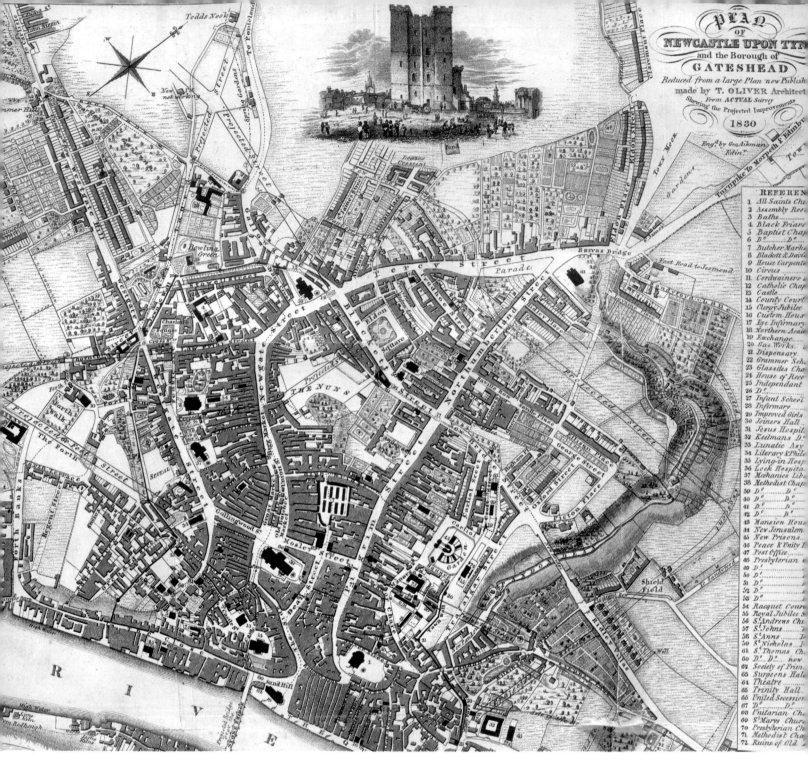

[Fig. 59] As his great map of
Newcastle was too cumbersome
for use out in the streets and
probably too expensive for many
possible purchasers, Thomas
Oliver produced this reduced
version, at 1 inch to 9 chains
(1:7128), or a third of the original
scale, and measuring a compact
27 by 34 cm. The Municipal
Boundary Commissioners used
it, and in 1836 it was also included
in Thomas Oliver's *A new picture
of Newcastle upon Tyne*. (CBTM 18641)
[British Library, 796.b.31]

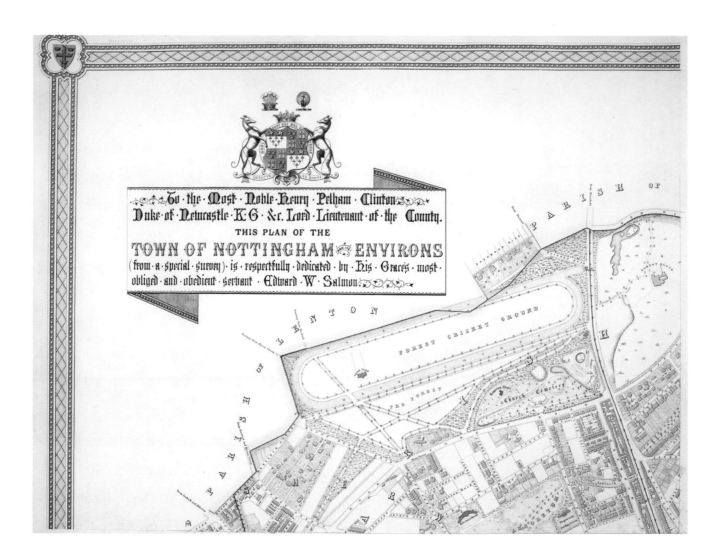

[**Fig. 60**] Few commercial large-scale maps of towns appeared after the late 1840s. An apparent exception is Edward Salmon's *Plan of the town of Nottingham and its environs (from a special survey)*, dedicated to 'the Most Noble Henry Pelham Clinton, Duke of Newcastle, K.G., &c, Lord Lieutenant', at a scale of 1 inch to 200 feet (1:2400), and published in about 1862 (CBTM 19829). In fact it is a reduction from a sanitary survey of Nottingham at 1:396 that had been made over the previous decade. Thus this late example of a town survey straddles both the old world of commercial cartography and the new world of survey for public health improvement that justified the Ordnance Survey's 'town scales'.

[British Library, Maps cc.2.h.5.]

[Fig. 61] Large-scale surveys of towns were far too cumbersome to be carried around in the street: their place was indoors, either bound into atlases or mounted up as wall maps. In order to provide for this element of display, outer edges only had a decorative border, often simulating wood or stone carving, with corner panels. An example of this style is to be seen on Beilby's map of Birmingham (1828). [See Fig. 57, p. 92.] (CBTM 20210) [British Library, Maps 197.d.2]

a series for Scottish towns between 1818 and 1827, which in 1828 were collected in a makeshift atlas. At least forty-eight towns were mapped, at scales varying from 1:1584 to 1:15,840, and when the atlas was issued, proportionately many more detailed town maps had been published for Scotland than for any other part of the United Kingdom [Fig. 62].[46] Wood also mapped at least seventy-five towns in England and sixteen in Wales. Wood's work in England is concentrated in parts of the north of England, the west and east Midlands, and the South West. The pattern of dates and areas reflects his working practice of establishing a temporary local base to survey a group of towns, and then moving on. Thus in 1839 he mapped Market Harborough (21092), Melton Mowbray (21090) and Uppingham (21075), and in 1840, Exeter (18312), Tiverton (20611) and Taunton (21398). It is as though Wood came to a town, surveyed it, collected subscriptions and sales, and then moved on. The maps vary in content, but several of them name owners comprehensively, suggesting that property owners might constitute an important component of his market [Fig. 63, *overleaf*]. Others have detailed lists and locations of inns, suggesting that wall display for the guidance of visitors and commercial travellers was a possible purpose.[47] In terms of detail, if not in ornamental finish, Wood usually approached the level of detail exemplified in the Oliver and Padley maps of Newcastle and Lincoln. His planimetric accuracy

BRITISH TOWN MAPS

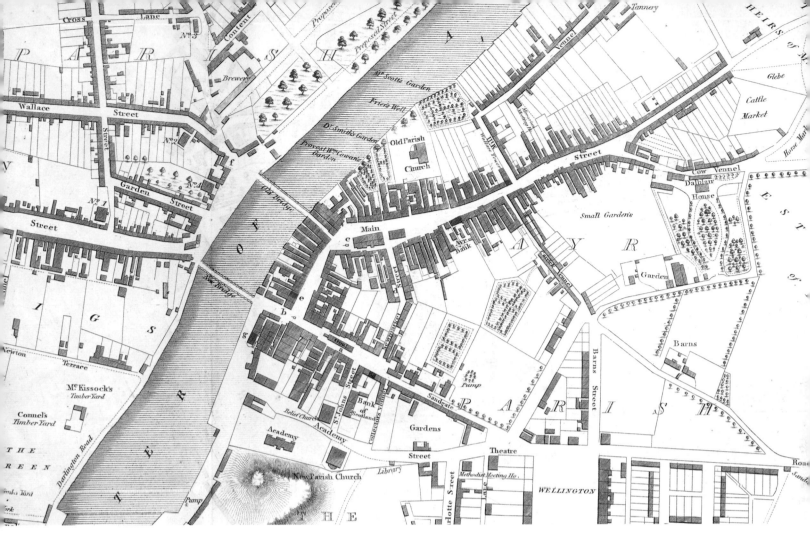

awaits detailed investigation, although he did occasionally confess, as on the maps of Hexham (19915) and Morpeth (18799), that 'the environs are sketched'. Almost all John Wood's Scottish maps are engraved; some of those of England and Wales used the new and much cheaper technique of lithography. His few maps, all in Scotland, that appear to derive from earlier work were included in order to complete the national urban atlas. Sometimes, as at Sunderland and Newcastle, there is a lack of detail in the more closely built-up parts, but this hardly detracts from Wood's overall achievement. He published his last known map, of Airdrie, in 1846 (21773); it was actually a reworking of

[Fig. 62] John Wood was by far the most prolific producer of town surveys in Britain in the first half of the nineteenth century. His earlier activities were mostly in Scotland, and culminated in the issue of an atlas of Scottish town maps in 1828. As this extract from the map of Ayr of 1818 shows, they are finely detailed, with careful attention to the shapes of buildings. It is possible that some of these maps were bought for display in inns and business premises. (CBTM 22032) [Detail: British Library, Maps c.21.e.4]

[Fig. 63] In addition to his work in Scotland, John Wood produced around ninety maps of towns in England and Wales. A striking characteristic of many of them is the naming of owners or occupiers, as here in the map of Berwick-upon-Tweed of 1822. Also named are incumbents of churches and chapels, banking firms, and landlords of inns.

(CBTM 19677) [British Library, Maps 183.q.1.(28)]

his earlier survey, published in 1825 (21971). In the same year the Ordnance Survey published its first 1:10,560 (1:10,560) sheet in Britain, opening a new chapter in British map history.

Wood was unique in the extent of his work, but a loose partnership of map-makers – signing themselves variously Kemp, Kemp & Nichols, Dewhirst, or Dewhirst & Nichols – produced maps which display a strong homogeneity of style [Fig. 64, *overleaf*]. In contrast to Wood, they are relatively small-scale and correspondingly generalised (1:7040–1:19,008, with the latter scale being more typical). Data on Parliamentary representation are commonly provided. As with Wood, there are county groupings: the largest, six in number and dated 1838–9, are of boroughs in Lincolnshire. Again, many survive only in single copies and so there may well be lost maps

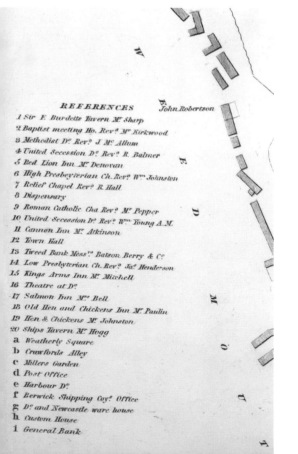

REFERENCES   John Robertson

1 Sir F. Burdetts Tavern Mr Sharp
2 Baptist meeting Ho. Revd Mr Kirkwood
3 Methodist Do Revd J McAllum
4 United Secession Do Revd R Balmer
5 Red Lion Inn Mr Denovan
6 High Presbeyterian Ch. Revd Wm Johnston
7 Relief Chapel Revd R Hall
8 Dispensary
9 Roman Catholic Cha Revd Mr Pepper
10 United Secession Do Revd Wm Young A.M.
11 Cannon Inn Mr Atkinson
12 Town Hall
13 Tweed Bank Messrs Batson Berry & Co
14 Low Presbyterian Ch. Revd Jas Henderson
15 Kings Arms Inn Mr Mitchell
16 Theatre at Do
17 Salmon Inn Mr Bell
18 Old Hen and Chickens Inn Mr Paulin
19 Hen & Chickens Mr Johnston
20 Ships Tavern Mr Hogg
a Weatherly Square
b Crawfords Alley
c Millers Garden
d Post Office
e Harbour Do
f Berwick Shipping Coys Office
g Do and Newcastle ware house
h Custom House
i General Bank

of other places. Unlike Wood, this 'partnership' did nothing, as far as is known, in either Wales or Scotland.

In the second half of the nineteenth century new town surveys were derived either from mapping prepared for sanitary planning, or from evidently rapidly executed 'skeleton plans' that had a similar municipal-administrative nature. Thomas Spooner's Burton-upon-Trent of 1857 (20458), reworked in 1865 (20800), is an example of these. Where Ordnance Survey base-mapping was available it was possible to publish street or general reference maps at low cost: both the Bartholomew-Heywood maps of Blackpool (19623) and York (19778) of *c.* 1869 and 1871 respectively [Fig. 65, Fig. 66, *p. 101*] are of obvious Ordnance Survey derivation, yet the growth of Blackpool in the twenty-five years or so between the official survey and the commercial publication was such that considerable unofficial revision was necessary. The source of these revision data has not yet been identified.

One avenue for commercial map publishers was to collaborate with borough engineers and surveyors. Sometimes this became a long-lasting association: Bartholomew's plan of Dundee (21752) was revised by the borough engineer from the start in 1876, and was still being revised in 1949 [Fig. 67, *p. 103*]. This was especially valuable where, as at Dundee, Glasgow and Edinburgh, maps were issued regularly, often annually, in directories or yearbooks. It is unclear how extensive this practice was: it may be that map-makers applied

[Fig. 64] More modest than those by John Wood are the maps produced variously by Kemp, Kemp & Nichols, Dewhirst, and Dewhirst & Nichols between 1832 and 1841. The purpose of this mapping is unclear: it is less elaborate than that of John Wood.

Were the maps simply intended to appeal to local patriotism? As this extract from the map of Cambridge shows, the producers were interested in population and administration. (CBTM 21195) [Detail: CUL Maps.aa.53.84.1.]

[Figs 65 and 66] *Although from the 1840s the Ordnance Survey provided a basic framework for commercial map-makers to offer derivatives, for growing towns it was necessary for the publisher to carry out his own updating if the map was to be credible. This certainly happened in the late 1860s with Abel Heywood's handy plan of Blackpool & Southshore – price sixpence. The map was prepared by the Edinburgh firm of Bartholomew, and is extremely useful for indicating the extent to which Blackpool had developed since the Ordnance Survey had mapped the nascent resort in the early 1840s.*

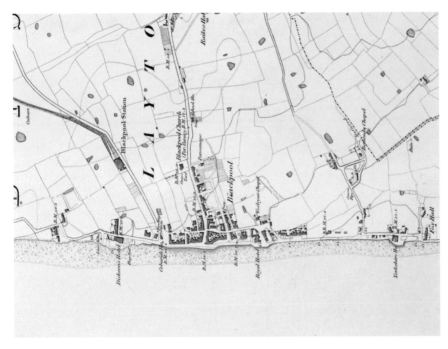

[Fig. 65] Blackpool as mapped by the Ordnance Survey in 1844.
[British Library Maps OS Lancashire 1:10,560 first edition sheet 50.]

[Fig. 66] The Bartholomew-Heywood mapping of 1869: the considerable expansion in the built-up area from the 1840s to the 1860s can be seen. (CBTM 19623)
[British Library Maps 3230 (3)]

to borough engineers for information on new streets and other developments, and that some were found co-operative and others were not. This was certainly Phyllis Pearsall's experience when she was preparing the *A–Z Atlas of London* around 1935–6.[48] Although after 1939 the Ordnance Survey revised more frequently, it was only from about 1970 that 'continuous revision' covered most towns with a population above about 15,000, and so there was still scope for extensive unofficial revision.[49]

[Fig. 67] The Bartholomew six-inch map of Dundee was based on Ordnance Survey mapping at the same scale, but was regularly revised with assistance from the borough engineer. One of its functions was to illustrate Mathew's annual directory of Dundee, and so it can provide useful data on annual growth between Ordnance Survey revisions. (CBTM 21752) [*Plan of Dundee revised to date by Wm Mackison, C.E., F.R.I.B.A. Burgh Engineer 1899, facing title page in* The Dundee directory 1899–1900*..., Dundee: James P. Mathew, 1899: National Library of Scotland*]

PLAN OF
DUNDEE

Revised to date by Wm Mackison, C.E., F.R.I.B.A.
Burgh Engineer
1899

SCALE OF HALF A MILE

F I R T H   O F   T A Y

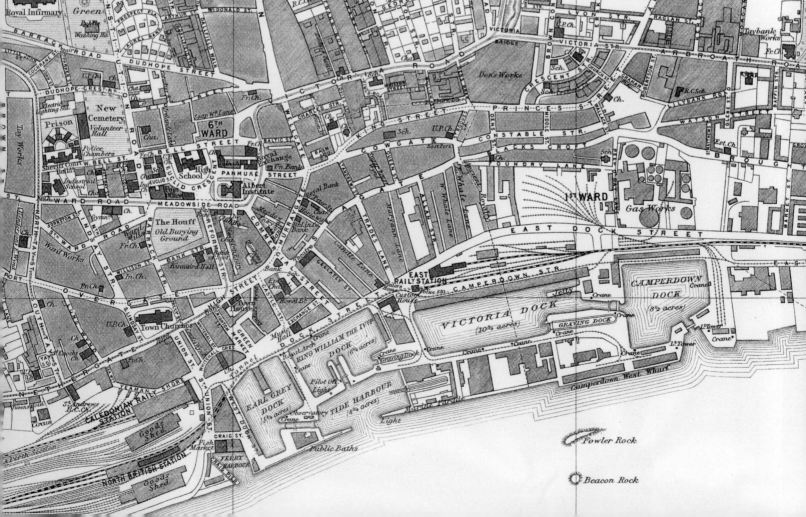

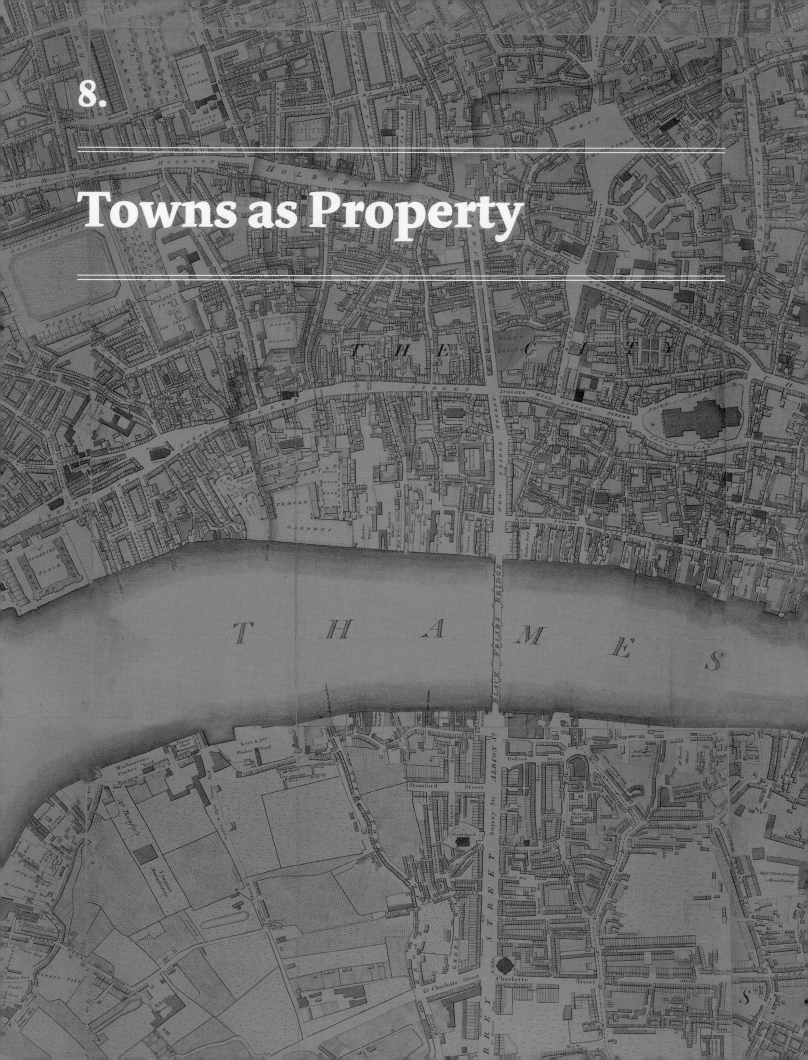

8.

Towns as Property

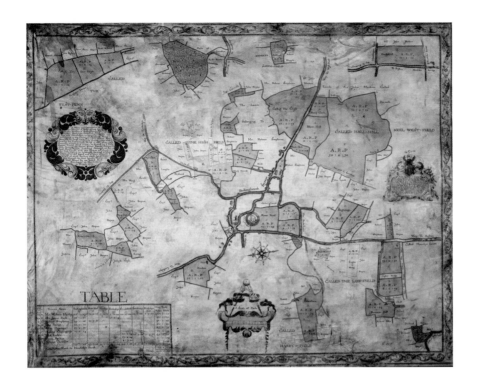

Estate maps

Estate maps depict the property of a particular individual or institution, and first appear in the cartographic record in the sixteenth century.[50] As the purpose of the map was to portray an individual's property ownership, estate maps depicting towns occur where places were in single or dominant ownership. Notable early examples are Ralph Agas's map of Toddington, 1581 (20665) [Fig. 42, *p. 74*], Ralph Treswell's map of Kettering, 1587 (20775) and John Norden's map of Higham Ferrers, 1591 (20694). Maps such as these might be made to facilitate the management of estates, or to record property that had recently been acquired. They might also be made for display, to serve as a substitute for the actual landscape [Fig. 68].

[Fig. 68] Estate mapping is by its nature focused on a particular owner's land, and this could be reflected in the incidental mapping of towns. Part of [Old] Bolingbroke in Lincolnshire was owned by the Duchy of Lancaster, and Duchy estates there were mapped by Jarred Hill of Canterbury in 1719. The Duchy land is coloured green: by this time it evidently excluded much of the town, and so, although the built-up part is indicated pictorially, there are no details of the plots occupied by the buildings. (CBTM 18591) [Detail: from The National Archives, MPC 1/118.]

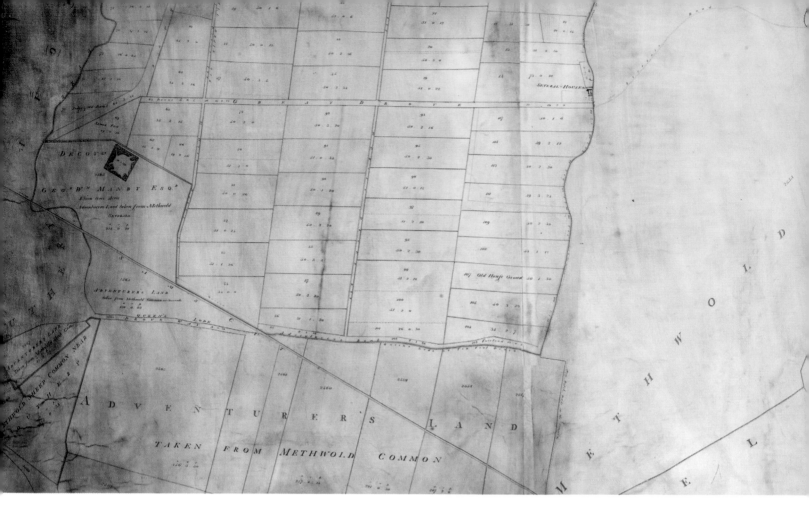

As estate maps are private and thus not subject to any degree of legal protection and, moreover, are overwhelmingly manuscript rather than printed, survival is very much a matter of chance. Sarah Bendall has catalogued 785 Cambridgeshire estate maps made before 1836, and estimates that there may have been 1,000 or more originally. For this county, investigation is helped by many of the maps having been made for Cambridge colleges, which might be expected to be more preservation-minded than individuals. It is possible, therefore, that rates of loss in other counties were much greater.[51]

The mapping of towns as a by-product of estate management presents, therefore, a fragmentary

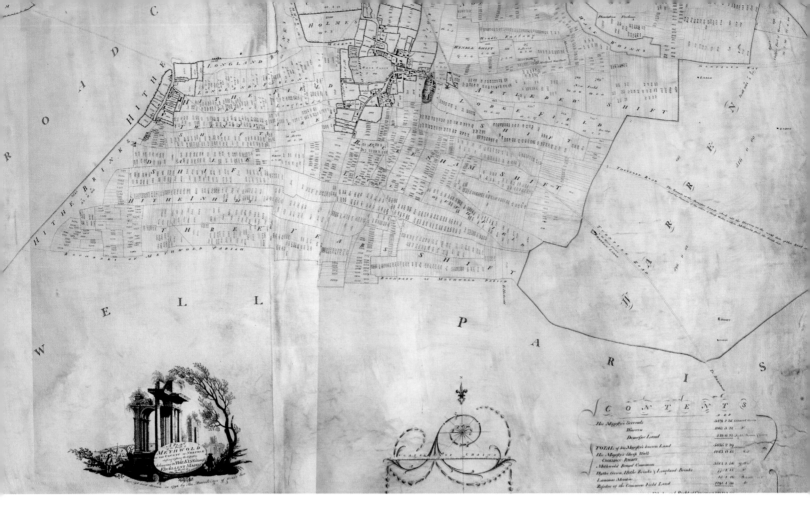

record of urban Britain, in time as well as in space. For some smaller towns, often the only known map up to the first third of the nineteenth century is an estate map, but it is exceptional to find a wide temporal spread of estate mapping of a particular town [Fig. 69].[52] Woburn in Bedfordshire, with six examples between 1661 and 1868, is quite unusual; it was part of the Bedford estates. Downton in Wiltshire has six examples between about 1740 and 1865; Huddersfield has ten maps between 1716 and 1850.[53] In contrast, another town dominated by the Dukes of Bedford, Tavistock in Devon, has no similar long sequence of estate maps. The only substantial map of Tavistock is of 1867, at 1:1152 (18249).

[Fig. 69] 'A plan of the parish of Methwold in the county of Norfolk distinguishing the estates belonging to the King's most excellent majesty in right of his Duchy of Lancaster' by Thomas Bainbridge was made in 1796. As it was necessary to map the whole parish, the whole of the small town was mapped. Buildings are shown in plan, other than the church which is shown pictorially: such relics from an earlier tradition in map-making would continue far into the nineteenth century.
(CBTM 18628) [Detail: The National Archives, MR 1/207]

Enclosure maps are closely related to estate maps – they are manuscript maps in the main and mostly produced by the same type of private land surveyor. As with estate maps, the portrayal of a town is incidental to the main purpose, which in this case was to serve as an instrument to effect parliamentary enclosure. This was a process of rationalisation of rural properties and land rights that ran through the eighteenth century and into the nineteenth.[54] Unlike estate mapping, which was fairly evenly distributed across Britain, enclosure maps which include portrayals of towns are almost all concentrated in Midland counties and the east of England, which reflects the pattern of Parliamentary enclosure itself. This is a genre of town maps unknown in Wales and Scotland.[55] Enclosure was a once-for-all process, but the maps produced might be reused for other purposes.

Many small market centres in England counted as 'towns' for our purposes had extensive open fields that were enclosed between 1750 and 1850. Because enclosure was often accompanied by commutation of tithe, which affected already enclosed areas, the whole parish was mapped, including the town. The type of detail shown is similar to that for estate maps [Fig. 70]. As with estate maps, enclosure maps may well be the only extant detailed map of a town produced before Ordnance Survey large-scale maps after 1840.

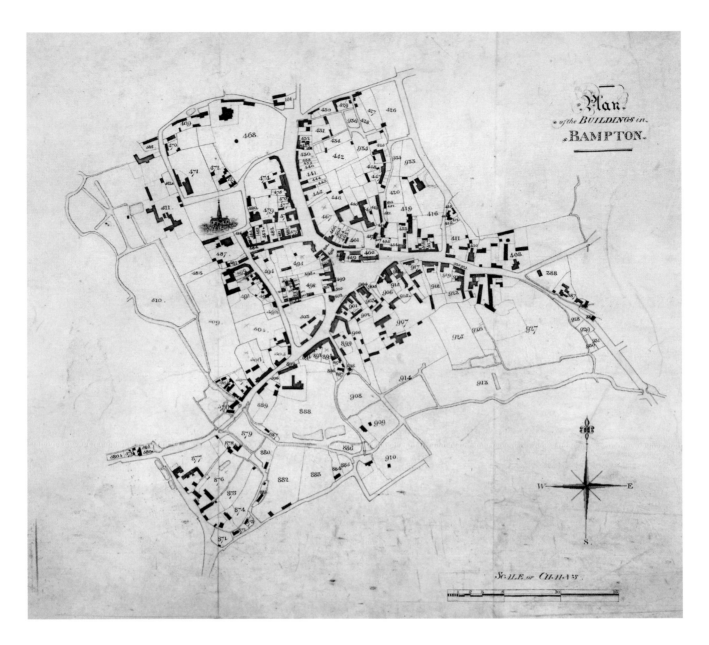

[Fig. 70] Although the avowed purpose of enclosure mapping was the division of commons and open fields, often the old enclosed areas were included. Such mapping is often the first extant of some smaller market towns. One such is Bampton in Oxfordshire, where enclosure was completed in 1821. The main enclosure map is at 1 inch to 6 chains (1:4752), but the town is mapped at 1 inch to 3 chains (1:2376). Building shapes are generally shown in some detail, but the church is shown pictorially. (CBTM 12396). [Detail: The National Archives, MR 1/703]

Many towns, even if they were not affected by open arable fields, did have commons on which townspeople had rights. These commons often adjoined built-up areas and acted as a constraint on urban expansion. The outstanding example of this is at Nottingham, where enclosure of the open fields and pastures around the town was enacted in 1845, and where the final award of twenty years later is characterised by a layout of streets ready for building, and with some sewerage and other infrastructure indicated (17252). Earlier examples are at Bolton in Lancashire (1807: 15252), Croydon (1800: 18363) and Portsmouth (1822: 14568), though at these places the pressure on land was rather less and the development process more protracted than at Nottingham. The resulting maps show the division of common into lots, but before building started.

Rating maps

A second type of map that appeared in the late eighteenth century was for the assessment of rates for poor law and other purposes.[56] These differ from estate and enclosure maps in that, although again the mapping of urban areas per se was not the primary purpose, where they cover towns these urban areas are portrayed in considerable detail. Comparatively few such maps survive, but they include a significant number for parishes in the City of London. Rating maps comprise two broad categories: maps of whole

parishes made to assist poor rate assessment, and maps of areas subject to drainage rates. The latter occasionally include small towns and, once again, this may represent the only pre-Ordnance Survey large-scale mapping of a town. The most extensive drainage map of all is of the Bedford Level, mostly in Cambridgeshire, made by Lenny & Croft of Bury St Edmunds, at 1:23,760, and lithographed in 1842. It includes plans of several towns, including March and Ely, which lay outside the area to be drained (14409).

A notable early example of a map being used for the assessment of poor rates is that of Nantwich (1794: 15322); others are Hodnet (Shropshire) (1815: 15364) and Bishops Stortford (1823: 14161). Making and using rating maps in England and Wales was greatly encouraged by the Parochial Assessment Act of 1836, which was a logical consequence of the Poor Law Amendment Act of 1834. The 1836 Act provided for more equitable assessments and reassessments for poor-rating; its application was not compulsory, but the Poor Law Commissioners could make orders for reassessment, and these might – but did not have to – involve making a map [Fig. 71, *overleaf*].

Although numbers of extant rating maps are very small by comparison with other categories of property maps, they make a proportionately larger contribution to the urban mapping record than do these other categories. This is particularly so for London, where between 1775 and 1914 about forty maps of parishes

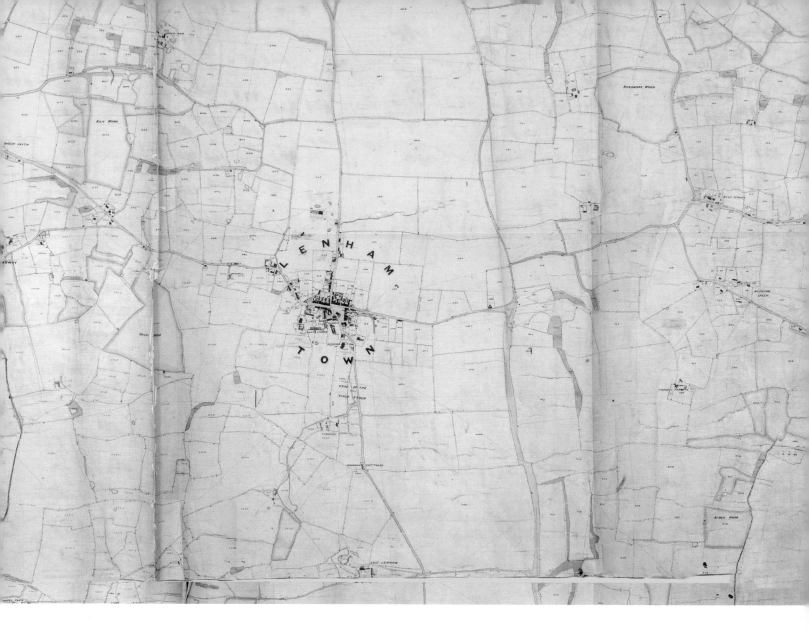

[Fig. 71] Although every holding had to be assessed for poor-rating purposes, there was no compulsion to make a map, and consequently the cover of towns by rating maps is patchy. Those rating maps that were made are often the most detailed map of a place before the large-scale Ordnance Survey in the second half of the nineteenth century. An example is the survey of Lenham in Kent, made by Thomas Thurston of Ashford in 1838, at the 3-chain (1:2376) scale. The mapping was used for both rating and for tithe commutation purposes. The mapping is neat and functional rather than intentionally decorative: inhabited buildings are infilled carmine, and uninhabited ones are infilled grey. (CBTM 03834) [Detail: The National Archives, IR30/17/220.]

are known to have been made, with rating purposes often a significant, if not the only, motive.[57] Maps used for rate assessment might also be used for other purposes, such as recording boundaries or general reference as a 'parish map' or 'vestry map'. What might originate as a rating survey might be developed into a general smaller-scale reference map, as was the case with a map of Lambeth engraved and published in 1841 (18212). Outside London extant maps are very unevenly distributed. Rating maps are unknown in Scotland.

Tithe maps

Tithe maps constitute the largest group of manuscript maps for which town mapping was an incidental by-product. They cover some three-quarters of England and Wales and are very variable in scale and content. For very many smaller towns the tithe survey is the first extant large-scale map.

Some tithe, the traditional 'tenth' of a farmer's income paid to support the established Church in a parish, had been commuted for money or land by enclosure or other local acts in some parishes, but tithe dues were still a considerable burden on the landowning interest in England and Wales when the Tithe Commutation Act was passed in 1836.[58] The object was to commute payments in kind or by custom into a fixed money rent-charge. Tithe was agricultural in its incidence but, as with enclosure, it occasioned some urban mapping, either because towns very often

contained titheable land in the form of gardens or dairies or because a built-up area was mapped as part of a parish as a whole.

Tithe maps display some local homogeneity, for example where a group of parishes was mapped by the same surveyor, but overall there is considerable heterogeneity of scale and detailed content. All tithe maps show the boundaries of holdings and of titheable areas. Most portray details of individual fields and a minority depict land use in considerable detail. All are accompanied by an apportionment which sets out in some detail the owners, occupiers, description of premises, land use and acreage. This information is also sometimes provided for tithe-free land, particularly for the built-up parts of villages and small towns.

[Fig. 72] As with estate and enclosure maps, tithe maps sometimes include towns, but the extent of cover is variable. The most extraordinary of the tithe maps that include an urban area is that of Brighton, where only some cowsheds remained titheable: hence this strangely diagrammatic depiction of 1851. (CBTM 08811) [Brighton tithe map, The Keep, Sussex]

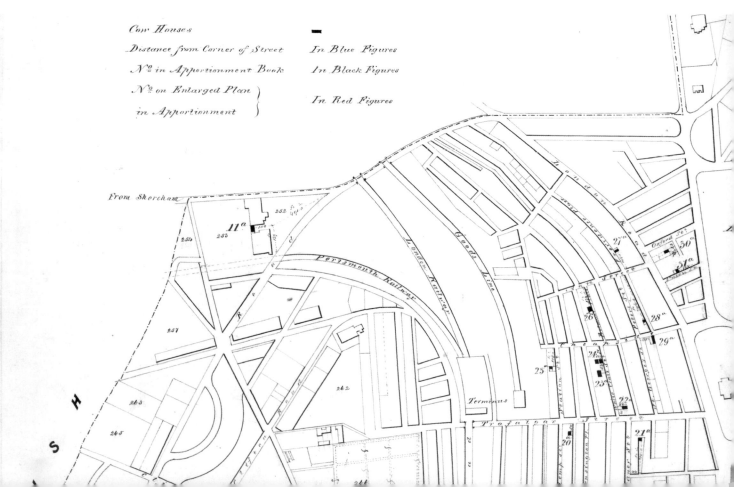

Small towns might be mapped in their entirety on tithe maps, while larger places are mapped either fragmentarily (for example, some London suburbs, such as Paddington: 04968) or not at all. Particularly odd is the mapping of Brighton, where the only remaining tithes *c.* 1840 were collected from urban cowsheds, which were mapped in detail in semi-diagrammatic form (08811) but related to an overall 'key' map of the town [Fig. 72]. Swansea (11523) and Whitehaven (01293) were exceptional in that they were mapped in great detail, at 1:1584 and 1:792 respectively, with careful attention to building shapes, and divisions in terraces of buildings. It is to be suspected that both of these tithe maps were derived from earlier surveys made for other purposes, as yet unidentified [Fig. 73].

[Fig. 73] For a few towns tithe maps were made in considerable detail, as at Swansea, surveyed at 1 inch to 2 chains (1:1584) in the early 1840s. Churches and other public buildings are emphasised by heavier shading, as they often are on printed town maps. (CBTM 11523) ['Plan of the Town of Swansea Glamorganshire'. The National Archives, IR30/51/122]

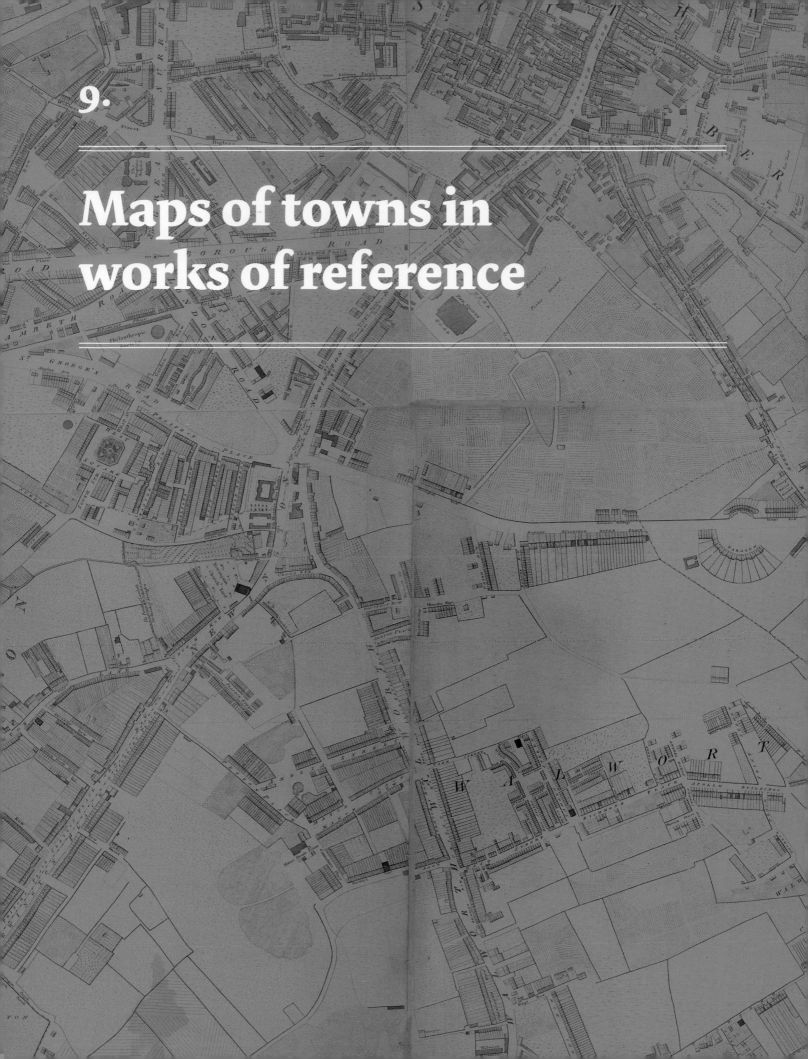

9.

Maps of towns in works of reference

IN SECTION 6 WE NOTED that some of the earliest maps of British towns are found in books, both manuscript and printed. These include the early manuscript maps of London (19876) and Bristol (23271), which illustrate works that can be at least broadly classed as histories [see Figs 34, *p. 63*, 35, *p. 65*]. The first printed map of a town outside London, Cuningham's Norwich of 1559 (20570), is unique in that it illustrates a text on surveying [see Fig. 38, *p. 69*]; the next, Richard Lyne's of Cambridge of 1574 (20684), proved to be part of a modest trend, of maps that illustrate books that, if not outright histories, at any rate have a strong historical theme [see Fig. 40, *p. 72*].

The Norwich and Cambridge maps were originally printed to illustrate particular texts. The very fact that they were printed gave them a circulation unthinkable for any manuscript map, and thus facilitated their emulation. John Speed's county maps provided materials for others, particularly on the continent where collections of town plans and town views were an established genre. Braun and Hogenberg began publishing their monumental *Civitates orbis terrarum* in 1572 and issued the sixth and last volume in 1618. They included ten depictions of British cities and towns: that of London (18462) can be traced directly to the Copperplate Map [see Fig. 39 *p. 71*]. The final volume appeared late enough to include three maps derived from Speed. Other collections including derivatives of Speed's maps

were published by Daniel Meisner (1631), Rutgur Hermannides (1661), Johann Christoph Beer (1690) and Vincenzo Coronelli (1706) [Figs 74, 75, 76 and 77 (overleaf)]. Together these perpetuated increasingly outdated or planimetrically distorted views, from Cuningham's Norwich onwards, far into the eighteenth century. Coronelli actually published two versions of Cuningham's Norwich, as mediated via Speed (22114, 22119) in 1706, notwithstanding that a new survey of the city had been published by Thomas Cleer in 1696, in two versions (20573, 20574).

There are scattered examples of maps as illustrations in books through the seventeenth century. An early example is a Spced derivative of Bath in Thomas Johnson's *Thermae Bathonicae* of 1634 (22505), and another Speed derivative, of Coventry, appears in William Dugdale's *The Antiquities of Warwickshire*, 1656 (18322). More appeared in the eighteenth and early nineteenth centuries. The most elaborate in terms of cartographic illustration is John Strype's edition of John Stow's *Survey of London*, published in 1720, which includes forty-seven plates of parish and ward maps, as well as general maps of London and Westminster and numerous illustrations of churches and other notable buildings [see Fig. 49, *p. 83*]. The maps mainly derive from Ogilby and reappeared in a further edition published in 1756, around the time that Rocque's survey was printed. The general approach was imitated in several later histories of

London, notably by William Maitland (1756), John Noorthouck (1772–3), and William Thornton (1784).[59] Away from London, perhaps the most elaborate collection comprises the six town plans in Thomas Hutchins' three-volume history of Dorset, 1773–5. The maps of Bridport (19341: **Fig. 78,** *p. 122*), Dorchester (19342), Poole (19339) and Wareham (19340) seem to have been specially commissioned for the work.

Not all county histories of the period include maps. Manning and Bray's monumental history of Surrey, 1804–14, is replete with line engravings of churches, country houses and other buildings, but has no maps of Surrey towns. By contrast some very local or single parish histories contain maps, as for Fulham (1813: 22276), Hampstead (1814: 21504), Tottenham (1818: 21505) and Kensington (1820: 22277) [**Figs 79,** *p. 123,* **80,** *p..124,* **81,** *p. 126,* **82,** *p. 127*].

Maps in urban histories are often found as frontispieces, where they could serve several functions. One is practical: it is easiest to find and handle a folding map at either the front or the back of a volume. One function might be for reference – to help locate places or features described in a text. They can also function as general illustrative views or visual prologues. The map in William Richards' *The History of Lynn*, 1812, faces the title page of the first volume (18339) [**Fig. 83,** *p. 128*]. Revd Charles Coats commissioned a map for the frontispiece to his *The History and Antiquities of Reading* of 1802 (19331). He wrote later that such maps

[Fig. 74] Berwick-upon-Tweed was mapped in the early 1570s for military purposes, but these plans were unpublished. Because of its situation between England and Scotland the town was of considerable strategic importance, and was at least comparable with a county town or cathedral city in status. It was thus a natural subject for John Speed, and his is the first published survey of the town, in 1611. Indications of its military significance include 'Kings Stables', 'Store Houses' and several named 'mounts'. (CBTM 18432) [British Library, Maps C.7.c.20

[Fig. 75] Berwick's strategic importance made it a natural choice when in 1661 Rutger Hermannides copied some of Speed's maps for *Britannia Magna*. In contrast to Speed's original, there is a marked lack of text.

(CBTM 21366) [British Library, 796.a.5]

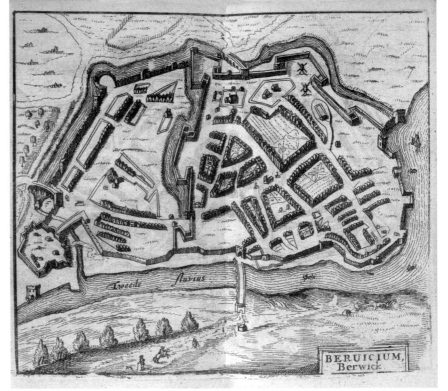

BRITISH TOWN MAPS

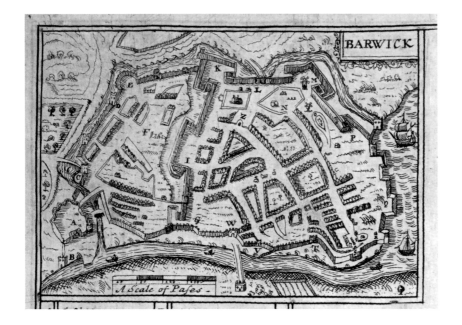

[Fig. 76] Though Saxton's county maps of the 1570s had official backing, it was left to Philip Lea to enhance their usefulness by including versions of Speed's town surveys. Lea shows the origin of the survey by including the 'Kings Stables', 'Store Houses' and named 'mounts'. (CBTM 21135) [British Library, Maps C.21.e.10, inset on Northumberland]

[Fig. 77] Though it may be disputed whether this map owes its origin to Matthias Merian c. 1650 or Johann Christoph Beer c. 1690, it is evident that it is another example derived from Speed's work. (CBTM 19732) [British Library, Maps c.27.e.3.(1)]

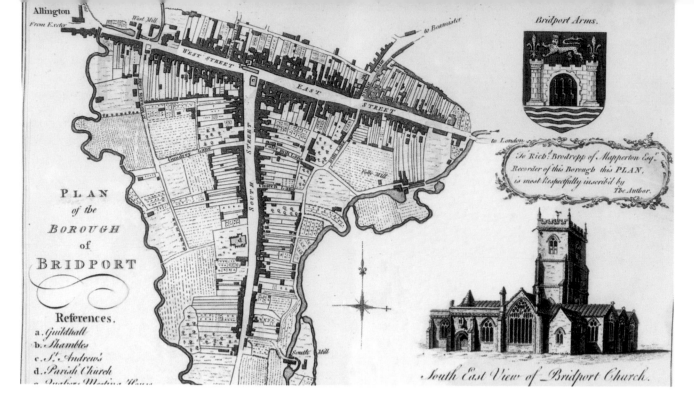

'are perfectly uninteresting except to the inhabitants; &... unless taken from actual survey, & upon a large scale, like the plan of Reading, in which you will see every alley & yard, & even gardens, correctly laid down under my own eyes, they are mere deceptions'.[60] He had been charged £40 for the engraving and thought this excessive, although the cost of the field survey was paid by Reading Corporation. Not everyone was able to draw on such resources: a small map illustrating a history of Malmesbury published in 1805 (23244) is as minimal as can be, showing little more than the principal streets, the church and some monastic remains [Fig. 84, p. 129].

The production of town and county histories reached a peak in the early nineteenth century. While town histories could be produced to reasonably manageable dimensions, county histories were invariably outsize in both price and bulk, and this

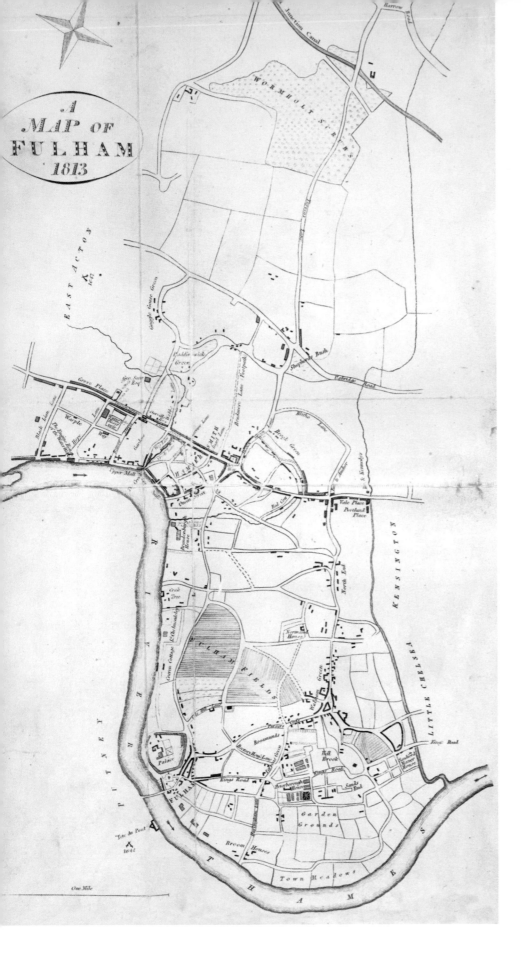

[Fig. 79] A map of the parish could be a useful addition to a narrative history, and several examples are known for places which in the early nineteenth century were on the fringes of London. This rather generalised example was included in Thomas Faulkner, *An historical and topographical account of Fulham*, of 1813. The map is engraved. (CBTM 22276) [British Library, 2366.cc.2]

[Fig. 80] The map at the opening of John James Park, *The topography and natural history of Hampstead*, of 1814, has a note 'Compiled from various surveys with sketched corrections'. Field boundaries appear somewhat incomplete. (CBTM 21504) [British Library, G.3783]

naturally restricted their market. Around the time
of the Napoleonic Wars, topography and history
were fashionable pursuits as can be seen in what
Nicholas Alfrey describes as 'growing awareness
of the precise and varied character of regional
landscape, made all the more poignant by the ever-
present fear of invasion'.[61] This interest is reflected
in two particular series of topographical works, *The
Beauties of England and Wales* of 1804–10 and *Magna
Britannia*, started before 1806 but abandoned in 1822.
The Beauties was published in parts by John Britton.
Parsimonious or local customers could content
themselves with their own county; others could build
up a topographical library piece by piece. The work
was liberally illustrated with both line drawings and
maps. Britton's maps, including all the counties of
England and Wales and twenty-one maps of towns,
were collected and issued in 1810 as *The British Atlas* by
a consortium of publishers, including Faden. In line
with the project's title, the urban maps are mainly of
cathedral cities and other historical centres, such as
Colchester, but include Liverpool and Manchester.
Maps were prepared to a uniform format – though
not scale – and to an excellence of finish unknown
since Speed. There is invariably a vignette; this might
include the cathedral, but might be an old bridge
(Chester) or abbey gateway (Colchester), the arms
of the town and, where relevant, of the bishopric
[**Fig. 85,** *p. 129*]. The choice of towns was not entirely

[Fig. 81] Another parish on the fringes of London that had its history illustrated with a map is Tottenham, in 1818. 'A map of the parish of Tottenham in the county of Middlesex from an actual survey' accompanies William Robinson, *The history and antiquities of the parish of Tottenham High Cross*. The acreages in fields are an unusual feature for a map of this sort. The detail depicts the southern part of the elongated built-up area at an enlarged scale.

(CBTM 21505) [British Library, 577.d.26]

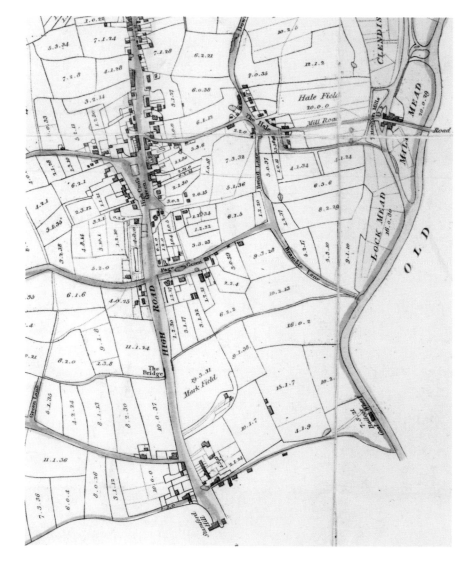

BRITISH TOWN MAPS

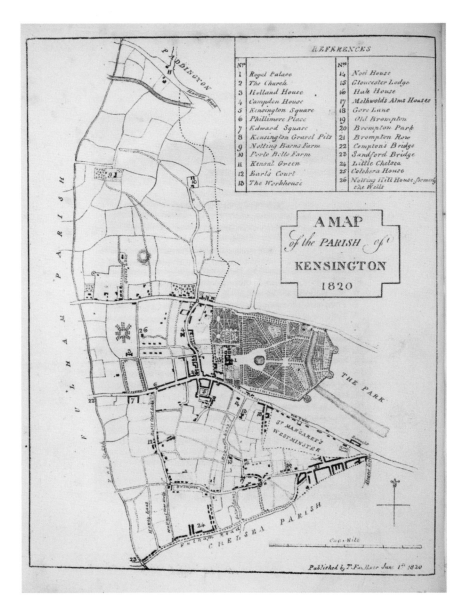

straightforward, though places such as Liverpool and Manchester can be explained by both their economic importance nationally and in terms of possible sales. It is notable that the cathedral cities of Ely, Lincoln and Peterborough are unrepresented, most likely because there was no up-to-date mapping of these places to serve as a starting point. *The Beauties* is essentially a work of compilation from published sources, rather than of original research.

[Fig. 83] It was quite common for town and county histories of the later eighteenth and earlier nineteenth centuries to be accompanied by maps. Kings Lynn in Norfolk was more frequently mapped than most towns, and the availability of existing maps may have helped the inclusion of this one as a frontispiece to William Richards, *The History of Lynn…* (1812).

Although the content is generally similar to the map of the town included as an inset on the Milne-Faden county map of 1797 (CBTM 18233), it is by no means identical: some updating is apparent. No street names are given, which may reflect Richards' views on the recent renaming of several of them by the town's Improvement Commissioners: he wrote that

they were 'most capriciously, childishly, and confoundedly changed'. As a radical he perhaps objected to the use of 'King', 'Queen' and the latest national hero, 'Nelson'. (CBTM 18339) [British Library, 10368.i.10]

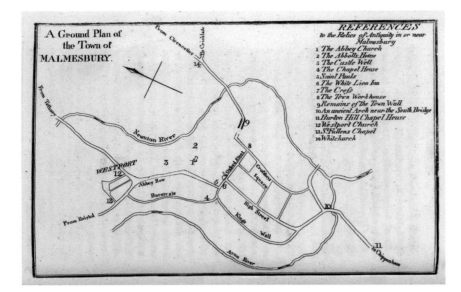

[**Fig. 84,** *left*] Maps to accompany histories are sometimes purely functional, as in this example, illustrating J. M. Moffatt's *The History... of Malmesbury* of 1805. Ordinary buildings are reduced to areas of hatching, and the few more significant buildings of this small town are identified by number. (CBTM 23244) [British Library, G.3929]

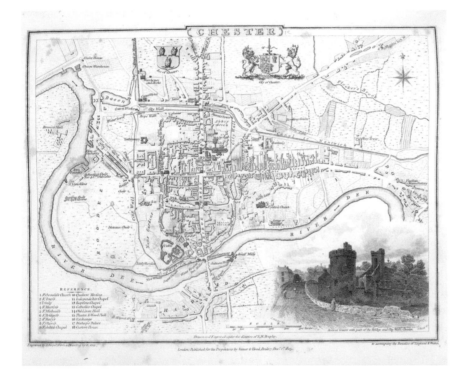

[**Fig. 85,** *above*] John Britton's *The Beauties of England and Wales* (1804–10) is a compilation rather than an original work of research, intended to appeal at least as much to those who yearned an aura of antiquarianism as to those who wanted scholarly accuracy. Production values are high: this is clearly apparent in the maps of towns, exemplified by this one of Chester, which includes the arms of the bishopric as well as of the city. (CBTM 18400) [British Library, Maps 11.b.3]

10.

Maps of towns
in directories

DIRECTORIES WERE PRODUCED from the mid-eighteenth century and had two quite separate functions: as indexes to businesses, and as catalogues of residents.[62] They often combined these functions with history and topography, and this echo of the county history and guidebook declined only slowly. It was still a feature of the best-known series, Kelly's Directories, in the 1930s.

Directories vary in physical size: by the later nineteenth century some locally produced ones were quite attractively bound and suitable for display in a reception room, whereas bulkier directories for whole counties and larger cities, culminating in the massive, near-cubic format of Kelly's directory for London, were probably destined for the office or library shelves. The inclusion of maps in directories had parallels with county histories and guidebooks, and the distribution of places mapped is likewise erratic. It is only in the second half of the nineteenth century that maps appear in directories for some larger places, notably Bristol (1852: 21061), Birmingham (1863: 20389), Bradford (1872: 21358) and Cheltenham (1892: 21548). By contrast directory maps appear for a number of smaller places markedly earlier: Perth (1837: 22920), Dudley (1839: 20916), Worcester (1841: 23275) and Reading (1842: 22517). It seems that while a map appended to a directory might be useful, particularly in a smaller town where perhaps there was no published street map, it was not an essential

[Fig. 86] The inclusion of maps in directories was novel when Edward Baines included plans of four Yorkshire towns in his *Yorkshire*, published in 1822. The 'Plan of the town of Leeds with the recent improvements. Surveyed in 1821, by Chas Fowler, Leeds' claims to be an independent production, rather than derived from an earlier survey. The scale of the main map is 1 inch to 12.5 chains (1:9900): an extension to include the then-important potteries is at 1 inch to 24 chains (1:19,008). Several large areas are annotated 'Building Ground', with streets laid out and named. At top left, balancing the title, is a south-east view of the Philosophical & Literary Society's Hall. The enlargement shows part of the town centre around Briggate. The prominent building numbered '54' is the White Cloth Hall. (CBTM 19760) [British Library, Maps 7.c.23]

accompaniment to directory listings. A map could readily be provided if there was an existing survey to draw on, but the example of Birmingham shows that this practice was not axiomatic. Including maps was facilitated by the existence of fairly up-to-date surveys which could serve as a starting-point, but constrained by the cost of engraving a new plate.

What proved to be the nineteenth century's most elaborate group of directory maps of towns are two sets prepared for the directories of Yorkshire (1822: four maps) and Lancashire (1824: ten maps) published by Edward Baines.[63] The introductory sections of each of these directories are a mix of history and economic, statistical and administrative information. This compendium approach is echoed in the maps, a number of which were specially surveyed and are the first known maps of those towns. The advent of these finely produced maps seems to have had a catalytic effect elsewhere [Fig. 86]. The map produced for Pigot's directory of Manchester (19214) symbolises technology, commerce and modernity in every respect: in not only its topographical content but also in its embellishment. It was marketed both in this leading directory and as a separately sold street map [Fig. 87, *overleaf*].

By the 1870s Kelly's had emerged as the leading firm of directory publishers in Britain, although local directories continued. The first Kelly directory to include a street map was of London, in 1856. Gradually from about 1880 more of their directories were

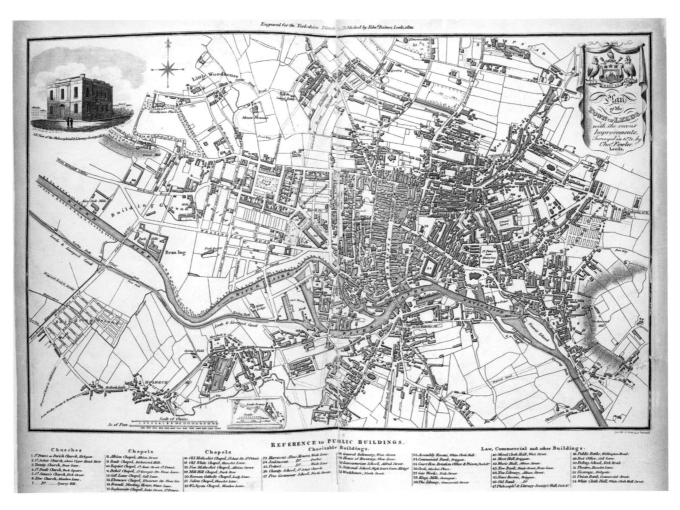

Engraved for the Yorkshire Directory. Published by Edw.d Baines, Leeds, 1822.

REFERENCE to PUBLIC BUILDINGS.

Charitable Buildings.

Churches	Chapels	Chapels		Law, Commercial and other Buildings.

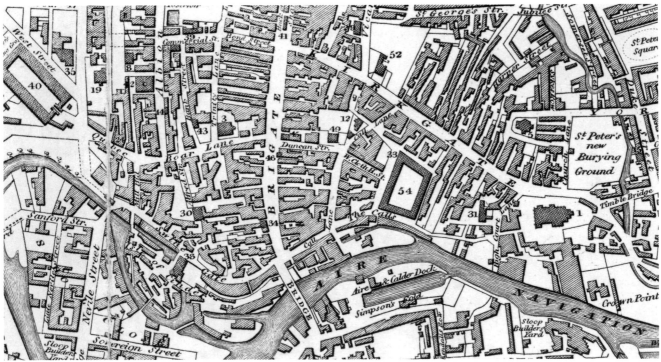

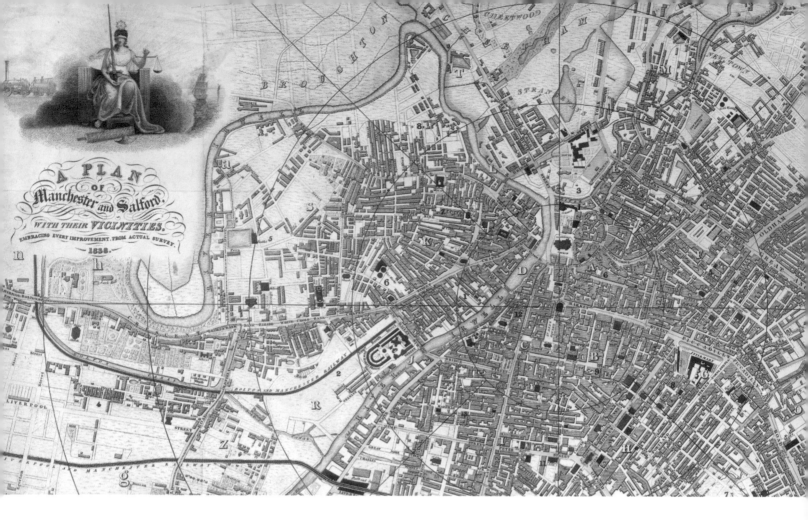

[Fig. 87] When Pigot included a map in their directory of Manchester of 1804, it was an unremarkable addition. The replacement of 1829 was much more distinguished: by 1836 it had been updated to include not only new streets and buildings, but also symbols of industry. The railway locomotive pictured to the left of the cartouche is of a type particularly associated with the Liverpool and Manchester Railway. (CBTM 19214) [Detail: Cambridge University Library, Maps bb.18.G.89 Maps.bb.18.G.89]

furnished with maps. Unlike guidebook maps, those in directories did not have to be suitable for the pocket and often took advantage of the full size practicable with litho-printing. Kelly's used a mix of mapping, some produced wholly in-house and some from other publishers, notably G. W. Bacon. At Liverpool they apparently took over a map originally prepared for a rival directory (19488). The multi-functionality of maps appearing in directories is illustrated by later nineteenth-century examples for Edinburgh (21736) and Glasgow (21328). These last were sold as ordinary folded maps and were also overprinted on several occasions to show proposed and actual administrative boundaries [Fig. 88].

The gradual decline of the street directory, particularly for residential information during the twentieth century, can be ascribed to the development of the telephone service with its accompanying directories, which supplied at nominal cost much of the core information, particularly about private residents, that had hitherto been the preserve of street directories. Kelly's struggled on, but finally gave up in 1974. New entrants to the field in the late twentieth century, such as Thompson's, were variations on the business section of telephone directories and do not include comprehensive street maps.

[Fig. 88] In 1865 John Bartholomew of Edinburgh produced six-inch (1:10,560) scale maps of both Edinburgh and Glasgow, for inclusion in the post office directories of those cities. Both are based on the Ordnance Survey mapping at that scale – only just published for Glasgow – but both were regularly updated in a way that Ordnance Survey mapping was not. Both cities were expanding in the later nineteenth century, and so the area of cover of the map had to be extended as well. Illustrated here is part of the Edinburgh map and the cover, as published in 1897. (CBTM 21736) [Detail: British Library, Maps 31.b.35]

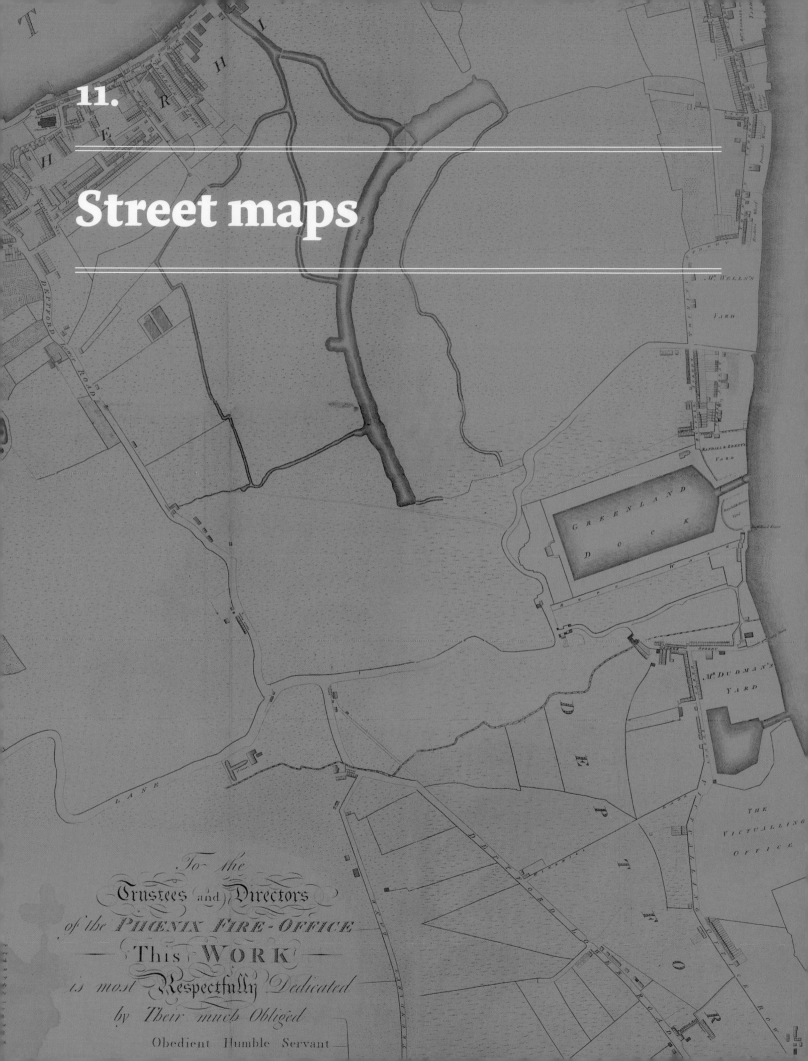

11

Street maps

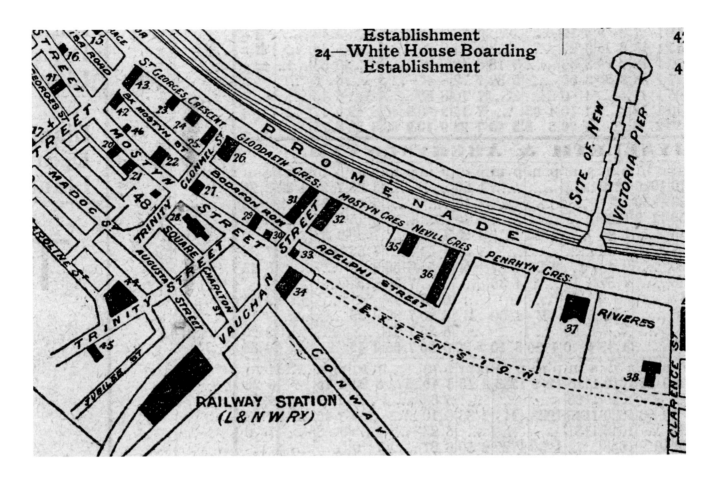

Establishment
24—White House Boarding
Establishment

[Fig. 89] For finding one's way on the ground certain features are essential. They are exemplified by this extract from *Plan of Llandudno* by T. T. Marks CE, Surveyor, Llandudno, and printed and published by W. H. Evans & Sons of Chester in 1900. Streets are named and public and other significant buildings are shown, but there is no indication of more ordinary buildings. (CBTM 22754) [British Library Maps 6453 (4)]

WAYFINDING IN AN URBAN CONTEXT requires a street map, and this in turn implies a certain minimum content: street names, buildings of general interest, transport infrastructure and open spaces [Fig. 89]. Street maps depicting both less and more than this have been published. Amongst the more elaborate are the Ordnance Survey 'Town Maps' of the early 1920s – an aesthetic but not a commercial success [Fig. 90, *overleaf*]. At the other extreme are skeletal maps which omit most public buildings [Fig. 91, *p. 139*]. Portability is an important attribute [Fig. 92, *p. 140*].

The same basic survey could provide the material both for a relatively comprehensive, though cumbersome, reference map and for a much more

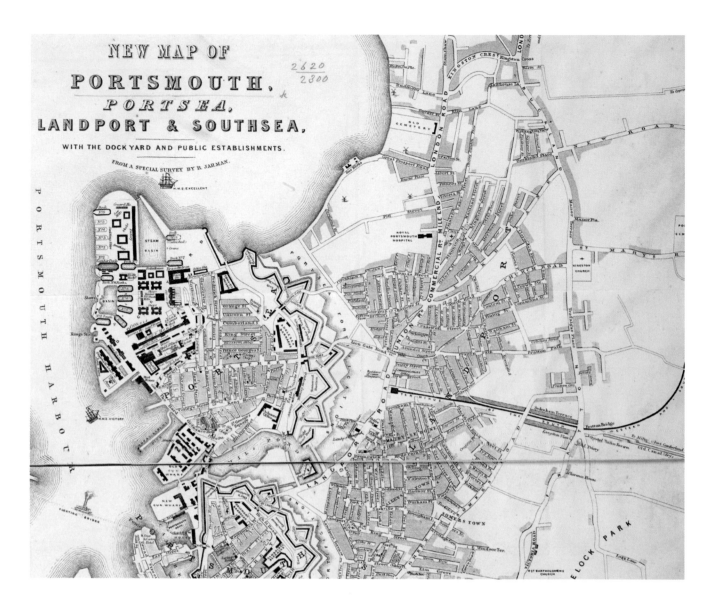

[Fig. 90, *opposite*] Perhaps the most elaborate 'street maps' produced in this country are those published by the Ordnance Survey. They reused basic material drawn for the national 1:10,560 map series, and enhanced it with the liberal use of colour: the detailed scheme owes as much to earlier estate mapping styles as it does to conventional ideas of street mapping. These maps were expensive to produce, comparatively few were sold, and the series was discontinued after 1923. This is an extract from the map of South Shields.

[Detail: British Library, Maps 4575.(3.)]

[Fig. 91, *above*] Although most street maps show more than streets, some show very little more! This is an extract from the *Map of Portsmouth*, published in 1881 by Curtiss & Sons, Railway & Shipping Agents, of Portsmouth and Ryde. It shows not much more than street names – and Messrs Curtiss's premises.

(CBTM 19850) [Detail: British Library, Maps 2620. (2)]

[Fig. 92] There are no theoretical limits on the minimum or maximum size of a map, but in practice street maps are constrained by two factors. On the one hand, they cannot be too bulky; but on the other, they cannot be folded so small that they are easily mislaid. This 'PopOut' map of London represents a combination of compactness with a cover – roughly postcard-size – and a map large enough to be displayed effectively. This example actually includes five separate maps, of Central London, the West End, Theatreland, bus routes and the Underground. [Compass Maps London PopOutmap (2011): worldwide patents granted and pending including EP 1417665, CN ZL 02819864.6 and CN ZL02216471.5]

compact and inexpensive street map. The Ordnance Survey exemplifies this very well. Its large-scale mapping has always enjoyed only limited sales in its original form, mostly to professional and business users, but it also provided the basis for inexpensive and accessible street maps, developed and published by commercial companies.[64] Similarly, commercial street maps might serve as a basis for more specialised mapping, as at Oxford [Fig. 93].

Most towns and cities in early modern Britain were relatively compact, and could be traversed on foot from one side to the other in twenty minutes or less. There was therefore not much obvious scope for maps for wayfinding on the ground at this early date. A stranger could always ask for directions. Indeed, those who travelled by stage coach were likely to be delivered to an inn from where they would be directed further to their destinations. The great exception in size was London, which dominated all other towns in

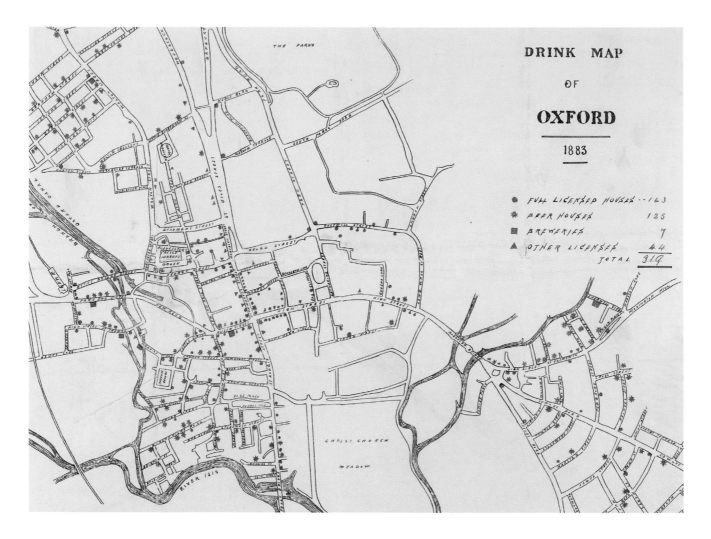

both population and economic influence. What was really a conurbation, drawing in Westminster and Southwark, had by the time of the Great Fire long since expanded beyond its walls; it had no obvious equivalent of a marketplace or other clear focus and had several centres. It is, therefore, unsurprising that London saw the birth of the wayfinding street map: John Norden's *A Guide for Cuntrey men In the famous Cittey of London by the helpe of which plot they shall be able to know how farr it is to any street. As also to go vnto the same without forder troble* (19512).[65] Two more appeared almost simultaneously in 1675–6: from

[**Fig. 93**] Street maps are primarily for wayfinding and general reference, but can also serve as a base for more specialised uses. Here a basic outline of streets has been used for a map showing the distribution of licensed premises in Oxford; it was issued in 1883 to draw attention to the large number of 'houses for the sale of intoxicants' and 'the pernicious effects of drink'. A number of such 'drink maps' were produced in the late nineteenth century to support temperance campaigners. (CBTM 22143) [Detail: BOL C17:70 Oxford (7)]

[Fig. 94] John Overton's *A New and Plaine Map of the Citty of London…*, dateable to 1675–6, is the earliest map of London that seems to have been suitable for carrying around by visitors. As this illustration shows, it is accompanied by explanatory letterpress. (CBTM 22183) [Bodleian Library, Gough Maps London 12]

Robert Green & Robert Morden (23327) and from John Overton (22183). Neither was explicitly described as a street map, but both were relatively compact – a mapped area of about 55 by 35 to 40 cm, supplemented in the Overton map by explanatory letterpress [Fig. 94]. These are by no means the first small-size maps of London, but they are the first not to be a book illustration or inset on a larger map. Several compact maps were issued in 1666–7 to illustrate the Fire of London, but these were in the nature of news maps rather than wayfinding street maps.[66] The mid-1670s was an opportune time for mapping London, as the city was largely rebuilt, and any earlier depictions could be dismissed as outmoded.

The actual demand for a compact visitor's map may have been relatively modest. It would depend not only on the number of visitors, but also on their purchasing power and their belief that a map would help them. The first map to carry an explicit hint that it is intended to be portable, and hence for wayfinding as opposed to reference, appeared in the mid-1720s: Thomas Bowles's *A Pocket Map of London* (22206). Other maps of London with similar titles followed [Fig. 95]. After 1800 the formula 'stranger's guide' was preferred. Either way, the purpose was clear and maps were published in sufficient quantity to indicate that there was a considerable market, although we are unlikely

[Fig. 95] In the eighteenth century maps of London for carrying about often announced their intended market by including the phrase *A Pocket Map* in their title. One such is Thomas Bowles's *A Pocket Map of the Cities of London, Westminster & Southwark...* of 1727. (CBTM 22206) [Bodleian Library, Gough Maps London 21]

ever to discover how many were actually printed and even less likely to know what proportion was carried about and used in practice.

Away from London the wayfinding street map was slower to develop, and when it did, it took two forms: either, as in London, as an independent map sold on its own merits, or included in a guidebook. Free-standing town maps that might have been useful for visitors appeared of Edinburgh in 1778 (22013) and Brighton in 1788 (18711), and Glasgow had a combined guide-with-map in 1797 (22101).

Through the nineteenth and into the twentieth centuries, further towns were furnished with basic street maps, and for a few places several were produced simultaneously. Apart from the special case of London, the best-served places tended to be those where street mapping had commenced relatively early – say before about 1830 – places such as Bath, Birmingham, Brighton, Edinburgh, Leeds, Liverpool and Manchester. Later they were joined by others. There was a boom in mapping at Bournemouth after 1880, which can be traced to its steady growth as an upmarket resort and also to the availability from 1872 of Ordnance Survey base-mapping.[67]

In the early 1920s the Ordnance Survey published twenty-one 'Town Maps'. They are multi-coloured and undeniably attractive, but they were also expensive, and a commercial flop [*see* **Fig. 26**, *p. 51*]. A subsequent monochrome series issued in the early 1930s went to the other extreme: the covers warned users that they were 'Produced by direct untouched transfer from the normal Six-inch Sheets and printed on cheap paper. Not suitable for joining up to other sheets and not reliable for Engineering or Survey purposes.' Actually, at a shilling (£0.05) each they were good value for money, and by 1939 a number had been reprinted. From 1979 the Ordnance Survey produced a further series, variously 'Town Map' or 'City Map' according to official status: not many were produced, apparently because they depended on local initiative. One of the first to be published, of Cambridge, was the last of these to survive. Though produced by Ordnance Survey, it was published by Heffers, a celebrated Cambridge bookshop.

A notable feature of many street maps is a reference system. This usually takes the form of an alpha-numeric grid, a method that is still familiar today. The first appearances of this device on urban maps that we have discovered date to 1720, when both Henry Overton and Thomas Taylor published 'squared' maps of London (18675, 19519) [**Fig. 96,** *overleaf*]. The system was especially useful when exigencies of space made it useful to number, rather than name, churches and public buildings on a map.

One of the applications of a reference system was in ascertaining distance. To this end a minority of maps were provided with distance-circles radiating from a central point. On a few maps these circles are

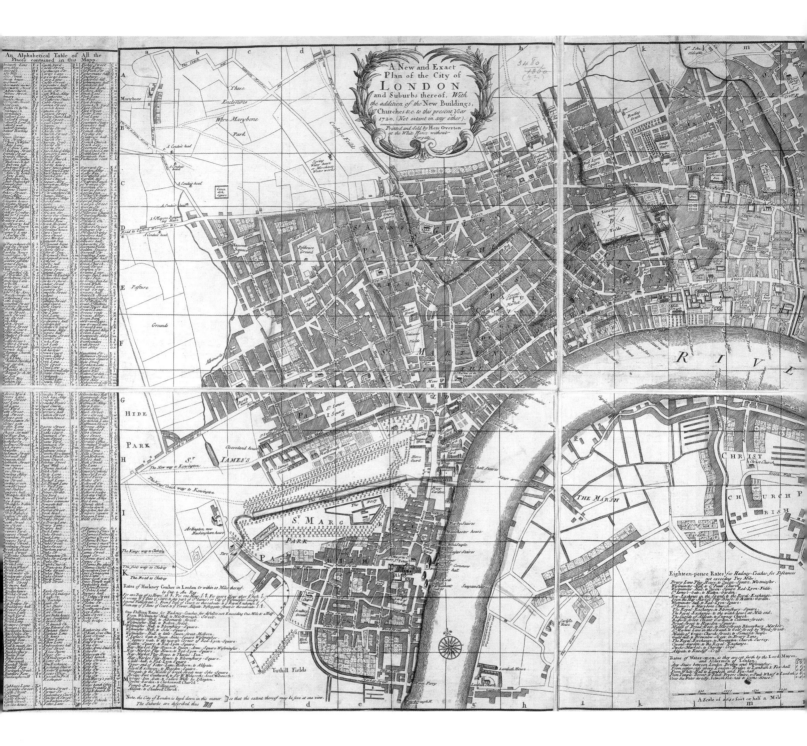

An Alphabetical Table of All the Places contained in this Maps

A New and Exact
Plan of the City of
LONDON
and Suburbs thereof, With
the addition of the New Buildings,
Churches &c. to this present Year
1720, (Not extant in any other).
Printed and sold by Hen: Overton
at the White Horse without
Newgate.

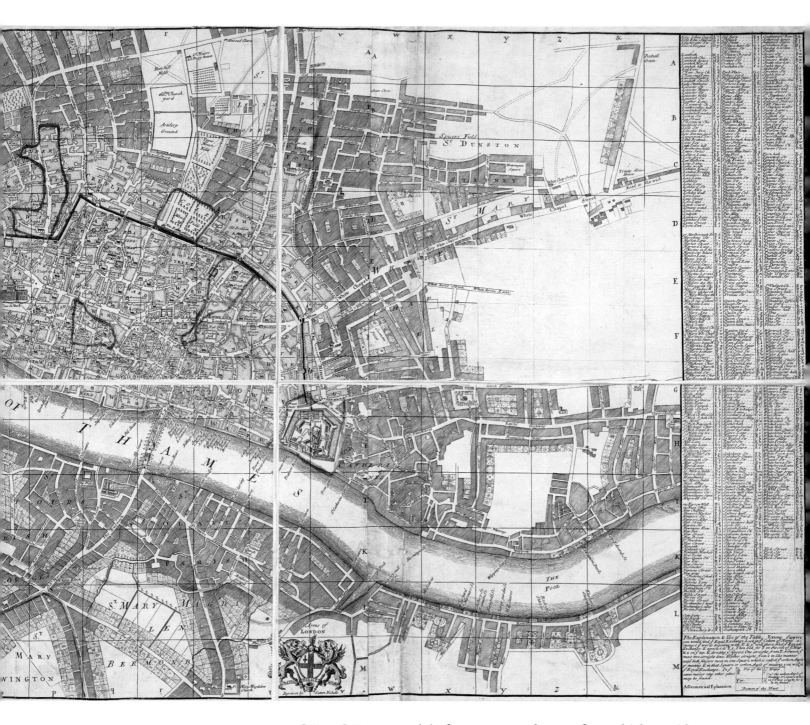

[Fig. 96] However original or otherwise the general topography may be on Henry Overton's *A new and exact plan of the city of London and suburbs thereof, with the addition of the new buildings, churches &c to the present year 1720*, it was innovative in one respect. This is the grid of squares on the map face, which provides a reference system and enables churches and other notable buildings to be identified using an alpha-numeric system. It might also be used to reckon distance. (CBTM 18675) [British Library, Maps *3480 (42)]

[Fig. 97] Distance circles were used by some map-makers as an aid to reckoning distance, but were never as popular as squaring systems. An unusual variation is the circle-and-radius method on Pigot's *New plan of London* of *c.* 1824. (CBTM 22642) [Cambridge University Library, Maps.c.71.82.20]

combined with squaring, as for example on Pigot's map of Manchester of 1829 (19214). Pigot's *c.* 1824 map of London (22642) uses a system of circles and radiating lines [Fig. 97].

Distance was of particular interest in calculating hackney carriage fares. Notional fares, together with watermen's fares on the river, are often cited on maps of London, but there was still scope for argument.[68] To subvert the practice of 'monstrous impositions practised by Cab-Drivers', J. Friedrichs published *The Circuiteer, or distance map of London* (19521) in about 1847, which was based on circles [Fig. 98]. Improved police regulations in 1853 removed most of the basis for such complaints in London, but

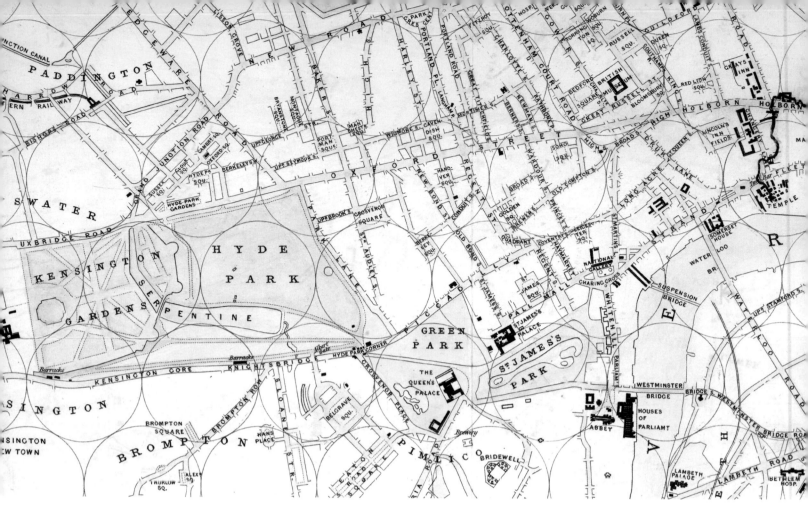

[Fig. 98] In about 1847 J. Friedrichs published *The Circuiteer, or distance map of London: invented by J. Friederichs, particularly adapted for cab conveyance,* which was based on circles. It is accompanied by a leaflet: 'J. Friederichs' circuiteer system; explained in a series of rules for the working out of an improved management of hackney carriages, and for the removal of existing complaints against the present mode of cab conveyance.' The 'Address to the public' inside begins: 'The monstrous impositions practised by Cab-Drivers upon the public have long been the subject of general complaint; but of all the plans hitherto suggested to remedy this abuse – and they have been many – not one has been found to answer the purpose. The Circuiteer, or Distance Map, at last offers a certain protection against such extortions, as the reader will be enabled to judge for himself from the following concise explanation. – The Circuiteer is a Map covered with circles, each of which is supposed to have a half-mile diameter; and by merely counting the number of circles between one point and another you have at once the distance travelled. As no fare under a mile is allowed, it is obvious that any minuter division of space is unnecessary.' If the idea caught on, Friedrichs proposed to add rules and regulations for cab hire in English, German and French. He reckoned that his innovation would both protect the public and help the cab proprietors 'by at least doubling the demand for their Vehicles.' (CBTM 19521) [British Library, Maps 3480. (15.)]

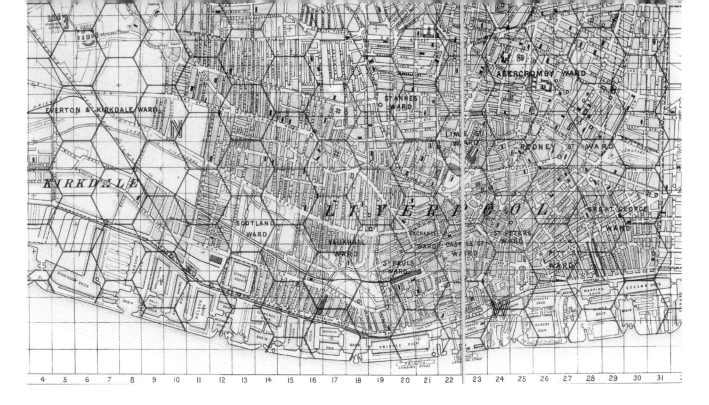

[Fig. 99] In 1868–9 Llewellyn Syers issued cab-fare maps of Liverpool, Manchester and Birkenhead, which used a system of hexagons to enable distances – and hence fares – to be calculated. This illustration is of part of the Liverpool map, dated October 1868. A note in red in the bottom margin, below the city arms, instructs users to allow 4 hexagons to 1 mile in calculating distance, thereby allowing for the winding of the streets. There is a letterpress reference to churches and public buildings, but not to streets. (CBTM 19621) [British Library, Maps 3200. (13.)]

Friedrichs republished *The Circuiteer* in 1862, perhaps hoping to cash in on visitors to the Exhibition at South Kensington, and announced his intention of publishing similar maps for provincial cities. This does not seem to have happened, but in 1868–9 Llewellyn Syers issued cab-fare maps of Liverpool (19621), Manchester (19633) and Birkenhead (19644), which use a system of hexagons [Fig. 99].

Growth in the publication of street maps mainly intended for wayfinding was accompanied by the development of a distinct 'street map style' which concentrates on essentials only. It is difficult to say exactly when this style began to evolve – the lack of detail on Rocque's maps in some ways anticipates it – but it can be seen clearly in the maps supplied by the firm of John Bartholomew for Black's *Guide to England and Wales* of 1864 [Fig. 100].[69] The essentials are street names and location of principal buildings – not

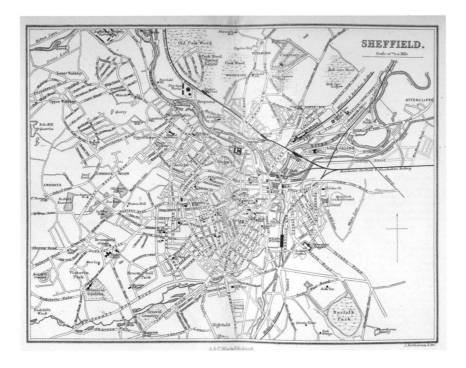

least the railway stations, through which many of the maps' users would pass. Bartholomew's mapping was produced to high standards of clarity by copper engraving [Fig. 101, *overleaf*]. Essentially the same sort of mapping, though less sophisticated in production, is exemplified by a group of three maps of districts around Manchester produced for Richard Collinson, 'Estate and Insurance Agent', in 1887 (19638–19640). The scale of 1:10,560 implies close dependence on the Ordnance Survey, but the details portrayed are greatly simplified, and the suburban growth which had taken place in the four decades since the Ordnance Survey's Town Maps were produced has been added [Fig. 102, *overleaf*].

A niche market for later Victorian street maps was provided by those people seeking to purchase houses. An early example is of Leeds, 1867 (19761).

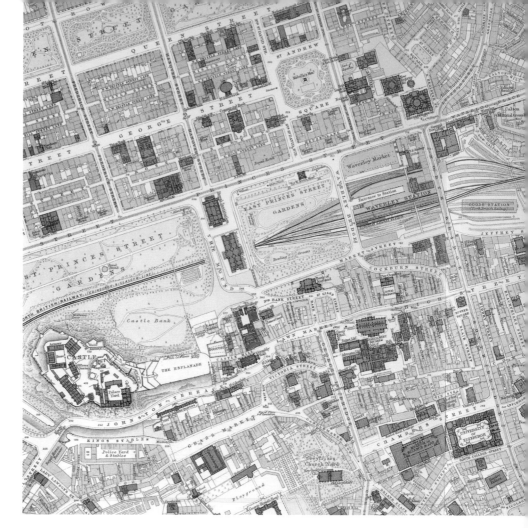

[Fig. 101] The last of a long line of town maps was also in some ways the most elaborate: Bartholomew's 15-inch map of Edinburgh, published in 1891. It was based on the Ordnance Survey 1:1056 survey, which had been revised in 1876, but was further revised with the assistance of the City Council. The last of the Bartholomews, John Christopher (1923–2008), described the map proudly as 'our finest engraved town plan'. It was printed in twelve sheets which were designed to be mounted together as a wall map, though many surviving copies have been bound as atlases. (CBTM 22847) [British Library, Maps 19.e.16]

[Fig. 102] Street maps are helpful for visitors, but they are also useful for new or prospective residents – indeed, in the twentieth century large numbers have been issued 'with the compliments' of estate agents. What seems to be a very early example of this genre is a group of three maps of districts on the south side of Manchester issued around 1887 by Richard Collinson, 'Estate and Insurance Agent'. This illustration is of Old Trafford: the basic survey derives from the Ordnance Survey, but many new roads and streets have been added by the compiler. (CBTM 19639) [Detail from Richard Collinson's plan of Old Trafford, Stretford and Chorlton cum Hardy: British Library, Maps 3230. (9.)]

House agents commonly acquired sets of maps from a producer and issued them to house purchase enquirers in customised covers to advertise their services. Similar thinking probably motivated publication of *The 'District Railway' Map of London*, first issued in 1873 (21334) in a form that seems intended for display as an advertising poster initially. Then it was republished in 1879 in a larger, more refined form, though still with the company's lines and connecting bus services shown very prominently in red (18283) [*see* **Fig. 24,** *p. 50*].[70]

A more explicit form of advertising was to produce a map expressly for that purpose, in which a basic street map is framed by advertisements, usually keyed to the locations of businesses depicted on the map. The standard of cartography and the degree of detail is invariably functional rather than decorative. Users might seek to be guided through the streets, but map producers wished rather to lead them to the advertisers. The earliest example known is of Leicester, dated 1877 (19827). By the 1890s the two leading advertising firms were both based in that city: Stephens & Mackintosh, and the Borough and County Advertising Company. A few early examples carry notes that the maps remain the property of the publisher. Examples are Mason's Birmingham, 1883 (22888) and Smith & Jabet's Coventry, 1888 (22220), which were presumably intended purely for display. The practice of issuing sheets folded in

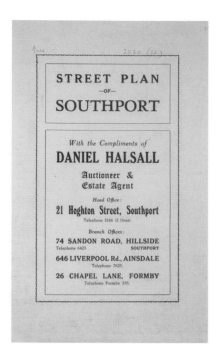

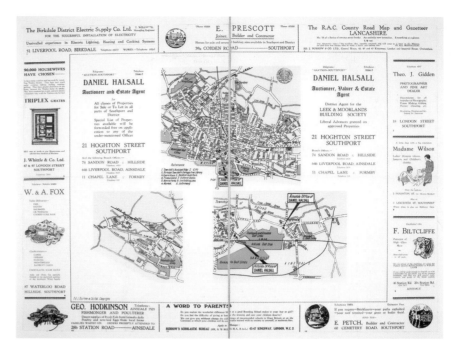

[Fig. 103] E. J. Burrow of Cheltenham originated in artistic publishing, but by the 1930s had become primarily an advertising and publicity business: maps of towns were a means to an end. Their map of Southport of 1931 is a typical example of their approach. [British Library, Maps 3230 (36.)]

covers indicates that sales to outsiders and to new residents were anticipated – tellingly, advertisements include those of removal firms. For the benefit of coal merchants there were standard blocks of railway wagons that could be customised with the advertiser's name and printed on a map. The same block often appears more than once on a particular map [*see* **Figs. 29 and 30**, *pp. 54–55*]. Comparatively few of these advertising maps survive, which underscores the ephemeral nature of basic street maps. Occasionally a map contains a statement specifying the number of copies printed. The Leicester Printing & Publishing Company's *New Business Map of Cardiganshire*, which includes ten inset maps of towns and larger villages, was printed in a run of 1,309 copies on 23 February 1909.[71]

In the early twentieth century other firms came to the fore and in the inter-war period J. W. Harding,

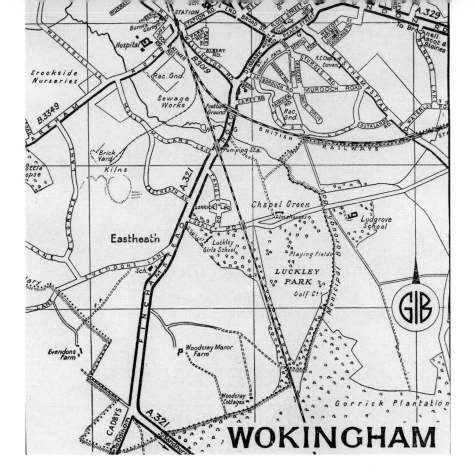

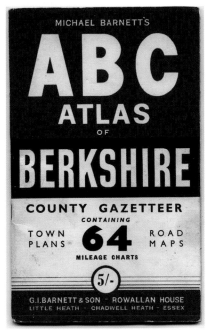

'Map Publishers and Advertising Agents', seem to have enjoyed a considerable trade, as did E. J. Burrows of Cheltenham, who also produced official guides for local authorities. Compared with the relative flamboyance of the advertisements themselves, the cartography was unremarkable [Fig. 103].

The maps by Burrows exemplify a new trend: for simpler, inexpensive monochrome or two-colour maps issued in an elaborate, often multi-colour cover. The cover 'sold' the product. This approach is exemplified by one of the leading firms offering such packages, G. & I. Barnett, founded in 1951. Today their website announces that they supply 'all good bookshops as well as garage forecourts, newsagents, and tourist information centres throughout the UK' [Fig. 104].[72]

[Fig. 104] G. & I. Barnett were often the first firm to publish a basic street map of a particular town for general sale. Their functional monochrome maps were mounted inside relatively austere but distinctive covers. This is exemplified by the map of Wokingham in Michael Barnett's *ABC Atlas of Berkshire*. Advertising in the atlas was an important part of the G & I Barnett business model. [Michael Barnett's ABC Atlas of Berkshire, n.d. [? 1965], private collection.]

12.

Street atlases

THE NAME 'A–Z' HAS BECOME synonymous with street mapping, and in particular with what for many people is 'the' atlas of London. However, A–Z was certainly no pioneer, and came relatively late in the development of the urban atlas in Britain.

As with sheet mapping, urban atlases divide into those for indoor reference and those for use in the street: the latter implies a size that is easily carried. The roughly octavo (15 by 23 cm) Bartholomew *Handy Reference Atlas of London and Suburbs* of 1908, and in its fourteenth edition by 1968, falls into the reference rather than the wayfinding category, based as it is on the firm's 1:18,495 mapping of London first issued in 1892 (19577).

The atlas format has a number of potential advantages over the individual sheet map for large urban areas. First, the use of a larger scale for the more complicated central area recognises that the use of a common scale – necessary on a single-sheet map – means either that the more complex central parts look congested, or that the more outlying parts have a skeletal appearance. An atlas also economises on paper and bulk. The irregular shape of all urban areas means that a sheet street map of a whole town is bound to include empty areas which cannot always be used up by including cartouches or other non-cartographic matter. An atlas can focus on the built-up area with only minimal waste of paper. The relative compactness of an atlas means that it is possible to offer continuous

[Fig. 105] One of the most successful maps in terms of longevity was that of London and its suburbs at 1:15,840, first published by George Washington Bacon c. 1874. Its general style is very conservative. However, Bacon had a flair for promotion, and this enabled the wide circulation of many of his maps. (CBTM 18282) [Detail: British Library, Maps 24.aa.9]

[Fig. 106] Although G. W. Bacon died in 1922 his name continued to appear on maps for another fifty years. This is an extract from *Bacon's Atlas of London*, in its 1963 edition: although the building infill has been replaced by colour, street names and other details are still recognisable from the 1874 parent map. [British Library, Maps 47.a.50]

map-cover for both the central part of a large town and for the various suburbs where many users might be expected to live. It is also possible to incorporate a comprehensive gazetteer of streets and places of interest. Atlases can be neatly packaged between covers, but this does limit a synoptic view to a page-opening and perhaps explains the relative popularity of sheet maps up to the first third of the twentieth century.

The first successful atlas of London was for reference rather than for wayfinding, and derived from existing sheet mapping. This is George Washington Bacon's *New Ordnance Atlas of London & Suburbs*, which was first issued in 1879. It uses 1:6732 mapping originally prepared for Cassell and the *Weekly Dispatch Atlas* in 1861–2 (19574) for central London and 1:15,840 mapping of 1874 for outlying parts [Fig. 105].[73] Although these are very definitely reference atlases, the inclusion of 1:15,840 mapping demonstrates once again how street mapping can be multi-functional. It also served as the basis of a wall map measuring some 215 by 180 cm.[74] Bacon's 1879 atlas was very long-lived; a drastically reworked version of the 1:15,840 map enhanced by the use of colour was still being offered in 1963 in *Bacon's Atlas of London* [Fig. 106].

Although with claims to be 'the market leader', and certainly the best-known urban atlas series in Britain, the A–Z was anything but the first portable street atlas. That was H. G. Collins's *Atlas of London*,

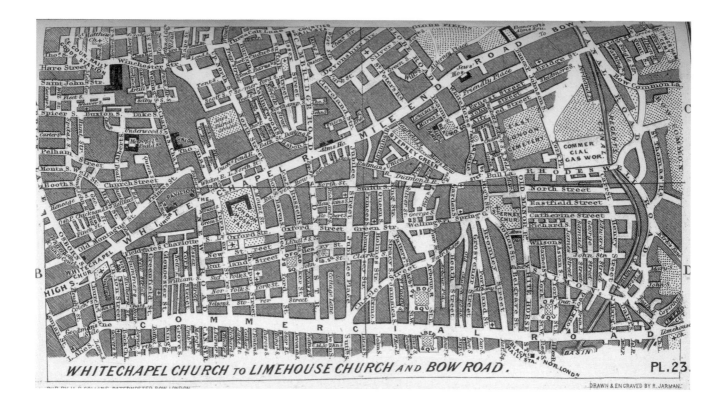

WHITECHAPEL CHURCH TO LIMEHOUSE CHURCH AND BOW ROAD.　PL.23.

PUB. BY H. G. COLLINS, PATERNOSTER ROW, LONDON.　　DRAWN & ENGRAVED BY R. JARMAN.

[Fig. 107] The first street atlas of London was issued by H. G. Collins in 1854. At the start is a note: 'If the reader has ever seen an unfortunate stranger in one of our busy thoroughfares examining, almost hopelessly, the square yard of paper, with its complicated network of streets and houses, which (if we except the "River Thames", lying like a large eel on its surface,) is the principal idea to be gathered at the moment from the "Map of London" before him, – if the reader has ever seen this, he will be quite ready to acknowledge that some more convenient guide is necessary for use in the streets.' The cartography of Collins's street atlas is clear, but the pages are orientated so that the direction of routes out of the centre appear towards the top of the page. This cannot have been very easy for those moving around other than radially; nonetheless there were several reissues up to 1862. Here is page 23, oriented north (CBTM 19549) [British Library, Maps 28.BB.22]

1854 (19549) [Fig. 107]. While this atlas is innovative in presenting street mapping in page-sized sections, it is distinctive in that the orientation varies from one section to the next, as main routes radiate from the centre. It is, therefore, not necessary to turn the map when going towards the suburbs, though it is necessary to hold it upside down when returning. This rendered it of limited use other than for radial movement. Because of the different orientation of the various sections, it had to be newly drawn, rather than able to make use of lithographic transfers from existing plates. The atlas was reprinted a few years later, but did not supplant the sheet street map. Much the same applies to other portable street atlases of London produced before about 1900, such as those by Reynolds (1859: 19541), Philip (1892: 19572) and Bacon (1894: 18282), the last using that publisher's hard-worked 1:15,840 mapping. In 1892 Bartholomew printed 5,300 copies of an atlas of London and 2,020 copies of its North London map (19577), so the demand for atlases was evidently not negligible, though comparatively few seem to survive.[75]

Between 1900 and 1925 pocket-sized atlases of London were issued by Philip, Bacon, Bartholomew and Geographia: all ran through several editions to 1939. Geographia's *Authentic Atlas* was issued in a French-language edition in 1922 and in Spanish in 1935.[76] Outside London, setting aside a curious reference atlas of Brighton and Hove at 1:5280 issued

by Bacon in 1882 (20764), street atlases developed only after 1918. By 1930 they had been issued for Birmingham, Bradford, Glasgow, Leeds, Liverpool and Manchester. All are based on existing sheet maps.

The A–Z atlas seems to have developed as a rival to the Geographia atlases. Geographia was founded in 1906 by Alexander Gross – anglicised from the Hungarian Sandor Grosz – but he was ousted from the company in 1923 and thereafter was based in the United States, using various front-persons in London for his continuing British operations. One such person was his daughter, Phyllis Pearsall. When Gross decided on the A–Z project in 1935 or 1936 she appears to have been instructed to compile the index and ensure the maps were up to date. The lack of recent Ordnance Survey revision meant resorting to borough engineers and estate agents and, when those failed, sketching new streets on the ground. The atlas was popular because it was up to date and inexpensive; early editions include maps of 'Shopping Centres and Parking Places' and 'Clubland' [Fig. 108].[77] As cartography, the A–Z was utilitarian, but the original drawings continued in use to the late 1970s. Although 'A–Z' is synonymous with street atlases, the firm created to handle the original London A–Z went on to publish both sheet maps and motoring maps.

Although in retrospect the A–Z can be seen as the culmination of the street atlas, there was a parallel context of seeking what might be described

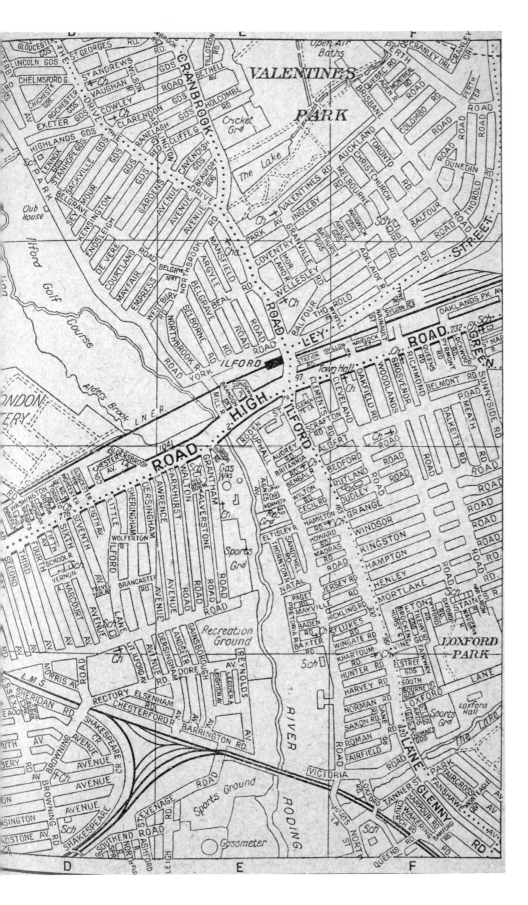

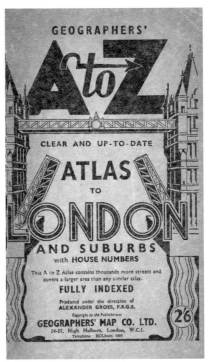

[**Fig. 108**] The best-known atlas of London is the A–Z, first issued in 1936. Its appeal lay in a mixture of its bold style, its comprehensiveness, its up-to-dateness and its low price. Omitting building infill both saved on production cost and made for a lighter-feeling, more user-friendly map. This extract is from the 1948 edition. [Geographers' A to Z Atlas of London and Suburbs [1948]; British Library, Maps 197.b.40]

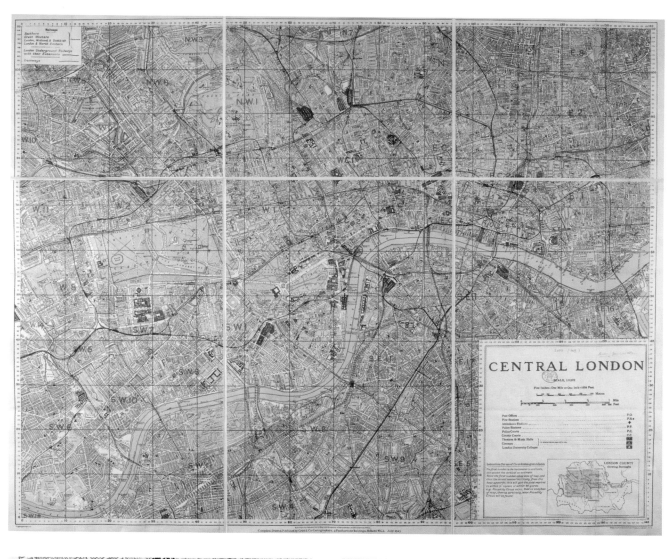

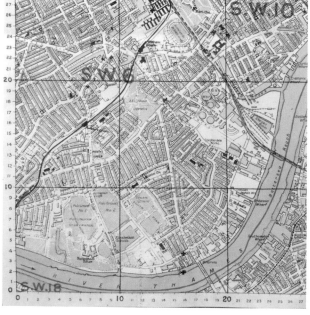

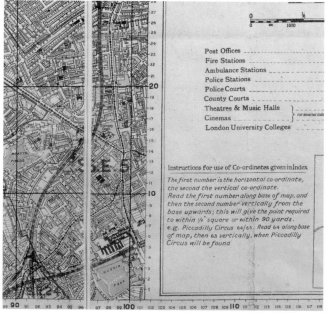

as 'efficient' mapping of London, which owed much to the development after 1914 of numerical grid systems.[78] One example is Cribb & Co.'s map of London of 1923, which was successful enough to be reprinted within the year: no doubt sales via the W. H. Smith high street chain of bookshops helped [Fig. 109].[79] The Ordnance Survey produced a three-inch (1:21,120) four-sheet map of London in 1933 employing a six-figure grid system, but it failed to catch on. The public seem to have resisted maps that were nominally expensive (the four-sheet Ordnance Survey map mounted as one cost ten shillings (£0.50). Ordnance Survey 1:21,120 mapping was used in 1934 for the *Lightning Plan* ('any street found in a few seconds'), which involves a complicated system of back-to-back street maps allied to numerical references. It was not a marketing success. The *A–Z* uses an ordinary alphanumeric system: when the maps were redrawn in the 1980s, Ordnance Survey's metric grid numbers were added to the maps, though not to the gazetteers.

It was the street atlas rather than the sheet map that finally brought basic street maps to every town in England and to most of those in the more populous parts of Scotland and Wales. These were produced on a county basis by the Ordnance Survey, which by the early 1980s was under considerable pressure from government to maximise its income and engage in commercial activities. County street atlases were not completely unknown – George Philip had produced

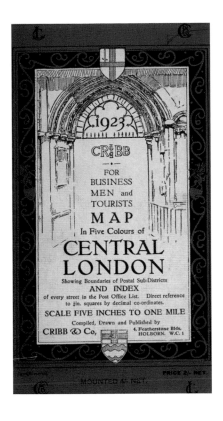

[Fig. 109, *opposite and above*] Messrs Cribb and Co. of 4 Featherstone Buildings, Holborn, published relatively few maps; one is their *Map in Six Colours of Central London* of 1923. It is accompanied by an eighty-two-page index, and reference to streets and places of interest on the map is by numerical referencing: thus the British Museum is to be found at 71/76. Although the map was reprinted in 1924, it appears not to have been a lasting success: perhaps the 'Direct reference to $^1/_4$ in. squares by decimal co-ordinates' was a little too sophisticated for the majority of contemporary map-users.
[British Library, Maps 3480. (349.)]

one of Surrey in 1966 – but they tended to be relatively bulky, better suited to the motorist than to the pedestrian. Ordnance Survey examples were first published in collaboration with Philip and were also quite bulky, but by the mid-1990s they were being issued at a smaller scale in pocket form. The nearest approach to a standard scale was around 1:25,000, although many rural areas were mapped at 1:50,000 and larger built-up areas at 1:12,500. This demonstrates a key flexibility of the street atlas that is denied to the sheet map. Since 1999, following a change in Ordnance Survey policy, the street atlases have been published exclusively by Philip, though the cartography remains unchanged [Fig. 110].

[Fig. 110] Comprehensive street-mapping of Britain had to wait until the late twentieth century, with a series of atlases jointly published by the Ordnance Survey and Philip. [*Cardiff, Swansea and the Valleys: Caerdydd, Abertawe a'r Cymoedd*, London: Philip, 2004. British Library, Maps 242.a.49]

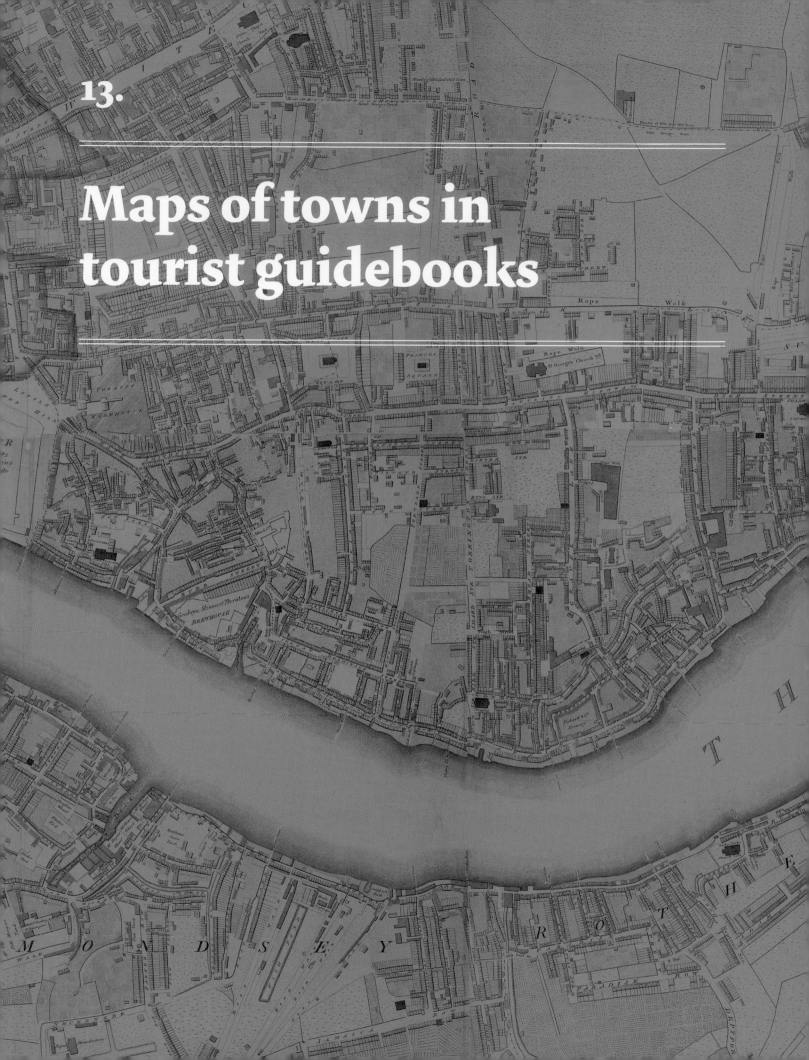

13.

Maps of towns in tourist guidebooks

GUIDEBOOKS WITH STREET MAPS were published
both for resorts and for commercial centres. The first
we have recorded are for Oxford in 1762, Cambridge in
1763 and Bath in 1773. Guides with maps followed for
Salisbury (1778: 22688), York (1785: 19697), Weymouth
(?1795: 22337) and Liverpool (1796: 20074). Elsewhere
they were a nineteenth-century development.
Scarborough, for example, had its first recorded guide
with a map in 1812 (19380). Birmingham had a street
map by 1792 (20193), but a guide and map was not
published until 1819 (23317). One of the constraints
on the production of street and guide maps was
availability of the basic data: it was much simpler to
copy an existing map than to commission a survey for
a new one, although evidently the market at Glasgow
in 1797 was considered good enough to justify the
latter course. These guidebook maps tend to be small
format, no doubt partly so as to facilitate folding
within pocket-sized books. The map accompanying
Walks in Oxford, published in 1817 (19104), is unusual in
that it could also be purchased separately, folded for
the pocket.

Whereas maps in early guidebooks appear to
have been specially created, later ones might reuse an
existing map. The Scarborough guide of 1812 is a good
example: it reuses a map that had first appeared in
Thomas Hinderwell's history of the town, published
in 1798 (19380). Up to about 1820 all these maps were
engraved on copper, but thereafter lithography was

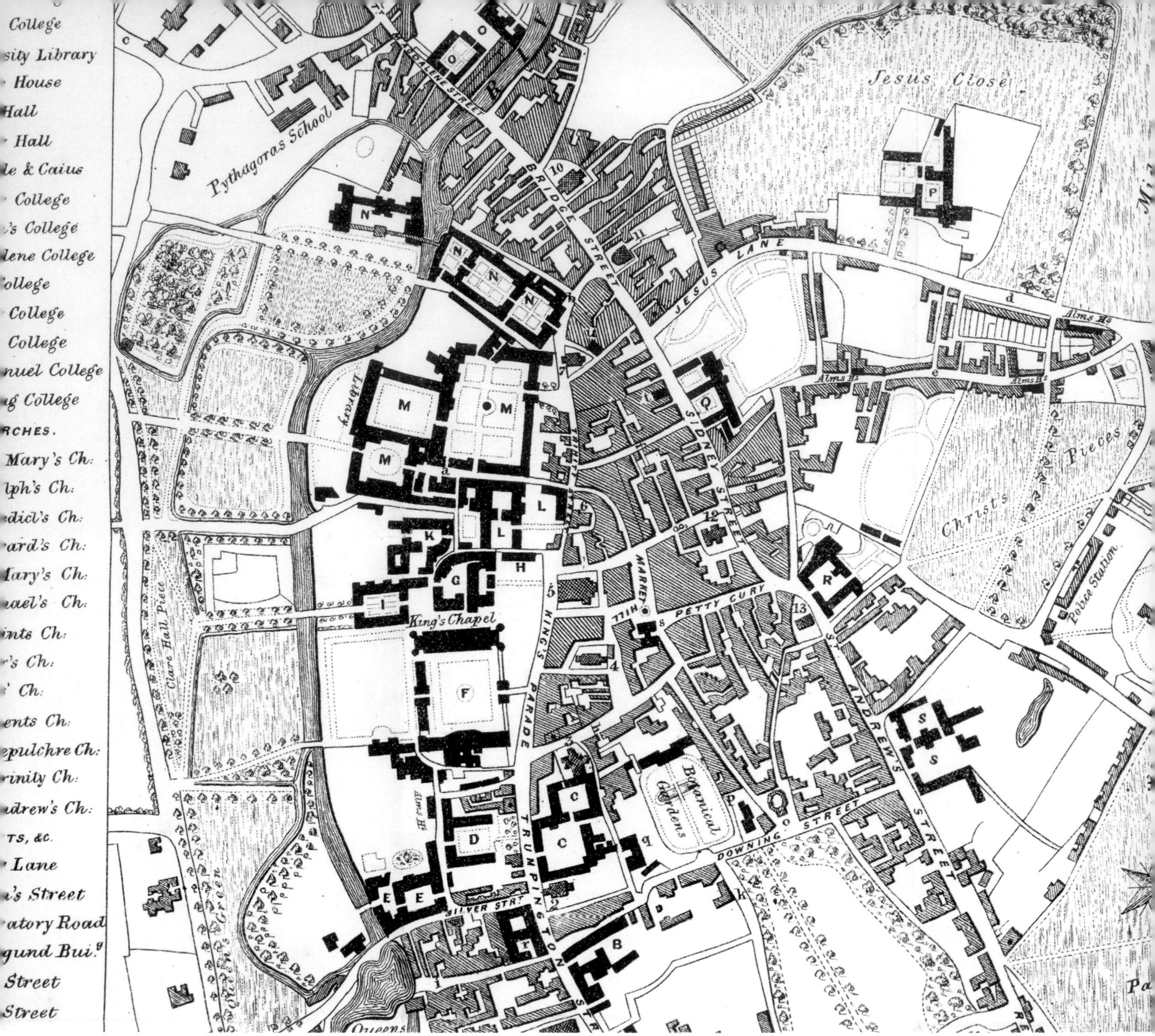

[Fig. 111] Until the 1820s the only way of duplicating an engraved plate of a map was by the labour-intensive procedure of re-engraving it afresh. Then came lithography, which in its original form entailed drawing an image in greasy ink on stone. This method was adapted so that a 'pull' from copper could be made in lithographic ink and laid down on stone, thereby avoiding redrawing. One application of this technique was for producing maps for guidebooks by using extracts from larger maps. This illustration is an extract from Richard Baker's map of Cambridge of 1830, which was used for a map in a guidebook of 1845. (CBTM 21178) [British Library, RB.23.a.21706.]

increasingly used. Lithographic transfer meant that by the late nineteenth century the same basic mapping might be encountered both as a street map, perhaps extending some way beyond the built-up area, and as a map in a guidebook, often cropped to confine it to the area most likely to be of interest to visitors. An early example is the reuse of the central part of Richard Baker's wall map of Cambridge, 1830 for a guidebook in 1845 (21188) [Fig. 111].

Early guidebooks usually focus on a single town and were published locally. A single map bound into the book was sufficient for those purposes. *A Guide to All the Watering and Sea-bathing Places*, published by Longman in 1810, marked the start of a new trend by including maps of Bath (21539), Brighton (21541) and Clifton (21540). Such wide-reaching guides flourished particularly as the railway system expanded after 1840. They included text on a number of towns and hence needed several maps.

The aristocrats of Victorian guidebooks are the *Handbooks for Travellers* published by John Murray. Town maps were introduced gradually through successive editions of the *Handbooks*. For example, the volume for Devon and Cornwall at first had only a small-scale map of south-west England, the fifth edition of 1863 added a woodcut map of Exeter (18740), and the sixth of 1865 added one of Plymouth (18741). These are illustrations in the text, rather than tipped in, and were replaced in the ninth edition of 1879 by

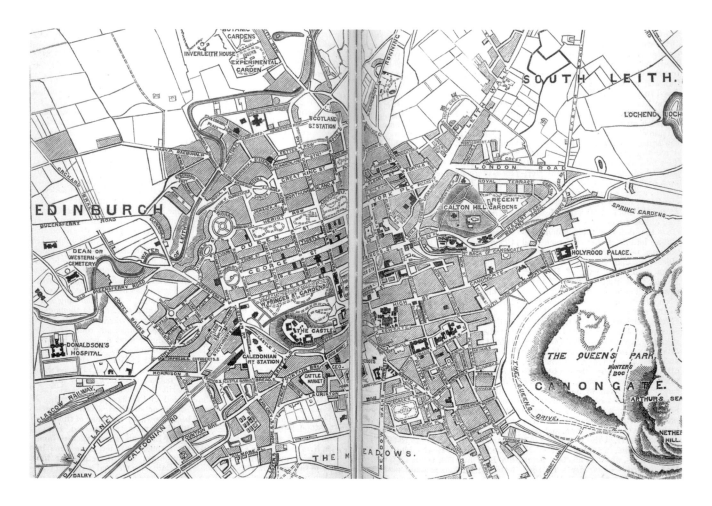

[Fig. 112] The series of *Handbooks for Travellers* published by the firm of John Murray at first included very few maps. Perhaps experience, and the relatively high cover price of the volumes, led to the decision to include street maps, such as this one of Edinburgh, in the 1867 edition of *Handbook for Travellers in Scotland*. The map is printed from a woodblock: this method had the disadvantage that the maps were hard to revise. (CBTM 23359) [British Library, 10028.cc.23]

much more sophisticated tipped-in lithographically printed maps by Edward Weller (18742, 18743). These in turn were supplemented in the eleventh edition of 1895 by maps of Ilfracombe (18745) and Torquay (18744). The Scottish volume went through a similar development: the first edition of 1867 includes woodcut maps of Edinburgh (23359) and Glasgow (23358); the third edition of 1873 replaced these with lithographed maps by Weller (23361, 23360 respectively); the fifth edition of 1883 added a map of Dundee (23362); the sixth edition of 1894 included Bartholomew plans of Aberdeen (22001), Inverness (22003), Oban (22002), Perth (22005), St Andrews (22004) and Stirling (22006)

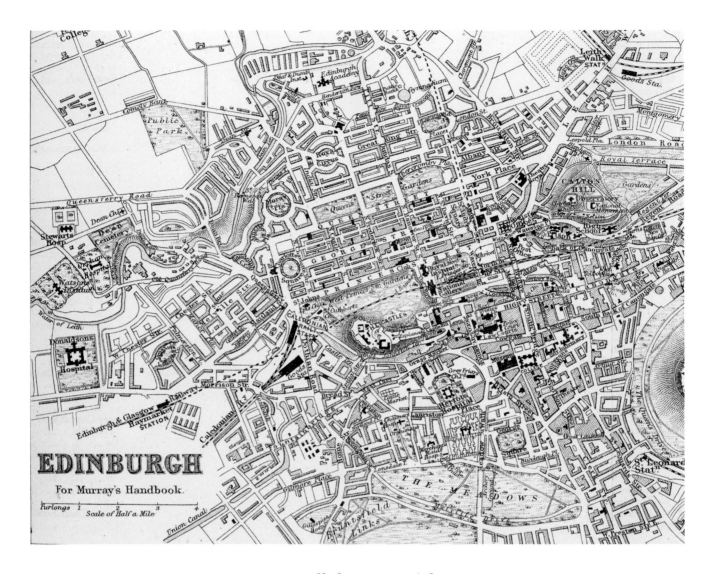

EDINBURGH

For Murray's Handbook.

Furlongs 1 2 3 4
Scale of Half a Mile

[Figs 112, 113, *opposite and above*, 114, *overleaf*]. All these Scottish town plans derived from Ordnance Survey maps. Bartholomew reused the town maps prepared for Murray for the *Atlas of Scotland*, 1895.

A similar series of guides, though intended for a wider market, was published by Black of Edinburgh. Their *Yorkshire* of 1866 is notable as probably the first guidebook to have all its town maps based on Ordnance Survey material (20424). The 1868 edition added a plan of Redcar (19025) [Figs 115, *p. 175*, 116, *p. 176*]. Inclusion of the Redcar plan is puzzling as the map

[Fig. 113] By 1873 Murray were sharpening up their approach: the map of Edinburgh included in the edition of *Handbook for Travellers in Scotland* published that year was by the well-known cartographer Edward Weller, and was probably printed by Edward Stanford. (CBTM 23361) [British Library, 10028.cc.24]

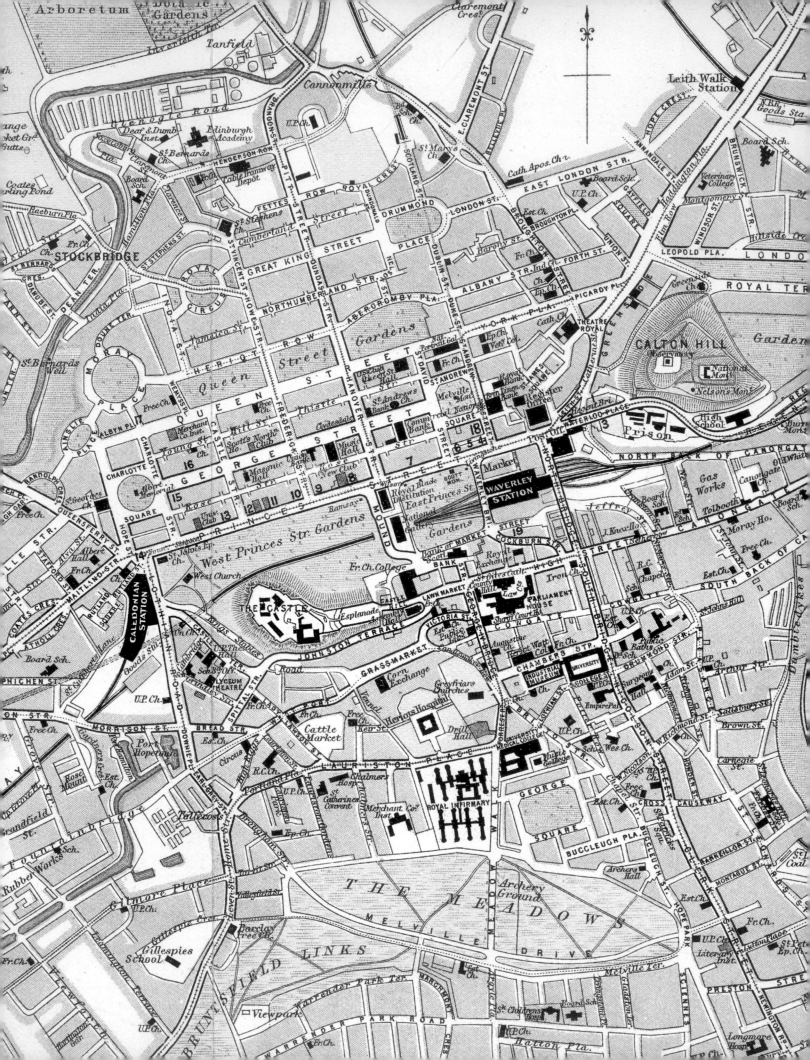

[Fig. 114, *opposite*] The 1894 edition of Murray's *Handbook for Travellers in Scotland* included an extended range of maps of Scottish towns, for which the publishers went to John Bartholomew and Son of Edinburgh. The map of Scotland's capital city derived from a plate that had originally been prepared in 1871, and was thus two years older than the map included in the 1873 edition of the Murray *Handbook*.(CBTM 21766) [British Library 10028.ccc.15, f.p. 37]

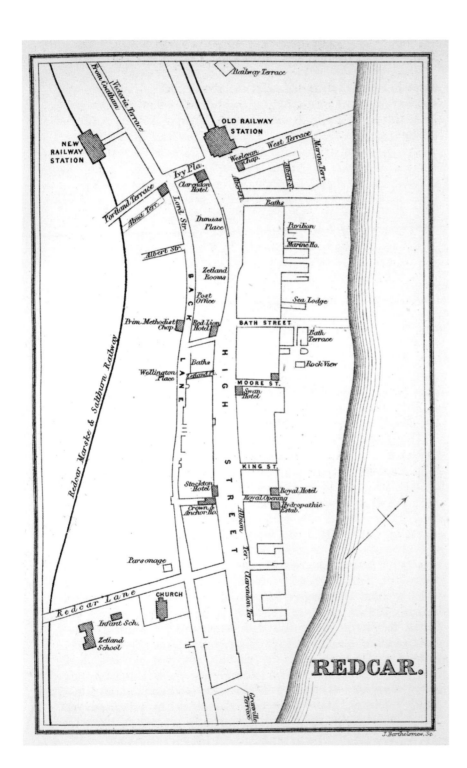

[Fig. 115, *left*] The provision of street maps in guidebooks of such large cities as Edinburgh or Manchester is easy to understand, but the inclusion of Redcar – practically no more than a single street – in successive editions from 1868 onwards of Black's *Guide to the County of York* is somewhat puzzling. The mapping was produced by Bartholomew. (CBTM 19025) [British Library 10347.bb.37, f.p.280]

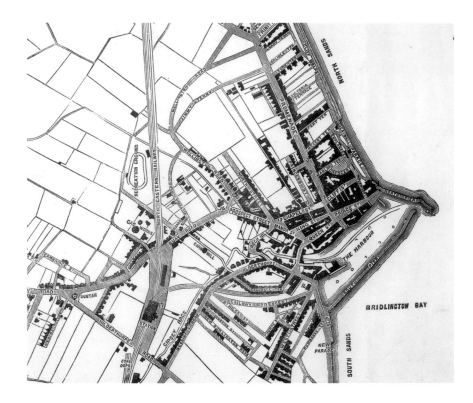

[Fig. 116] Although Bridlington in Yorkshire had been mapped by the Ordnance Survey in the early 1850s, and was both a prosperous port and a developing seaside resort, the town apparently had to wait nearly forty years before a commercial publisher issued a street map. The inclusion of field boundaries reflects derivation from Ordnance Survey mapping. (CBTM 19774) [Forster's plan of Bridlington Quay and district, c. 1891: British Library, 5985. (15.)]

reveals little more than a single long street. What was it that places like Saltburn, Filey or Bridlington lacked that caused the map-maker to pass them by but to favour Redcar? Though Black may have aimed the company's guides at a broader audience than Murray, both evidently counted on an increasing cartographic awareness in their readers.

Such awareness is indicated by the inclusion of maps, often not very sophisticated, from the 1880s onwards in what are very much bottom-of-the-market guides. Examples are those produced by Heywood of Manchester where the map is on a centre spread, with staples across its middle but printed on slightly better-quality paper than the rest of the guide. They are very different from the 'handy maps' issued a generation earlier by Abel Heywood, which were offered for

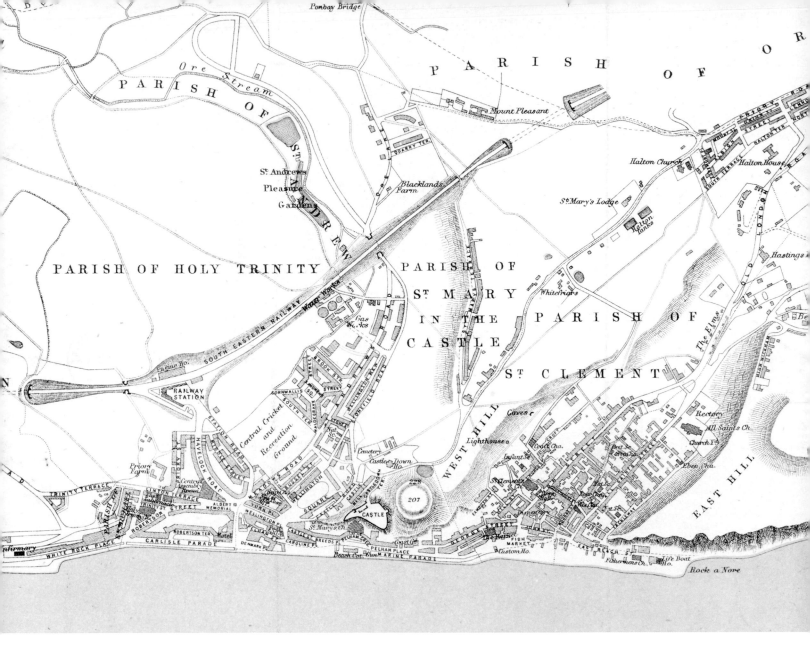

sixpence, colour-printed by Bartholomew [**Figs 117**, *above*, **118**, *overleaf*]. Maps of Hastings (1869: 18995; 1898: 22408) point the comparison.

Both the Murray and Black series, and a third series, Baddeley's *Thorough Guides*, were eclipsed after 1900 by a series published by Ward Lock, latterly known as the *Red Guides*, which continued and consolidated the role of street maps in guidebooks. The usual formula is 1:126,720 maps by Bartholomew

[**Fig. 117**] The Manchester firm of Abel Heywood issued a number of maps in the late 1860s and 1870s using material engraved from Bartholomew. This illustration is of Hastings, issued *c*. 1869. (CBTM 18995) [British Library, Maps 5460. (4.)]

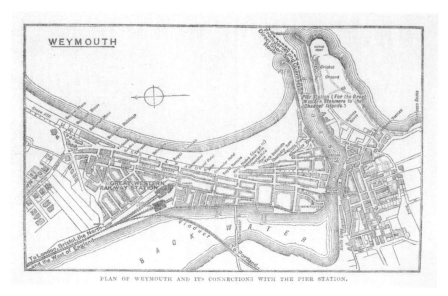

[Fig. 118] By the 1890s photo-lithography and photo-engraving had developed sufficiently to facilitate some easy inclusion of maps. *The Official Guide to the Great Western Railway*, published by Cassell in 1897, includes twelve town and city plans; this one is of Weymouth. (CBTM 21425) [British Library, 010351.I.3]

PLAN OF WEYMOUTH AND ITS CONNECTIONS WITH THE PIER STATION.

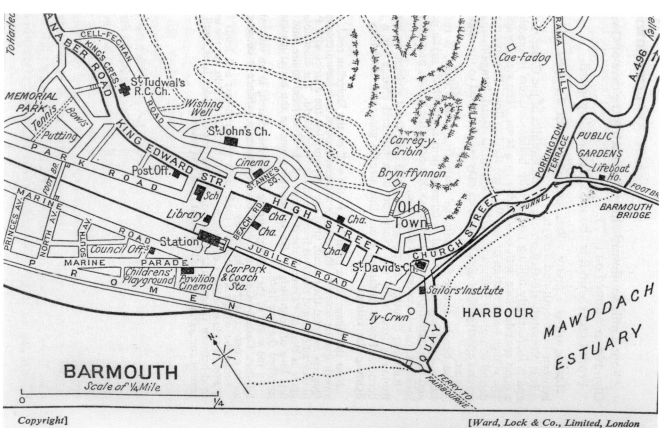

[Fig. 119, *above*] This street map of Barmouth appeared in the 1929 edition of Ward Lock's guide to North Wales. Although it appears much plainer than the Bartholomew example illustrated in Fig. 114, in fact it exemplifies a similar principle of concentrating essentially on streets and public buildings.

[British Library, 010347.de.131]

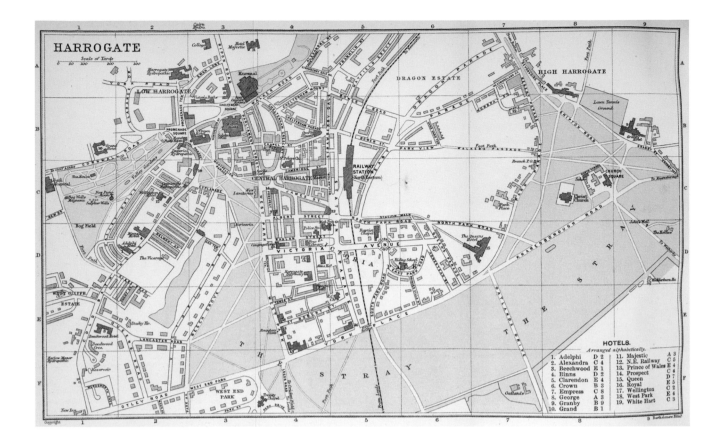

HOTELS.
Arranged alphabetically.

1. Adelphi	D 2	11. Majestic	A 3
2. Alexandra	C 4	12. N.E. Railway	C 5
3. Beechwood	E 1	13. Prince of Wales	E 4
4. Binns	D 2	14. Prospect	C 4
5. Clarendon	E 4	15. Queen	D 7
6. Crown	B 3	16. Royal	E 5
7. Empress	C 8	17. Wellington	C 2
8. George	A 3	18. West Park	E 4
9. Granby	B 9	19. White Hart	C 3
10. Grand	B 1		

supplemented by town plans, sometimes unattributed [Figs 119, 120]. By the time that this series expired around 1980, a somewhat different national series of unprecedented scope was popular. These are the volumes that began as *The Buildings of England* and are now, in recognition of their founder, known as the *Pevsner Architectural Guides*. The changing nature of maps included in the *Guides* followed a trajectory similar to that of nineteenth-century guidebooks. The early volumes have only basic county maps, but over time plans, first of cathedrals and then of town centres, were included.

[Fig. 120] By using colour Bartholomew were able to enhance their basic street map style and also to give an indication of the extent of building. This 1909 example illustrates their mapping of Harrogate, as used in the once well-known *Thorough Guides*. A delicate pinkish-brown infill is used for buildings. (CBTM 18993) [In M. J. B. Baddeley, Yorkshire (Part II) (Thorough Guide Series), 1909: British Library, 2366.a.19]

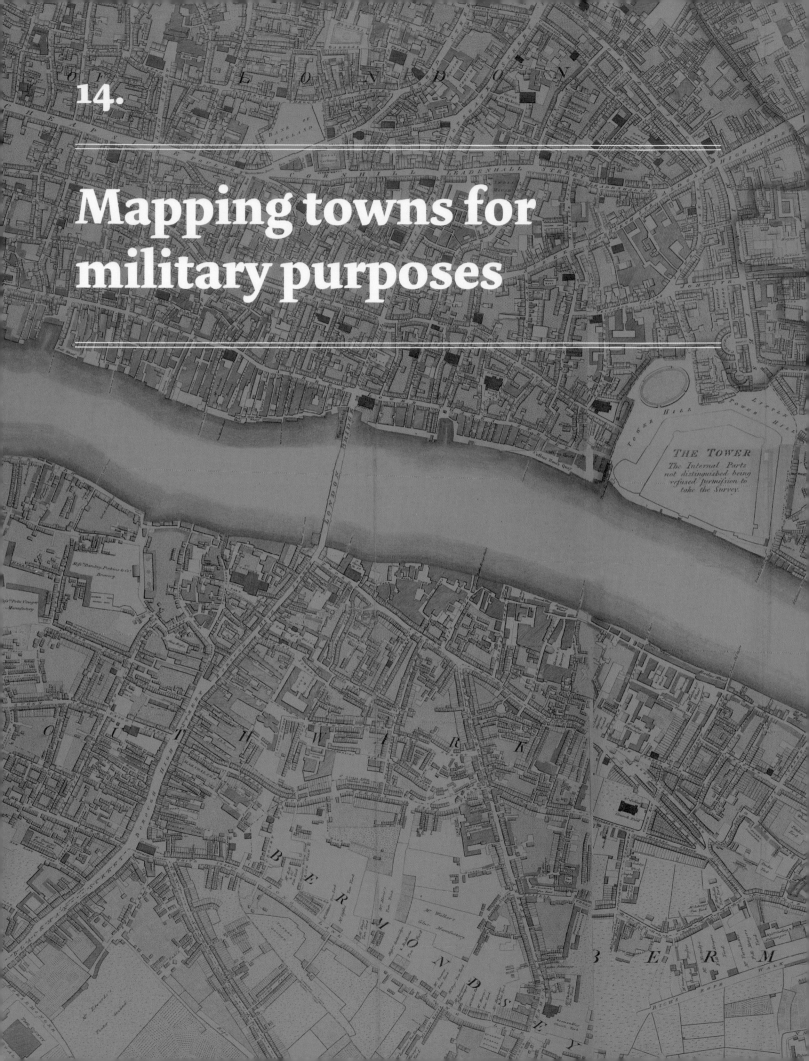

14.

Mapping towns for military purposes

THE TOWER
The Internal Parts
not distinguished being
refused permission to
take the Survey.

MAPS OF TOWNS produced for military purposes
are one of the most numerous genres of town map.[80]
They may well be the earliest, and often the only, map
of a particular town, but they may have comparatively
little to say about it, beyond the basics of street layout,
the principal church, and possibly the market hall and
one or two other public buildings. [81]

The 'military map' takes a number of forms, but
in the context of town mapping it is large-scale maps
for fortification planning and engineering that are
particularly relevant. Other forms of military maps,
such as small-scale topographic maps produced
for planning military movements and for studying
terrain, maps of opponents' positions, and maps
published as a record or for pedagogic purposes,
contribute to urban mapping only incidentally. In
contrast to many other genres, few military maps of
towns were produced after the late eighteenth century.
This decline in output can be traced to a shift in
emphasis during the eighteenth century from 'siege'
to 'battle' warfare. Whereas 'siege' warfare implied a
concentration on 'strong points', 'battles' might take
place almost anywhere.[82]

Both the military map as an identifiable genre
and maps drawn to true scale came to England in the
1530s. They can be linked to French and Italian military
engineers employed by Henry VIII, who introduced
the concept of the precisely surveyed map and plan.[83]
Henry and his circle of advisors were already map-

[Fig. 121] In England in the early sixteenth century there was a shift in emphasis from internal control to external diplomacy, and at the same time Henry VIII, King of England, was engaging with maps. There is a multiple interest to this map of Dover of 1532: it was drawn by an Italian brought to England by Henry, it shows an unrealised scheme for improving the harbour, and it was actually commissioned by Dover Corporation for presentation to the king, but it still has much of the bird's-eye view about it. (CBTM 21469) ['A Plott for the making the Hauen of Douer.', drawn by Vincenzo Volope, 1532: British Library, Cotton Augustus Ms.I.i.19]

minded, and the needs of coastal defence resulted in a series of picture maps not drawn strictly to scale but which nevertheless give a vivid depiction of the coast. Indeed, the lack of scale was in some ways an advantage as it enabled towns, castles, harbours and other points of particular interest to be shown in greater detail.

It is unsurprising, in view of its strategic position as the nearest point to mainland Europe, that Dover is possibly the earliest English town to be mapped in detail for military purposes. This happened c. 1530 for a projected improvement of the harbour (21469, 32155) [Fig. 121]. This improvement was not realised, but a long sequence of plans follows up to c. 1610; there is then a hiatus until the early eighteenth century. Although the town was, and still is, dominated by its castle, its main importance was as a port and base, and both sixteenth-century maps and then eighteenth-century remapping are associated with improvement of the port.

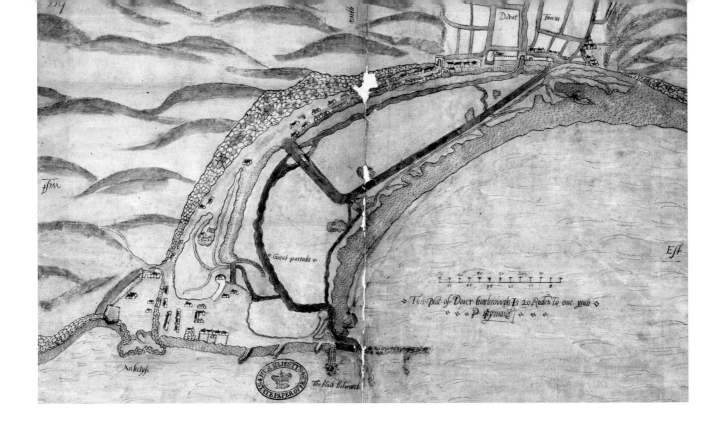

Bird's-eye and strict-scale concepts ran in parallel for some time. In the 1570s a number of schemes for new and improved fortifications at Portsmouth (18515, 18713, 19714), Berwick (19708–19711) and elsewhere were prepared by engineers such as Richard Popinjay. These are strictly plan drawings, whereas the near-contemporary proposals for works at Dover (18584, 18585, 19719) still have a good deal of the picture map about them [Fig. 122]. A sketch of defences at Scarborough dated 1586 (20197) is still entirely in the picture map tradition. On the other hand, a map of Harwich of *c.* 1600 (18563) is fundamentally planimetric, and looks forward to the more elaborately styled military mapping of the eighteenth century, in that it shows walls, streets and the church (still pictorial), but not 'ordinary' buildings.

[Fig. 122] By the 1570s the scale map was a well-established concept, especially for military engineering. Although apparently somewhat sketchy, the declared scale on this map of Dover of 1577 places it firmly in the category of scale plan rather than bird's-eye view. Characteristic of later military mapping is the treatment of the town, top right: this is reduced to streets with 'anonymous' tint between them. In contrast, buildings closer to the harbour are depicted in much more detail. (CBTM 18584) ['This plot of Dover harbrowoh Is 20 Rodes To one ynch. P. Symans', c. 1577: The National Archives, MPF 1/122]

[Fig. 123] The series of civil wars between the Crown and Parliament between 1642 and 1651 generated comparatively little mapping compared with later conflicts. Several towns were besieged, and some of these sieges are recorded in published maps. One such is Plymouth, a Parliamentary stronghold that was besieged by royalists for much of 1643. This map is the work of Wenceslaus Hollar, the celebrated engraver, and was originally prepared for *A true narration of the most observable passages, in and around the last siege of Plymouth*, London, 1644. There is a scale bar at the bottom of the map, but comparison with other maps shows that the scale is somewhat 'flexible'. (CBTM 18258) ['A True Mapp and description of the Towne of Plymouth and the Fortifications thereof, with the workes and approaches of the Enemy, at the last Siege, Ao.1643', by Wenceslaus Hollar: British Library, E.31. (15.)]

The English Civil Wars of 1642–51 seem to have generated very little new mapping; there was simply not enough time to plan and execute elaborate masonry fortifications. There are several maps of sieges and associated defences, including two maps of Oxford (22140, 22148) and others for Colchester (19335) and Newark (19820). That for Plymouth (18258) illustrated a Parliamentarian pamphlet [Fig. 123]. These maps were all published for sale, and are as much 'information maps' or 'news maps' as 'military maps'. However, they cannot be relied on as a record of what was actually on the ground, as defences portrayed may have remained projected rather than executed.[84] The lack of sieges in Britain after this period – a solitary map showing a battle outside Carlisle in 1746 (18313) is a striking exception – means that this sub-genre of maps effectively disappears.

One of two Oxford siege maps is the work of Bernard de Gomme, a Dutch expert on fortification who was in active employment in England from

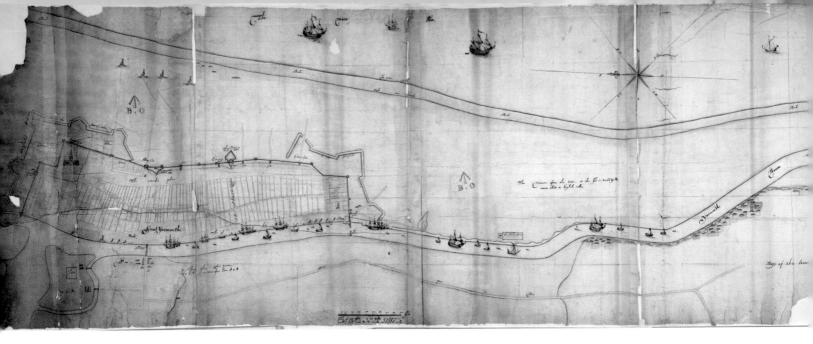

the 1640s to his death in 1685 [Fig. 124]. He represents the start of a second wave of continental European influence on successively English and, after 1707, British military engineering and map-making. This was maintained well into the eighteenth century by further influxes of Dutch, French and German practitioners, a process aided by both military alliances and by shifts such as Louis XIV's 1685 revocation of the 1598 Edict of Nantes (which had given some rights to Protestants in Catholic France). The infrastructure of warfare in Britain in the early modern period differed from that of Europe in that the fortified town was virtually absent, and the brunt of defence was borne by isolated forts and castles with no civil function and mostly located along the coast. At the same time the science of fortification was developing, with the advent of the 'zigzag' arrangement of bastions and ramparts devised by Vauban, with walls designed to afford maximum protection to defenders whilst at the same time

[Fig. 124] A paradox of English military engineering between the sixteenth and eighteenth centuries was that, although much of what was done had to do with war with continental powers, the engineering activity depended to a considerable extent on imported expertise from the continent of Europe. An example is Sir Bernard de Gomme, a Dutchman who came to England and served on the royalist side in the civil wars. In the late 1660s the Dutch were more the potential enemy than were the French: yet here is a map of an important port prepared by a Dutchman. Compared with Dover in Fig. 122, this plan of Great Yarmouth is more evidently 'scientific' in its approach, although it retains 'decorative' features, notably the pictorial depiction of shipping. (CBTM 18629) [Great Yarmouth by Sir Bernard de Gomme, 1668, original scale 1:1920: The National Archives, MR 1/487]

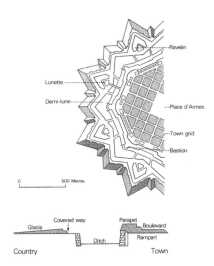

[Fig. 125] In the second half of the seventeenth century a more scientific approach to fortification came from Sébastien Le Prestre de Vauban; it was characterised by a zigzag arrangement to maximise cover for defenders and minimise opportunities for attackers. [A plan and cross-section of a typical Vauban defensive installation]

offering the greatest field of outward fire for artillery [Fig. 125]. However, such an arrangement was more suited to land warfare than to first-line defence against seaborne invasion. Vauban's influence in Britain is seen more in later, isolated forts, for example, Fort Cumberland east of Portsmouth (begun in 1746), than in replanned urban defences.[85]

Naval power rested on naval bases that needed strong local defence. The outstanding British examples are Portsmouth and Devonport. Portsmouth was an established naval base by the time of Henry VIII: the earliest maps of the town can be dated to c. 1545 and 1552 (23505), and more mapping is known from the 1580s (18515, 19713, 19714). There is then a gap until the mid-1660s, followed by a fairly regular sequence into the early nineteenth century, including one of c. 1691 produced for French troops fighting on behalf of William III in Ireland (19848).[86] Closely associated with Portsmouth was Gosport, for which there is a sequence of maps from the 1660s to the 1820s. Although the Portsmouth and Gosport area was intensively mapped for military purposes, the first published commercial civil mapping of Portsmouth appeared as late as 1833 (19111), and of Gosport in the 1870s (19851).

At Devonport the pattern was rather different. A greenfield site was selected for the new naval base in 1690, and over the next eighty years or so a planned dockyard with adjoining town – Plymouth Dock – was developed. The whole complex was enclosed by elaborate earthwork and masonry defences which on the landward side were the nearest approach in Britain to Vauban-style town defences.[87] There is a fairly consistent cartographic record from 1688 to 1793. In contrast to Portsmouth, detailed published civil mapping of Devonport appeared in the 1750s (19808, 19832). It was a proposal to augment the defences of Plymouth that resulted in a map at 1:10,560 in 1784–6 (18513). The proposal was narrowly defeated in the House of Commons, but this work was the earliest to be incorporated in a published Ordnance Survey map.[88]

Most manuscript military mapping, such as that of Portsmouth and Devonport, shows projected additions and alterations to existing defences. Elsewhere, military works were more in the nature of tactical obstructions to local attack, as at Sheerness and Harwich, rather than anything resembling a fortified town. Even at Portsmouth and Devonport the defences were aimed at protecting the dockyards rather than providing 'strong points' in their own right [**Figs 126, 127,** *overleaf*].

Few other places have anything representing the extended cartographic record of Plymouth-Devonport and Portsmouth-Gosport. Most closely comparable are the Medway towns, and Dover, Harwich and Kingston upon Hull. The nature of the mapping of each varies: at Kingston upon Hull the sequence is unusually long, from 1542 to 1840. The latest map (18710) is focused on

[Fig. 126, *right*] The planning of fortifications included both survey and scheming on the ground, and the consideration of ideas before the necessary substantial expenditure was incurred. This plan of Portsmouth was drawn in 1716 to show a projected fortification scheme. The ships can be interpreted as wholly decorative on a map that – on the evidence of careful penwork – was probably intended more for display, perhaps to a conference of officials, than as a working document. (CBTM 18520) ['A plan of Portsmouth with a design for securing the Dock, and naval stores, done by Talbot Edwards, his Majties. Second Engineer 1715/6', original scale 1:2400: The National Archives, MPHH 1/67 (2)]

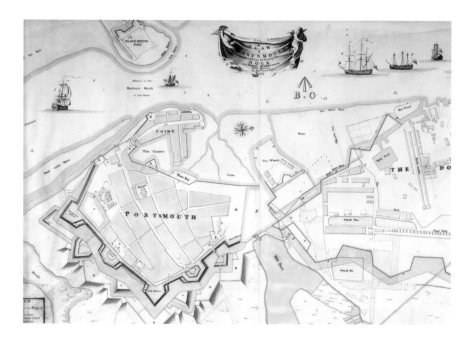

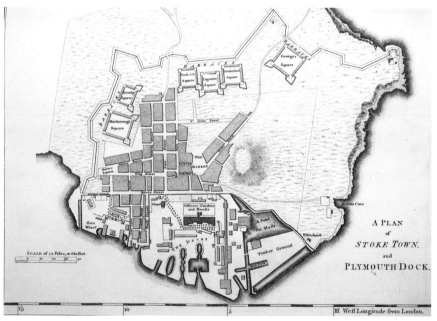

[Fig. 127, *above*] There is both military mapping of towns and maps of towns that were preponderantly military. One example of the latter is Plymouth Dock, later named Devonport. It is one of three towns in Devon that Benjamin Donn provided with a supplementary large-scale map on his one-inch survey of the county. (CBTM 18244) ['Plan of Stoke Town and Plymouth Dock', inset on Benjamin Donn, A map of the county of Devon, 1765: British Library, Maps 24.e.25]

BRITISH TOWN MAPS

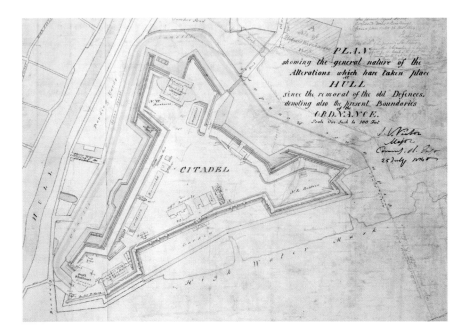

an imposing citadel, which stood outside the walls of the town and was demolished shortly afterwards [Fig. 128]. After 1800 it was much easier to defend Kingston upon Hull by various isolated forts and batteries further down the Humber.[89] At Harwich changes to the shoreline led to remapping at relatively frequent intervals in the eighteenth century [Figs 129, 130, *overleaf*, 131, *p. 191*].

Elsewhere in England, military mapping of towns was more spasmodic. Before 1603 Berwick-upon-Tweed was unique in that it was both a significant port and a frontier town, and there was intense mapping activity in the 1570s that complemented work on substantial fortifications. Thereafter Berwick declined in importance. Whereas Berwick was in a relatively exposed position and was characterised by masonry fortifications, Chatham was much more sheltered. Nonetheless, in 1667 a Dutch fleet sailed

[Fig. 128] Several streams of influence in the eighteenth century led to the creation of the Ordnance Survey. One of them was surveying military sites by the Board of Ordnance, as part of its responsibility for military infrastructure. These maps were made in a standard style, which was well established by the 1720s. The example illustrated here is an unusually late one. The scale, 1:1200, is a Board of Ordnance standard, and the mapping is in standard Ordnance style, both in general colour scheme and in detailed content: the citadel is shown in much more detail than the surrounding 'civil' areas. The map has a property ownership as well as an engineering function, and demonstrates that military mapping could be as much about territory as about ballistics. The map is signed by Major J. V. Victor, who twenty years earlier had been employed on the Board of Ordnance topographic survey in Scotland. (CBTM 18710) ['Plan showing the general nature of the alterations which have taken place at Hull since the removal of the old defences, showing also the present boundaries of the Ordnance', 1840, original scale 1:1200: The National Archives, MR 1/1228]

[Fig. 129] This map made in 1729 is concerned both with the defences of Harwich and with the problem of erosion of the soft cliffs. As usual with Board of Ordnance plans, far less attention is paid to the civilian than to the naval parts of the town. Reference letters refer mostly to damaged and repaired sea-defences. (CBTM 18587) ['Plan of the town of Harwich', 1729, original scale 1:2400: The National Archives, MPD 1/169]

[Fig. 130] Within the standard practices of the Board of Ordnance there was some scope for variation, as on this map of Harwich of 1752. Compared with Figure 129, street frontages are shown more sensitively, and particular attention is paid to the parish church – left of centre and identifiable by 'buttresses'. The indications of timber in what in 1729 was described as the 'Navy Yard' are quite striking. Most map-readers would accept that the disposition of timber stacks is more conventional than actual. (CBTM 18592) ['A survey of the cliff and town of Harwich shewing the incroachments made by the sea, since ye year 1709', original scale 1:1200, 1752: The National Archives, MR 1/1222.]

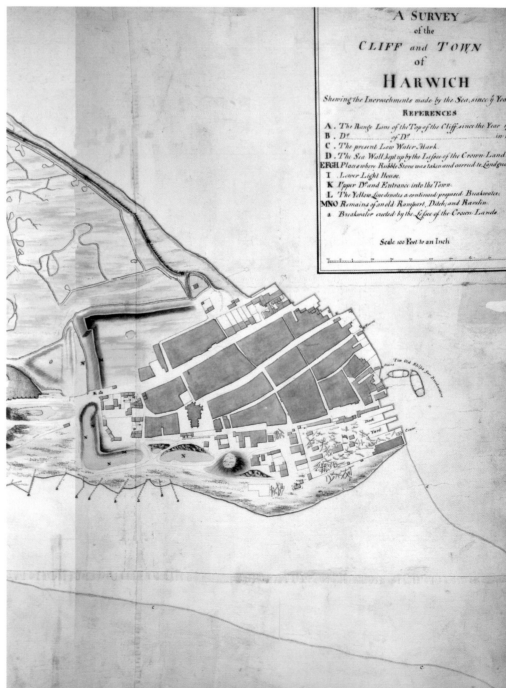

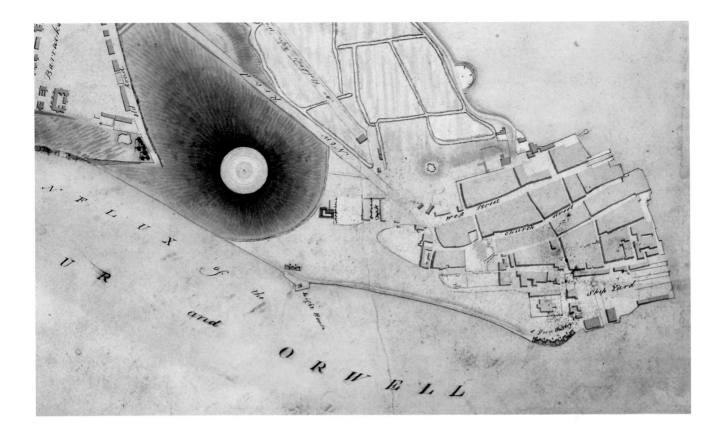

up the Medway and did much damage, regarded at the time as a catastrophe nearly on a par with the great plague in 1665 and the Great Fire of London in 1666. It is unsurprising that after this event there was close interest in the submarine details of the River Medway and in the erection at its mouth of defences to deter a hostile fleet from entering. For this reason, whereas much of the mapping of Berwick, Portsmouth and Kingston upon Hull is at relatively large scales for laying out fortification schemes – 1:2400 is representative – that of the Medway is at much smaller scales, typically around 1:18,000, and is related to lines of approach [Fig. 132]. There is no known mapping of Chatham comparable in scale with that of Sheerness, laid out as a dockyard in 1665. The early cartographic

[Fig. 131] Change on the ground often made new surveys of military sites desirable, and Harwich was no exception. It is seen here in 1808. The consistency of general approach, both in cover and style, is exemplified by the continuing summary treatment of the civil area, although two of the principal streets are now named. 'R.M.S.D.' stands for 'Royal Military Surveyor & Draughtsman', a military corps raised in 1800 by enrolling civilian Board of Ordnance staff. (CBTM 18794) [Extract from 'Plan of the Peninsula of Harwich surveyed by James W. Anderson R.M.S.D. 1808', original scale 1:2400: The National Archives, MPHH 1/299]

[Fig. 132] In 1667 a Dutch raid in the River Medway was highly destructive, and this led to increased attention to its defences. As part of this, a survey of the river was made by Grenville Collins in 1688: this explains not only the soundings in the river, but also the pictures of ships. This basic survey remained in use for a long time, and this copy dates from 1750: it illustrates both the urgency and the longevity of some military surveys. The map was drawn in the Board of Ordnance office at the Tower of London. The style is – the ships apart – standard Board of Ordnance, with buildings in carmine and associated gardens shown distinctly. This is one of four similar contemporary copies of this map, but is the only one to carry the name of its draughtsman. (CBTM 18503) ['A plan of the River Medway with the fortifications adjacent, &c.', by Thomas Chamberlain, 1750: original scale 1:19,800: The National Archives, MPHH 1/60]

record of Sheerness is relatively sparse. The earliest maps are a 1:4800 map of 1725 (20998) and a 1:2400 map of 1781 (20999). The dockyard was rebuilt in 1812–23, which generated a number of maps (18613–18617) [Figs 133, *below*, 134, *overleaf*]. Sheerness marks the last significant urban military mapping exercise before the advent of the Ordnance Survey large-scale map series.

Most of the extant military mapping of British towns was produced by map-makers employed by British state agencies. However, there is a significant minority of maps of French origin. One group of twenty-seven plans of towns is part of a manuscript atlas containing plans of northern European towns and cities; it appears to date from the mid-seventeenth century.[90] They are based on John Speed's town maps and show little more than town walls and churches. Their content suggests that they may have been intended as much for the armchair study of strategy as for any contemplated operations.[91]

[Fig. 133] The detailed cartographic record for Sheerness begins much later than for other naval bases in southern and eastern England. This may perhaps be accounted for in part by the rebuilding of the dockyard and associated defences in 1812–23. This is one of a number of maps of this town produced at that time: the ground-colouring indicates the various owners. Buildings are apparently shown according to the standard military convention based on whether they are of brick (red) or wooden (brown) construction. The elaborate mapping of individual buildings and plots in fact only covers part of the settlement. (CBTM 18614) ['Survey of Mile Town and ground in front of the new lines, Sheerness', by W. Chambers, R.S.D., 1815, original scale 1:2400: The National Archives, MPHH 1/599]

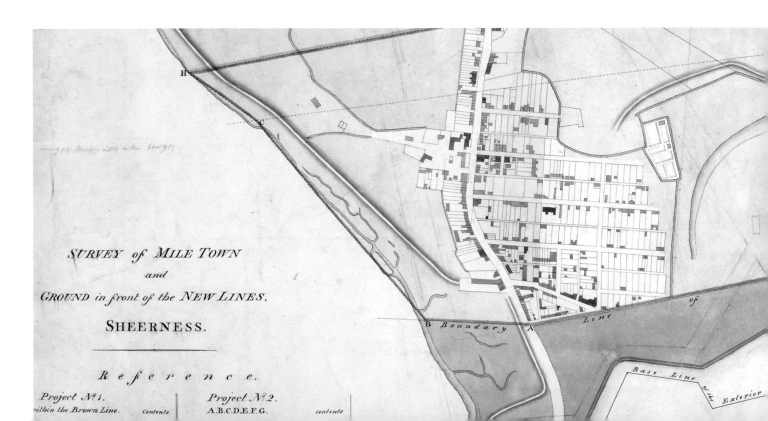

SURVEY of MILE TOWN
and
GROUND in front of the NEW LINES.

SHEERNESS.

R e f e r e n c e.

Project Nº 1.
within the Brown Line.   Contents.

Project Nº 2.
A.B.C.D.E.F.G.   contents

[Fig. 134] This map of the Blue Town district of Sheerness was produced in 1811 when the dock rebuilding was still at the planning stage. The detail in which dockyard areas are mapped contrasts with the much more generalised approach to the town, where basically only frontages are shown. The use of grey infill for buildings deviates from usual military practice. (CBTM 18613) [Untitled map of Blue Town, Sheerness, surveyed 1811, original scale 1:1200: The National Archives, MR 1/1214]

More directly connected to war is a small group of maps in J. N. Bellin's *Recueil des villes ports d'Angleterre*, published in 1759 during the Seven Years War. This has maps of several ports, including two inland ones (Oxford and York), but, significantly, not one of London.[91] More covert is a group of manuscript maps of ports along the south coast in 1768 with associated reports on defences [Fig. 135].[92]

French schemes for invasion were actively pursued a number of times between 1756 and 1805. In the event there were only a few coastal raids, really of no more than nuisance value.[93] In 1802 the *Bureau d'Industrie* produced an engraved map of London (23256) which might have been intended to facilitate an invasion.

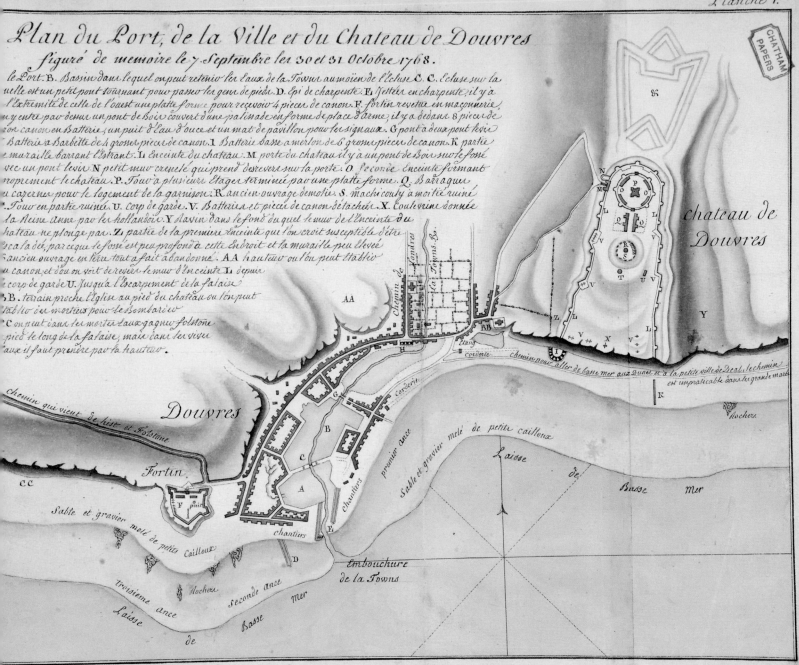

Plan du Port, de la Ville et du Chateau de Douvres figuré de memoire le 7 Septembre les 30 et 31 Octobre 1768.

[Fig. 135] The eighteenth century was dominated by warfare: even in peacetime there was continued suspicion of motives, and discreet preparations were made for another conflict. Such must be the explanation of this French map of Dover, accompanying a report of 1768, apparently made for espionage purposes. The set also includes the Tower of London and Windsor Castle. The style is broadly similar to that of the Board of Ordnance, but hills are given brown-sepia shading. This map illustrates the use of military mapping both for potentially hostile operations and as belonging to a generally 'European' rather than 'national' style. (CBTM 23496) ['Planche 1', 'Plan du Port de la Ville et du Cateau de Douvres....', 1768, original scale about 1:7500: The National Archives, MF 1/54]

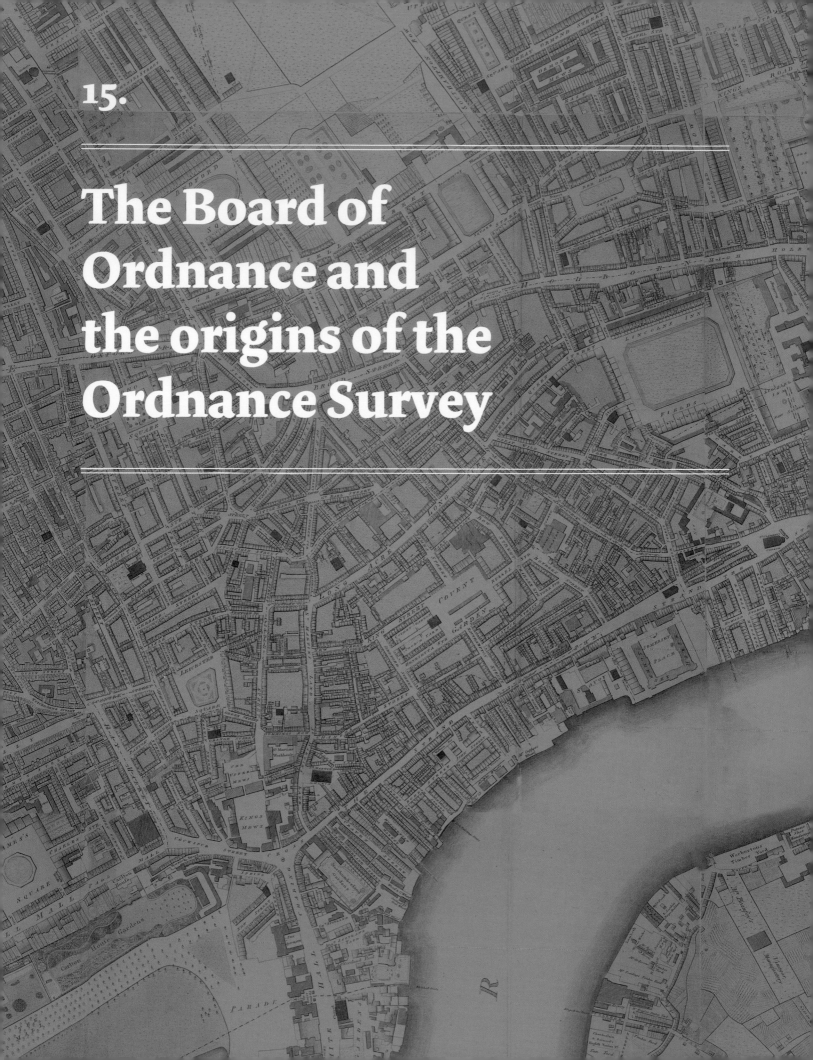

15.

The Board of Ordnance and the origins of the Ordnance Survey

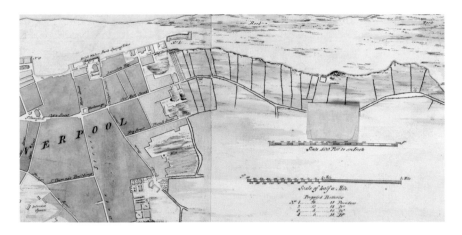

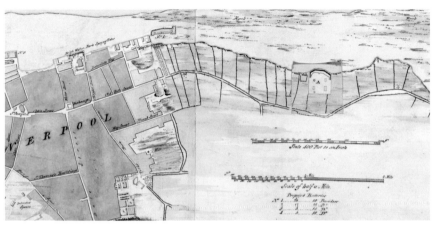

[Fig. 136] In the eighteenth century Liverpool was a fast-growing port, which made for both local prosperity and increased attractiveness for enemy raiding. Evidently by 1759 the hostilities that would later be known as the Seven Years War had been going on for long enough to justify investigating the building of a battery to protect the port. This map shows the site. The battery north of Liverpool proposed in 1759 is indicated by means of a flap overlaying the existing landscape – a 'before (above) and after (below)' technique perhaps better known in the landscape park designs of Humphry Repton. (CBTM 18619) ['A survey of the Town of Liverpool and River Mersey from thence to the Sea AD 1759', original scale 1:4800: The National Archives, MR 1/573]

THE BOARD OF ORDNANCE was ultimately responsible for most large-scale military urban plans from the late seventeenth century onwards. It was a military organisation separate from the War Office up to 1855 and was responsible for artillery, munitions and most military infrastructure. Away from established naval bases on the southern and eastern coasts, mapping activity occurred serendipitously as circumstances required. For example, Liverpool grew considerably as a port in the eighteenth century, and the Seven Years War of 1756–63 occasioned a fortification proposal in 1759 (18619) [Fig. 136]. The Board of Ordnance mapped Carlisle in 1716 (18610) and 1746 (18611, 18612) in the wake of the Jacobite uprisings.

Maps of Inverness (21800) and Stirling (21675, 21790) of 1725 have counterparts in England, for example at Sheerness (20998). A war with Spain was narrowly averted at this time, and the production of these maps can be clearly related to that political context.[94] The maps are very much the product of a mindset anticipating sieges rather than battles. With the exception of Fort William, the map record for other significant military centres in Scotland is both more fragmentary and more immediately connected with the Jacobite uprisings. The emphasis of 'defence' mapping in the two countries was therefore very different. In England military mapping was a response to an external threat. In Scotland such threat was mainly internal. Thus Inverness was mapped in 1718 (23133), 1725 (21800) and 1747 (21801). Perth was mapped in 1716 (21788, 22918, 22919), 1746 (21789) and 1765 (22912) and Stirling in 1725 (21675, 21790), 1740 (22778) and 1745–6 (21799, 22817). The maps of Stirling are notable for identifying the houses of rebel leaders and for the relative detail in which the town, as well as the castle, is mapped. An unusually late map of Inverness of 1802 (22815) is remarkable for the minuteness with which divisions between buildings are shown. At 1:1200 it anticipates in content, if not lineal development, the mapping of Irish towns at 1:1056 by the Ordnance Survey from the late 1820s onwards [Fig. 137]. Edinburgh was a centre of Hanoverian loyalism, and in September 1745 the *Gentleman's*

BRITISH TOWN MAPS

The following labels appear in the map and its legend:

TOWN o
with
FOR:
and Remain's
E:
A . FORT GEORGE
B . The Governours Ho
C . The Officers Barra
D . The Soldiers Barra
E . The Chappell
SCAL.

EAST STREET
CASTLE STREET
KING'S STREET
CHURCH STREET
ving Ground
S
S
ROA

Magazine published a map of the city (22014) because of the topicality of the uprising. It was mapped as part of the Military Survey of Scotland 1747–55 a few years later, and a map at 1:10,800 was prepared in 1807 showing the earthwork defences against Napoleonic invasions (22812).[95]

Board of Ordnance mapping is characterised by a high degree of uniformity of both presentation and scale. That said, as with other specialised mapping, the nature of maps produced for military purposes was conditioned by the need for, and circumstances of, their production, regardless of whether the 'corporate maker' was the Board of Ordnance, the Quartermaster General's department, or any other. More than some other specialised cartography, military mapping was focused on particular needs, and there is usually a sharp division between the levels of military and civic detail. Military structures are recorded in far greater detail than are

[Fig. 137] Although the Board of Ordnance had a standard approach to the colouring of its maps, the non-military content might vary, as is demonstrated by this remarkable map of Inverness of 1802. While the overall style is a good example of that standardised by the Board of Ordnance, a striking feature is the great detail in which buildings and the boundaries of plots are mapped. More characteristic of Ordnance mapping is a particular absence of building names, and there is nothing explicit to show that the large building, bottom centre, is in fact the main church in the town. It is unclear why the town was mapped at this unusual level of detail. (CBTM 22815) ['A plan of the Town of Inverness with the ruin's of Fort George and remain's of Olivers Fort' [sic], c. 1802, probably by J. S. Sedley, original scale 1:1200: The National Archives, MR 1/1053]

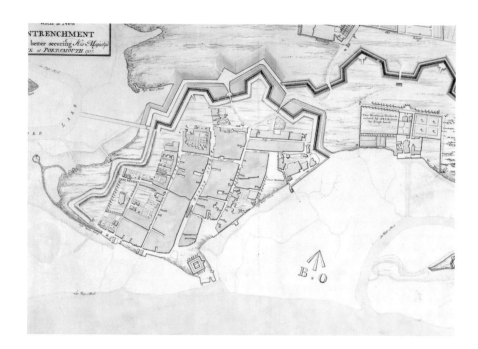

civilian components. Ground cover was of particular military interest, and from a military point of view civic buildings are simply another form of ground cover. Even churches are treated as just another area of building [Fig. 138].

This depiction of different categories of structures at different levels of detail is well exemplified by the mapping of towns such as Devonport, Gosport, Harwich, Kingston upon Hull and Plymouth, where frontages are mapped in detail, indicating the varying widths of streets, but otherwise building is reduced to an abstraction [see Fig. 138, above]. Although the Board of Ordnance maintained a high degree of uniformity in presentation and scale, it is apparent that the Ordnance was less successful in maintaining absolute uniformity of content. Inverness, for example, is mapped in detail unprecedented for purely military purposes.

As will be recounted in sections 17 and 18, the main work of the mature Ordnance Survey would be at scales of 1:2500 or larger, that is broadly similar to the scales used by the Board of Ordnance when mapping towns for military purposes.[96] However, the actual origins of the Ordnance Survey as a mapping institution lie in two quite different initiatives in the 1780s. One was the establishment of a national triangulation network that served both scientific and military purposes, and the other was mapping of mainly coastal areas that were of particular military importance. The military mapping was at first made at the six-inch (1:10,560) scale; later the three-inch (1:21,120) and two-inch (1:31,680) scales were used. It was the two-inch scale that dominated the national survey that was ordered in 1795, and became the basis for a published one-inch (1:63,360) map. However, it was the six-inch mapping that provided the inspiration for a survey of Ireland that was put in hand in 1824, to serve as the basis for a reform of local taxation. In turn, the survey of Ireland inspired a change in 1840 to the six-inch scale for the as yet unsurveyed northern half of Britain. As the six-inch was found inadequate in Ireland for mapping towns, the five-foot (1:1056) scale was adopted for larger urban areas; this practice, too, was imported into Britain after 1840.[97]

Thus although it had a military organisation, the Ordnance Survey developed after 1815 in response to civil, not military, considerations: and most of

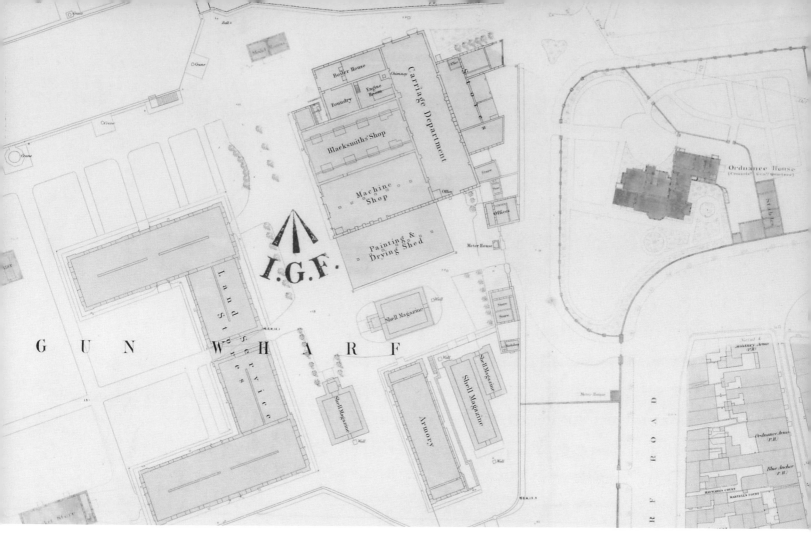

[Fig. 139] In the same way that several developments in the eighteenth century had led to the formation of the Ordnance Survey, so did a number of influences lead towards the Ordnance Survey's 'town scale' mapping. Although the range of scales was standard across the kingdom, the timing of some of the work was due to military considerations. One instance of this effect was at Portsmouth, where the town was one of a number mapped at 1:500 'out of turn' in the early 1860s, as part of planning a response to the perceived ambitions of the French Emperor, Napoleon III. Even after Napoleon's downfall in 1870, Portsmouth continued to be the most important of naval bases, and this no doubt explains the exceptional measure of revising its mapping in the late 1870s. This set of the town's maps with revisions added in manuscript is an unusual survival. The added work, in carmine and pink, readily stands out from the unchanged earlier work, printed in black. While this demonstrates how published Ordnance Survey mapping could be annotated for specific individual purposes, the reason here is probably the War Office's anxiety for up-to-date mapping sooner than it could be engraved by the Ordnance Survey, as this revision subsequently appeared on the published sheet. [Ordnance Survey 1:500 Hampshire sheet 84.11.4, with revision added in manuscript, 1879: The National Archives, WO 78/2315]

BRITISH TOWN MAPS

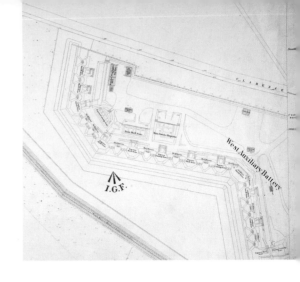

its relatively unskilled military mapping work was performed by civilians under military supervision. However, the rise of Napoleon III in France from 1848 prompted a series of large-scale surveys that were similar in purpose albeit different in content to those of the eighteenth century. In 1854–8 the Ordnance Survey made large-scale surveys of Aldershot, Gosport and Dover at War Office behest for training and fortification purposes. A more elaborate fortification programme started in 1859, soon to be dubbed 'Palmerston's follies', which spawned the largest number of post-medieval 'castles' in Britain.[98] In preparation for this the Ordnance Survey mapped large areas around Harwich, south London, the Medway, Newhaven, Portsmouth, the Isle of Wight, Portland, Plymouth, Milford Haven and also Cannock Chase. This last was to be the location of a central arsenal far removed from the vulnerable coast. These maps mark the effective end of military mapping as a distinct contributor to urban cartography. Henceforth, schemes to construct and augment defences were plotted on standard Ordnance Survey sheets, the only difference being that maps of areas of military interest were often prepared in two editions, one 'For War Department Use only' showing all details, and the other for general sale with fortifications omitted [Figs 139, 140]. The previously highly distinctive genre of military mapping was subsumed within a civilian Ordnance Survey discussed in Sections 17 and 18.

[Fig. 140] Although 1:500 maps of dockyard towns such as Portsmouth were made to a national standard designed to serve both civil and military users, security considerations led to some sheets being published in two editions, one being for very restricted official use. Thus the 1879 mapping of this battery at Portsmouth seems to show almost everything except for the gun mounts, and would no doubt have been of great interest to the French general staff. [Extract from Ordnance Survey 1:500 Hampshire sheet 84.16.1, 'For War Department Purposes Only': The National Archives, WO 78/2315]

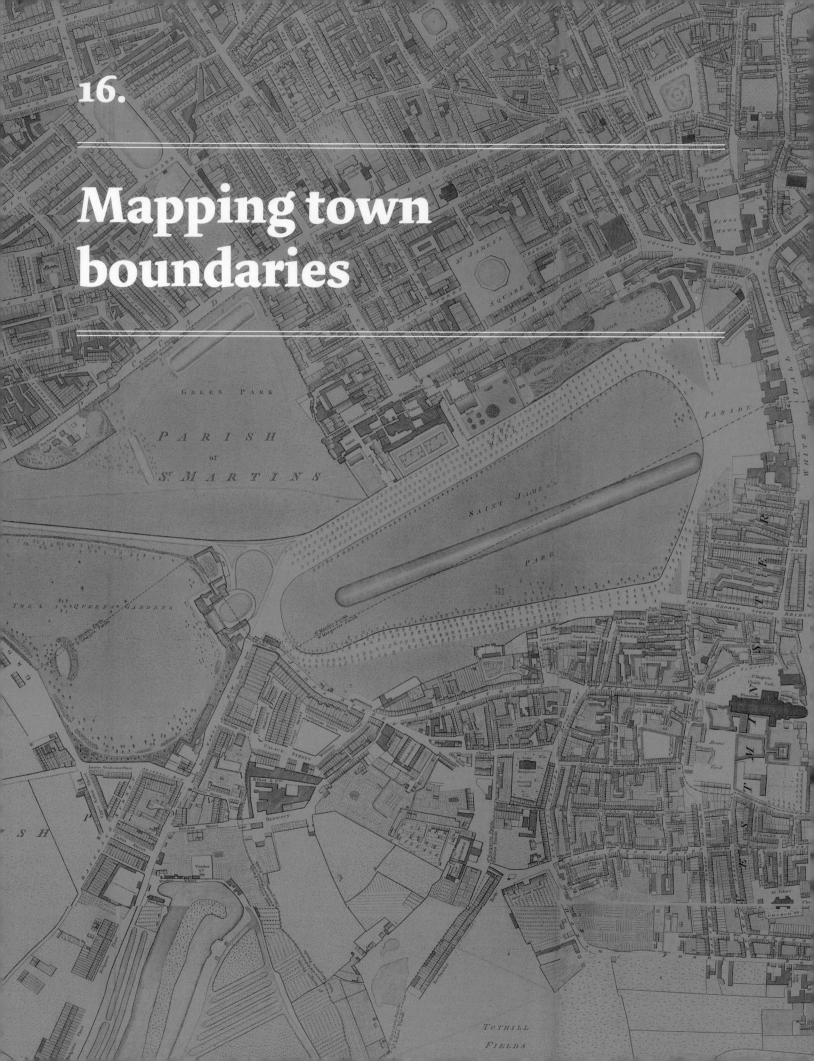

16.
Mapping town boundaries

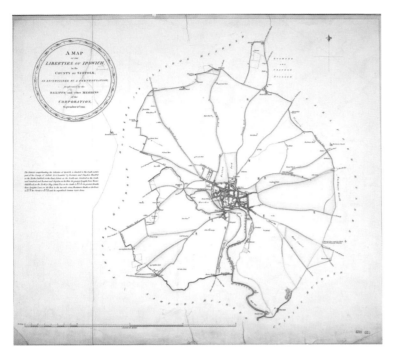

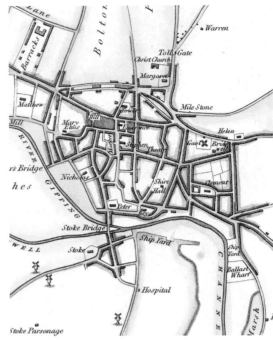

[Fig. 141] *A map of the liberties of Ipswich in the county of Suffolk, as ascertained by a perambulation performed by the baliffs and other members of the Corporation, September 17th. 1812.* The emphasis here is on boundaries rather than the town: such a map says more about the context of the urban environment than about the environment itself. (CBTM 18795) [Detail: British Library, Maps 5210. (11.)]

MOST OF THE KNOWN EXAMPLES of detailed urban boundary maps are from the City of London, and are complementary to rating maps. Although the number of London parishes known to have commissioned various types of boundary map is small, they account for about half the total of this genre of map known in Britain.[99] The maps are usually manuscript, but there are occasional published examples outside London, for example of Ipswich (1812: 18795) [Fig. 141] and Rochester (1822/31: 19124).

A variation on the parish boundary map peculiar to the City of London is the mapping of wards. Ralph Hyde has found over a hundred of these maps, dating from between 1720 and 1858.[100] Most were produced to accompany histories and are derived from other, general-purpose maps. Thus the first set, produced for Strype's edition of Stow's *Survey of London*, clearly

Enlarged from the Outline Maps
of the Ordnance Survey.

[Fig. 142] The mapping of the whole City of London by Samuel Angell and Michael Meredith, made between 1855 and 1858, was overall the most sophisticated and detailed before the making of the Ordnance Survey five-foot scale mapping in the early 1870s. The Angell and Meredith maps are at a scale of 1 inch to 10 feet (1:528) and are based on an enlargement and infilling of the Ordnance Survey 'skeleton' survey of 1848–50. This is Bassishaw Ward. (CBTM 23195) [London Metropolitan Archives, Secondary's Plan no.4]

derives from the Ogilby & Morgan survey of the 1670s [see Fig. 49, pp. 80–81]. By far the most elaborate is the final set of thirty-two maps at 1:528, produced by Samuel Angell and Michael Meredith in 1855–8, and used for electoral registration purposes [Fig. 142].[101]

The most far-ranging changes to urban boundaries in the nineteenth century were in connection with Parliamentary reform. Existing borough boundaries were recorded and then new ones set out on maps. The first such exercise was undertaken in 1831–2. Commissioners were appointed to conduct local investigations of boundaries, and maps to illustrate their work were produced under the superintendence of Lieutenant Robert Kearsley Dawson, seconded from the Ordnance Survey of Ireland. Base maps were compiled from a variety of sources. Some are enlargements of manuscript field-drawings, mostly at the two-inch (1:31,680) scale,

made for the published Ordnance Survey one-inch map. English boundary maps were lithographed and printed at 1:31,680, while those of Scotland are more sophisticated and are engraved at the six-inch (1:10,560) scale [Fig. 143].

There was a further wave of urban boundary recording in England and Wales following the passage of the Municipal Corporations Act in 1835. Once again commissioners visited the towns and maps were made to illustrate their recommendations, a process again supervised by Dawson. The end result is more sophisticated than in 1832. Most of the detailed mapping is at the four-inch (1:15,840) scale and is engraved [Fig. 144, *overleaf*].[102] Parish churches are usually the only buildings distinguished, together with

[Fig. 143] The mapping of Scottish parliamentary boroughs for the reform of 1831–2 was more sophisticated than was the corresponding operation in England and Wales. In Scotland a larger scale – the 1:10,560 – was used, and the maps engraved rather than lithographed. This is the map of Aberdeen; it is similar in style to others in the series, with buildings generalised. Very few buildings are identified by name. (CBTM 21604) [Report upon the boundaries of the several cities, burghs, and towns in Scotland, British Parliamentary Papers (House of Commons Series) session 1831–2 (paper 408) British Library, Maps 145.c.27. (2.)]

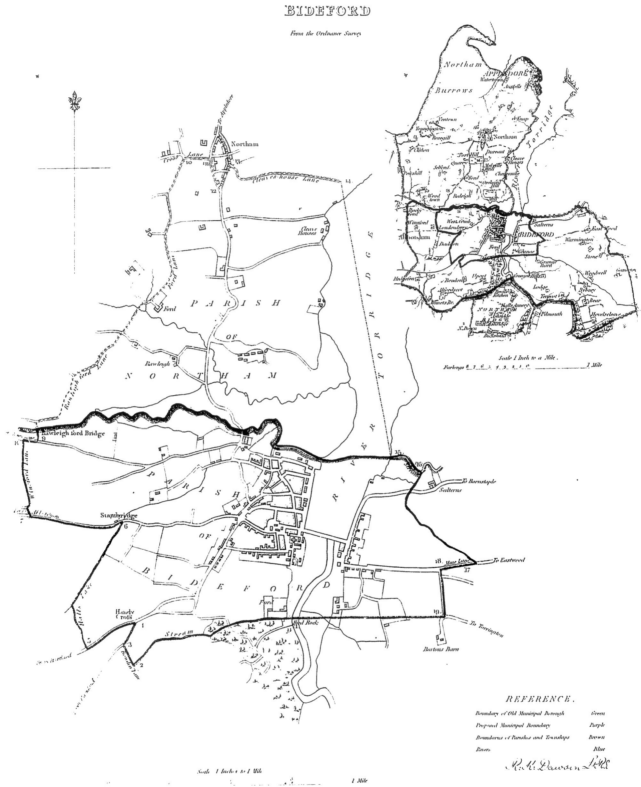

BIDEFORD

From the Ordnance Survey

REFERENCE.

Boundary of Old Municipal Borough	Green
Proposed Municipal Boundary	Purple
Boundaries of Parishes and Townships	Brown
Rivers	Blue

Scale 1 Inch to 1 Mile

1 Mile

Scale 1 Inch to a Mile.

1 Mile

occasional landmark windmills. Other buildings are shown in an anonymous, generalised way. Although there was no equivalent Act for Scotland, a few 'local' burgh boundary maps were produced after 1832, including Inverness (1841: 22925), Oban (1846: 21850), Aberdeen (1862: 22933), Arbroath (1863: 21921) and Dumbarton (1869: 21928). The last two are burgh extensions, and the Dumbarton map is derived from the Ordnance Survey 1:2500 survey.[103] Another is Kirkcaldy, where boundaries were mapped in 1840 for the implementation of a Prisons Act (22800). There were further reforms to Parliamentary boundaries in 1867–8 which reused a mixture of 1830s maps and available Ordnance Survey Maps. [104]

The real growth of towns during the nineteenth century made the division of ancient parishes desirable, and from 1835 the Ecclesiastical Commissioners had powers to make orders designating new ecclesiastical parishes. The orders for these new parishes were accompanied by maps, but these are remarkable only for their minimalistic and derivative approach, using whatever was to hand: Ordnance Survey 1:10,560 maps where available, otherwise tithe or similar maps. The intention seems to have been to show boundaries simply for general illustration, but not in such a way that boundaries depicted could be reconstructed on the ground by reference to the maps.

[**Fig. 144,** *opposite*] The reform of the House of Commons enacted in 1832 was followed by further reforms: one of these involved the reorganisation of municipal corporations. It was necessary to define the boundaries of the reformed corporations, and some boroughs were divided into wards. Often, as at Bideford in Devon, there was both a 1:63,360 map of the outer boundary and a 1:15,840 map of the town itself, with both derived from the same Ordnance Survey material. (CBTM 18878) [Map of Bideford in Report of the Commissioners... upon the boundaries and wards of certain boroughs and corporate towns..., British Parliamentary Papers (House of Commons Series) session 1837 (paper 238)]

17.
Sanitation maps and Ordnance Survey town plans

SANITATION LAY AT THE CORE of urban improvement. In the later eighteenth and earlier nineteenth centuries some towns obtained Improvement Acts, which provided for paving and lighting as well as some drainage and water supply works. These piecemeal improvements resulted in a limited amount of urban mapping. The map of Exeter by John Coldridge, 1819 (18291), is typical in that it is at a large scale – one inch to 1 chain (1:792) – but shows only streets and sewers. There is a lack of behind-frontage detail.

Sanitation was intimately connected with poverty. Growing discontent with the burden of poor rates led to the passing of the Poor Law Amendment Act of 1834 and establishment of the Poor Law Commissioners. Their secretary was Edwin Chadwick, who believed that a main cause of poverty was ill health. Improved sanitation, he argued, would lead to improved health and less poverty. Money spent on sanitary works would be more than recouped in lower poor rates. This is the underlying message of Chadwick's *Report on the sanitary condition of the labouring population*, issued in the autumn of 1842.[105]

We explained in Section 15 that the 1:1056 scale was adopted in Ireland as it was needed to provide extra detail for valuation of urban areas. The Treasury minute of October 1840 that authorised the change to the 1:10,560 scale made no mention of the use of any larger scale for towns. The use of the 1:1056 scale in

northern Britain was at first simply a survey practice, and there was certainly no authority for publishing the 1:1056 mapping at national expense.[106] In 1843 the Ordnance Survey was approached to supply tracings of 1:1056 mapping of Leeds and Manchester, an estimate was supplied for mapping London likewise and, with some prompting by Prince Albert, a 1:1056 survey of Windsor was put in train.[107] Other towns expressed interest in 1:1056-scale mapping, but in the short term action was frustrated by the Treasury's unwillingness to grant any funds for other than 1:10,560 production. At about the same time a Health of Towns Commission was appointed. Its reports in 1844 and 1845 emphasised Edwin Chadwick's belief that there must be proper mapping before any schemes were devised. The reports stated that appropriate maps – to include buried pipes and sewers in addition to the surface details hitherto customarily recorded by the Ordnance – could be obtained economically whilst Ordnance Survey personnel were at work in northern England. But the Treasury and the Home Office continued to argue that those towns wanting copies of the maps should pay themselves. Eventually engraving of 1:1056-scale mapping was authorised in December 1846. Wigan was the first town to be completed, in September 1848 [Fig. 145].

In 1847 the Metropolitan Commissions of Sewers were reformed, and in 1848 the newly reconstituted Commission proposed to procure a 1:1056 survey

[**Fig. 145**] The 1:1056 scale was first used by the Ordnance Survey in Ireland in order that urban plots could be mapped with sufficient clarity for local taxation assessment purposes. The scale was introduced to Britain after 1840 as a working practice, but it soon justified itself as a tool for planning sewerage and other urban sanitary reform. The demand for copies was such that, unlike in Ireland, it was worthwhile to engrave the mapping produced at this scale in Britain. Wigan was the first town to be completed, in 1848. Details shown include divisions between buildings, ground floors of public buildings, and functions of buildings within industrial premises. [British Library, OST 100 – Wigan sheet 5]

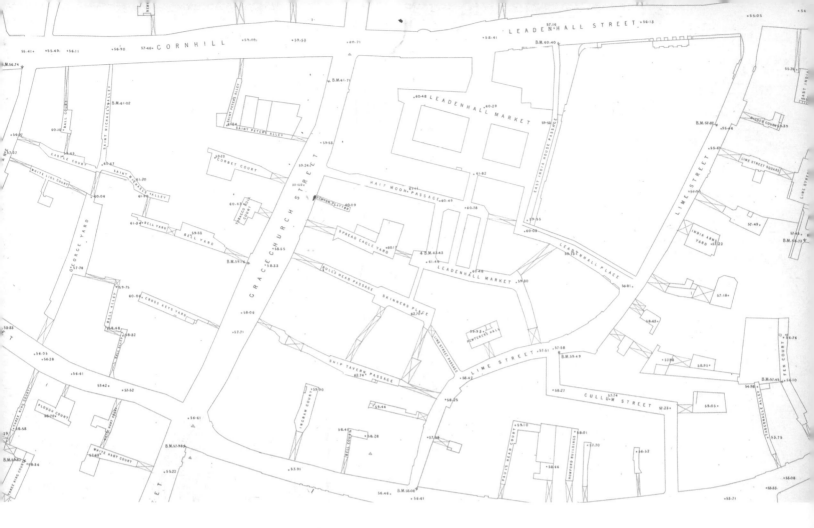

[Fig. 146] In the 1840s the main work of the Ordnance Survey was in northern England and Scotland, but in 1848–50 it made a 'skeleton survey' of London for the Metropolitan Commissioners of Sewers. As this extract shows, the maps depicted little more than building frontages, street names, and altitudes. It was intended that they would provide a framework for the Commissioners' own surveyors to 'fill in', though in fact very few such surveys seem to have been made. [British Library, Maps OST 61–76: sheet 449]

of London from the Ordnance Survey. This was obstructed in the House of Commons by James Wyld, a map publisher who had obtained the plates of Horwood's map of London and proposed to update them to provide a map of the Metropolis for sanitary work. The Commissioners got around this by commissioning the Ordnance Survey to produce a 'skeleton' plan of London, extending somewhat beyond the built-up area, that would show levels and frontages only [Fig. 146].[108]

A Public Health Act of 1848 confined to England and Wales established a central General Board of Health, and enabled towns where either the death rate was excessive or where sufficient ratepayers petitioned

[Fig. 147] The 1:528 scale was adopted by the Ordnance Survey at the behest of the General Board of Health. The Board's advisers thought that the 1:1056 scale was inadequate for sanitary planning so towns which set up Local Boards of Health following the Public Health Act of 1848 had no choice but to commission a survey at the 1:528 scale. Some of these surveys were made by the Ordnance Survey, and a few were engraved and published as part of the standard range of national mapping. This is an extract from the survey of Barnard Castle, made in 1852. Details portrayed on these maps include sewer grates (SG), dustbins (DB), pumps (o P), piggeries (Py), brew houses (BH), cow houses (CoH) and stables (ST): all of these had sanitary implications. Public houses are indicated, but not beer houses.

[British Library, OST 16 – sheet 1]

to set up local boards of health. The Chadwick precept was to be followed – a large-scale survey had to be made before a sanitation scheme could be planned. Surveys were done at the larger 'ten foot' scale (1:528). The Ordnance Survey itself produced twenty-nine new surveys, and three more by enlargement from the smaller, 1:1056 scale.[109] These maps produced under the superintendence of the General Board of Health in the early 1850s and including sanitary details – both those directly related to sewerage, such as privies and cess pits, and other hazards or potential nuisances, such as dustbins, brew houses, coach houses and cow sheds – marked the high point of detailed representation of towns by the Ordnance Survey [Fig. 147].[110]

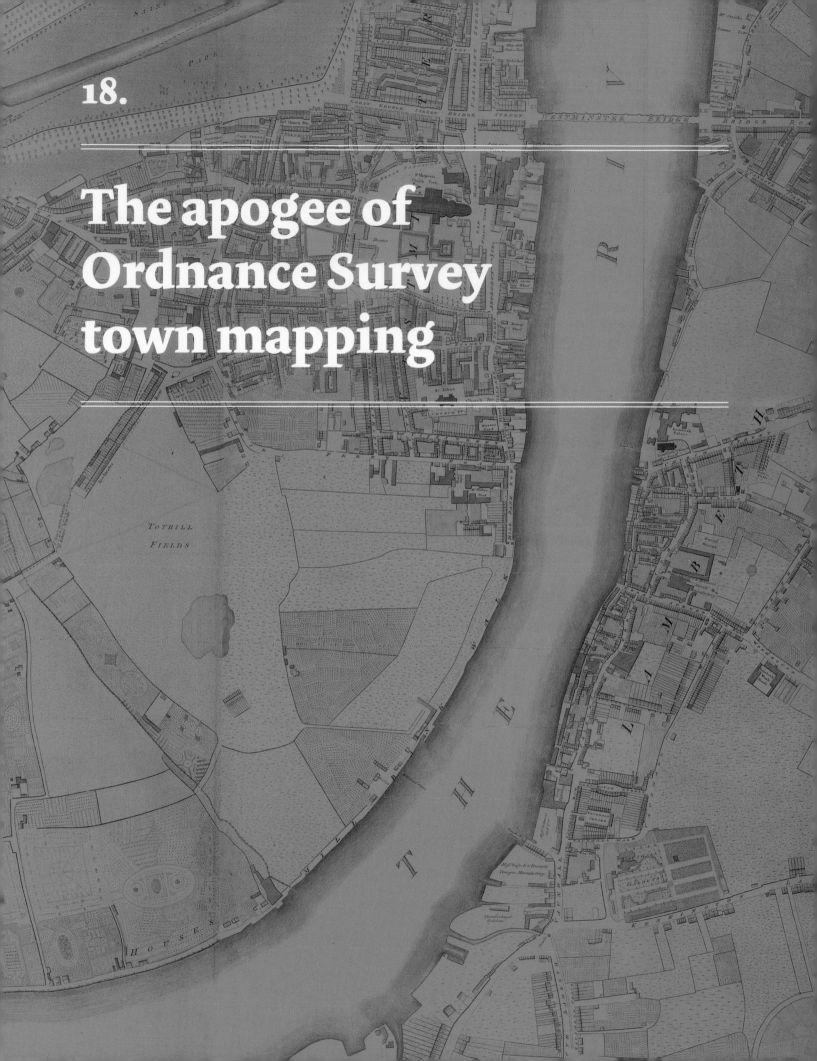

18.

The apogee of Ordnance Survey town mapping

DISCONTENT WITH THE SLOW PROGRESS of the
1:10,560 survey in northern Britain by 1851 sparked
off a series of inquiries that resulted in a Treasury
decision in May 1855 that the standard rural scale
should be 1:2500, and 1:500 for urban areas. The
argument was that the detail to be recorded at 1:2500
and 1:500 involved little extra work as compared with
that for the 1:10,560 and 1:1056 scales, but that the
larger scales had many more potential applications
than did the smaller ones; smaller-scale mapping
could always be produced by reduction.[111] Thus the
'sanitary scale' of 1:500 – a 'rational' version of the 1:528
– would eventually be available to all towns of over
4,000 population yet to be surveyed by the Ordnance
Survey. In practice in the late 1850s and early 1860s
only towns in the far north of England and in southern
Scotland benefitted, but in 1863 a resurvey of southern
Britain was authorised. By 1894 1:500 surveys covered
nearly 400 towns and cities. This includes a number
of maps of towns that had been surveyed before 1855
at the 1:1056 scale.[112] London mapping was completed
in the mid-1870s and was the last to be engraved. From
the late 1850s zincography was increasingly used. The
standard specification for the 1:500 resembles that
for the 1:1056. Both record buildings and associated
divisions, to the extent of indicating the thickness of
garden walls, and above-ground sanitary and utility-
related features such as sewer-grates and lamp-posts
[**Figs 148, 149, 150, 151,** *overleaf*].

[Fig. 148] In 1855 the Ordnance Survey substituted 1:500 for 1:528, as the 'rational' scale accorded better with the scale of 1:2500 adopted for rural survey at that time. The established technique of engraving on copper continued to be used for some of the early 1:500 mapping, such as that of Gateshead (1857) illustrated here. Details such as 'SG' (sewer grate), 'WP' (water plug) and 'GP' (gas plug) are unusual on 1:500 mapping, as is the note 'Ruins of buildings destroyed by the fire of Octr. 6th. 1854'. [British Library, Maps OST 20 – sheet 4]

[Fig. 149] Engraving on copper was expensive, and the cheaper zincographic process was increasingly used for reproducing 1:500 map sheets, as for Guildford, surveyed in 1870. These zincographed maps were usually issued hand-coloured: brick and stone buildings were infilled light carmine, wood and iron buildings were infilled grey, and a rich carmine was used to infill walls. The ground floor layout of the County Police Station is shown, complete with the water closets. [British Library, Maps OST 48 – sheet XXIII.16.19]

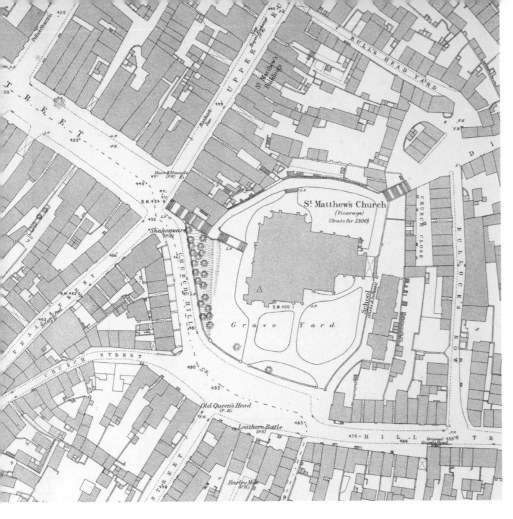

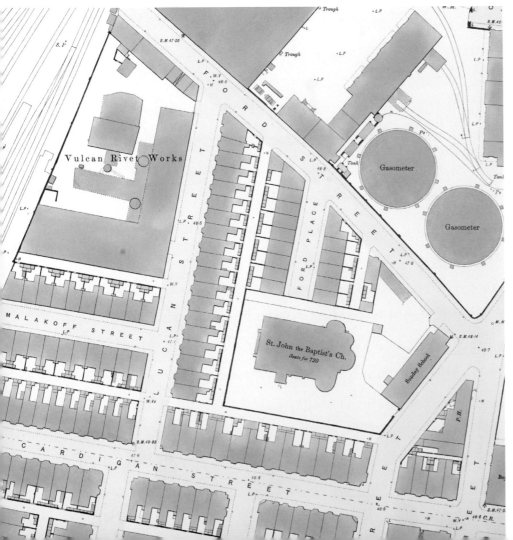

[Fig. 150] Hand-colouring was labour-intensive, and after the early 1870s was little used. Instead buildings were hatched, as here at Walsall, which was surveyed at 1:500 in 1883–4. [British Library, Maps OST 154 – sheet LXIII.11.6]

[Fig. 151] For reasons that are unknown, hand-colouring was revived in the late 1880s for the remapping of towns in Lancashire and Yorkshire at 1:500, as here at Stockton-on-Tees, surveyed in 1891–2 and published in 1893. This sheet was published at a time when the continuing usefulness of the 1:500 was being questioned, and early in 1894 the 1:500 was discontinued as a state-funded scale. Stockton was actually in County Durham, but was mapped as part of the Yorkshire operation because of the way that its suburbs straddled the county boundary. [British Library, Maps OST 232 – sheet L.12.18]

[Fig. 152] Although in the 1880s the standard 1:500 style used hatched buildings, and therefore did not indicate the structural nature of buildings, this information continued to be shown on the 1:2500, as here at Aberystwyth in 1885. [British Library, Maps OS – 1:2500 Cardiganshire, first edition, sheet VI.9]

In the mid-1850s the need for sanitation had seemed to make a scale of 1:500 logical for built-up areas, but by the time that the '1:1056 towns' were being remapped at 1:500 in the early 1890s the force of the sanitary argument was less apparent. In mid-century there had been a backlog of sanitary works. By 1890 setting out water mains and sewers was a natural concomitant to laying out and constructing new streets. The need for elaborate retrospective action had passed, and with it the essential role of the 1:500 maps.

A review of the Ordnance Survey in 1892 was prompted by concern that much Ordnance Survey mapping was not as up to date as it could be. The review found that 1:500 sales were very poor and concluded that were the 1:500 to be discontinued, a much-needed 1:2500 revision could proceed much more cheaply and expeditiously [Figs. 152, 153 and 154]. In January 1894 the Treasury ruled that in future

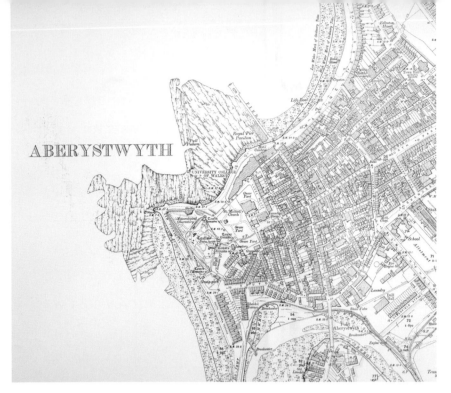

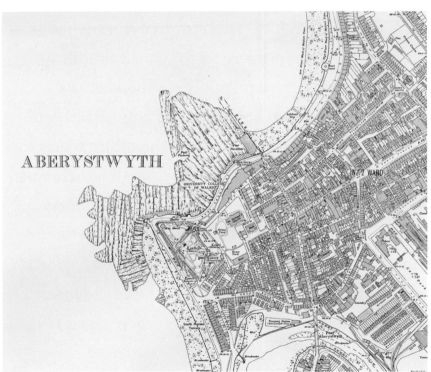

[Fig. 153] The revised sheets of the Ordnance Survey 1:2500 were issued with hatched buildings, but for a while they continued to include a subtle indication of the structure of buildings: 'shading' – the thickening of lines – was used on the south and east sides of brick and stone buildings. Such 'shading' is quite obvious on this map of Aberystwyth, revised in 1904. [British Library, Maps OS – 1:2500 Cardiganshire, second edition, sheet VI.9]

[Fig. 154] The trickle of 1:500 sheets revised at local expense dried up completely after 1910, and the 1:2500 was the largest scale at which the urban cartographic record was continued by the Ordnance Survey. After 1914 revision was impeded by financial stringency, and the Survey's revisers only returned to Aberystwyth in 1937–8. [British Library Maps OS – 1:2500 Cardiganshire, revised edition, sheet VI.9]

mapping at 1:500 was only to be undertaken on a repayment basis. By 1909 only fourteen places had taken up the offer of a revised 1:500 by repayment.[113]

London stood apart from the picture elsewhere. Land registration on transfer was made compulsory in

London in 1900. Ordnance Survey 1:1056 sheets were partially revised in order to provide a basis for Land Registry index-maps, and in 1906–9 a considerable extension of the area of London mapped at a 1:1056 scale, including the whole London County Council area, was undertaken by the Ordnance Survey – at national expense. Much of the extension area was still undeveloped and so the ground survey cost was relatively modest.

In 1910 the revision policy adopted in 1894 was called into question by the advent of a new tax on increase in land values. This required a base valuation of hereditaments (properties) for which up-to-date Ordnance Survey mapping was needed as a framework on which hereditament boundaries could be mapped. For most urban areas the solution was to photo-enlarge 1:2500 maps to 1:1250 so that there was sufficient space on the surface of the map to carry manuscript annotations of boundaries and reference numbers. Although the immediate need was for land valuation purposes, a considerable number of 1:1250 enlargements were produced for general sale into the 1920s.[114]

After 1914 the Ordnance Survey was subject to considerable restrictions on its funding, and by 1935 the backlog of revision led to a further review of policy. Unofficial revision of 1:500 maps had been going on in a number of towns, land registration justified the 1:1056 scale in London, and this no doubt helped a tentative recommendation that ad hoc mapping at 1:1250 should be experimented with – once the backlog of 1:2500 revision had been cleared.[115] In the event it was decided that it would be much cheaper to survey from the start at 1:1250. Experiments began in Bournemouth and Edinburgh in 1943–4, and from the mid-1940s to the later 1950s, 1:1250 scale maps account for a majority of Ordnance Survey effort, and for a significant amount thereafter [**Fig. 155,** *overleaf*]. The introduction of 'continuous revision' addressed the problem of currency, at any rate at 1:1250 [**Fig. 156,** *p. 225*]. By the time of the Ordnance Survey's official bicentenary in 1991 some 58,000 1:1250 sheets had been published. The development of digital mapping from the late 1960s onwards led to the 1:1250 series and its portrayal of British towns being subsumed within a vast topographic database, in which map scale has been replaced by data resolution.[116]

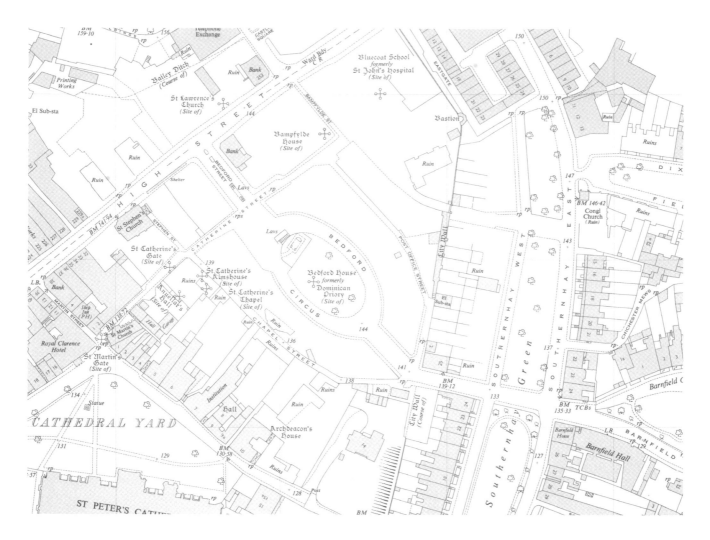

[Fig. 155] From 1911 the Ordnance Survey made large numbers of photo-enlargements of the 1:2500 scale to 1:1250; these enlargements contain no more information than does the parent mapping, but they do provide extra space for annotation. A desire for something to replace the 1:1056, 1:528 and 1:500 scales of the nineteenth century, together with the value of 1:1250 for land valuation purposes, led the Ordnance Survey to embark in 1943 on a resurvey of larger urban areas at 1:1250. The content of the new series was influenced more by the 1:2500 than by the 1:500, but it was surveyed to very rigorous standards of accuracy, so that the basic data could be enlarged to 1:500 if required, though this seems to have been done but rarely. The priority for resurveying towns was decided in consultation with the Ministry of Town and Country Planning. Towns taken up early in the resurvey programme included those where redevelopment or slum clearance were urgent, and those where reconstruction had been forced by air raid damage during World War II. The centre of Exeter was badly damaged in a 'Baedeker' raid in May 1942, and so the city was an obvious candidate for attention at 1:1250 from 1947 onwards. The Bedford Circus area had been cleared by 1948, but redevelopment had yet to begin. [British Library, Maps OS 1:1250 National Grid series, sheet SX 9292 NW, edition 'A' (c. 1949)]

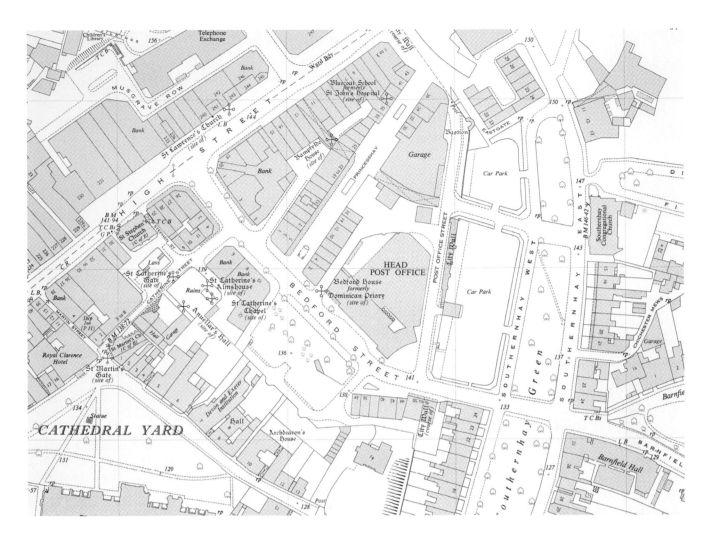

[Fig. 156] The 1:1250 was distinguished from previous Ordnance Survey series by being subject to frequent revisions. By 1959 redevelopment in this part of Exeter was largely complete.

[British Library, Maps OS 1:1250 National Grid series, sheet SX 9292 NW, edition 'E' (c. 1959–60)]

19.

Fire insurance maps

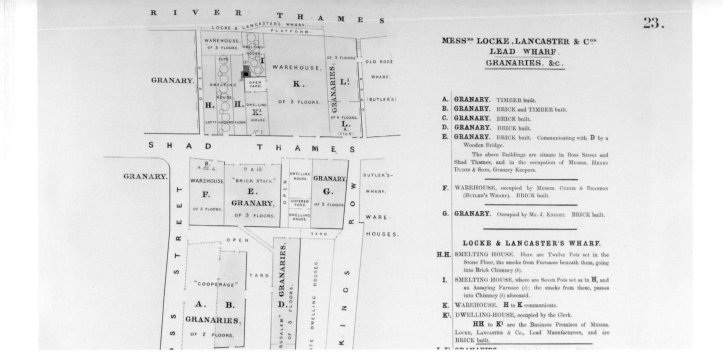

R I V E R   T H A M E S

LOCKE & LANCASTER'S WHARF.
PLATFORM.

WAREHOUSE.
OF 3 FLOORS.

SMELTING
HOUSE.

POTS

GRANARY.

SMELTING
HOUSE.

H.   H.

I

OF 3 FLOORS

WAREHOUSE,

OLD ROSE
WHARF.

OPEN
YARD.

K.

L¹

(BUTLER'S)

OF 3 FLOORS.

K¹
HOUSE.

DWELLING
HOUSE

LOFTY GROUND FLOOR.

OF 6 FLOORS.

L.
A.
(1 TO 4)

G R A N A R I E S .

S H A D   T H A M E S

GRANARY.

8.
4.½2. 6

WAREHOUSE

F.

OF 3 FLOORS.

9 & 10

"BRICK STACK."

E.
GRANARY,
OF 3 FLOORS.

DWELLING
HOUSE.

COVERED
YARD.

DWELLING
HOUSE.

OPEN

GRANARY.

G.

OF 2 FLOORS.

BUTLER'S—

WHARF.

WARE—

HOUSES.

OPEN

YARD.

YARD.

"COOPERAGE"

GRANARIES.

A.   B.

GRANARIES,

OF 2 FLOORS.

"JERUSALEM"

OF 3 FLOORS.

D.

PRIVATE DWELLING HOUSES.

K I N G S   R O W

MESSᴿˢ LOCKE, LANCASTER & Cᵒˢ
LEAD WHARF.
GRANARIES, &c.

A.	GRANARY.	TIMBER built.
B.	GRANARY.	BRICK and TIMBER built.
C.	GRANARY.	BRICK built.
D.	GRANARY.	BRICK built.
E.	GRANARY.	BRICK built. Communicating with D by a Wooden Bridge.

The above Buildings are situate in Boss Street and Shad Thames, and in the occupation of Messrs. HENRY DUDIN & Sons, Granary Keepers.

F.	WAREHOUSE,	occupied by Messrs. CURTIS & BRANDON (BUTLER'S WHARF). BRICK built.

G.	GRANARY.	Occupied by Mr. J. KNIGHT. BRICK built.

LOCKE & LANCASTER'S WHARF.

H.H.	SMELTING HOUSE.	Here are Twelve Pots set in the Stone Floor, the smoke from Furnaces beneath them, going into Brick Chimney (b).
I.	SMELTING HOUSE,	where are Seven Pots set as in H, and an Assaying Furnace (c); the smoke from these, passes into Chimney (b) aforesaid.
K.	WAREHOUSE.	H to K communicate.
K¹.	DWELLING-HOUSE,	occupied by the Clerk.

HH to K¹ are the Business Premises of Messrs. LOCKE, LANCASTER & Co., Lead Manufacturers, and are BRICK built.

L. L. GRANARIES.

ALTHOUGH SANITARY MAPPING by the Ordnance Survey in the early 1850s represented the high point in terms of the detailed mapping of whole towns, maps for fire insurance purposes provided yet greater topographical detail for particular parts of towns. The pre-history of this nineteenth-century fire insurance mapping is shrouded in some degree of mystery. Edmund Petrie's *Ichnography of Charleston, South Carolina* published in London in 1790 specifically states that it is 'for the use of the Phoenix Fire-Company of London'.[117] The dedication by Richard Horwood of his map of London of 1792–9 to the Phoenix Fire Insurance Company might imply that a 'cartographic solution' for assessing fire risks was in use by the end of the eighteenth century. Be that as it may, the earliest avowed British fire insurance map is *Loveday's London Waterside Surveys*, of 1857 [Fig. 157], which was aimed at insurance assessors, merchants and others concerned with the risk of fire in warehouses along the River

[Fig. 157] *Loveday's London Waterside Surveys, for the use of fire insurance companies, merchants, brokers, agents, wharfingers, granary keepers &c. Showing… the whole of the wharves & granaries with the buildings connected therewith, situate on the banks of the Thames… With a description of their occupancy – construction – use – and internal & external risk… This is the first printed insurance plan known to have been produced in Britain: it dates from 1857, and its scope is adequately covered by its somewhat wordy title.* (CBTM 22212) [From Bodleian Library, G.A. fol. A 75]

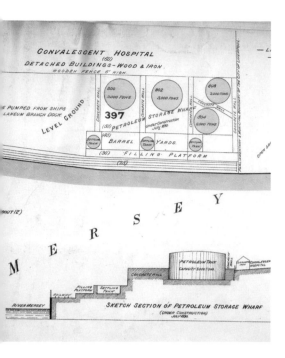

[Fig. 158] The insurance mapping published by Charles E. Goad was mostly based on Ordnance Survey 1:500 mapping, but included details that neither the Ordnance Survey nor any other map-maker had hitherto recorded. Conventional information in plan was sometimes supplemented by cross-sections through buildings that presented particular fire hazards, as here at Liverpool in 1888. (CBTM 21239) [British Library, Maps 145.b.1.]

Thames below London Bridge (22212). This seems to have been an isolated example for nearly thirty years.

The modern fire insurance map may not have been invented in North America, but it certainly developed there: various firms exploited the market in the United States, and in Canada Charles E. Goad was dominant. In the mid-1880s Goad extended his activities to Britain and he was no doubt helped in this by the availability of Ordnance Survey 1:500 maps.[118] However, Goad's scales related inches to feet: 1:480 – 1 inch to 40 feet – was the Company's standard for detail mapping, with scales such as 1:2400 – 1 inch to 200 feet – used for indexes [Fig. 158]. In detail Goad began where the Ordnance Survey 1:500 left off by adding a record of building materials to the maps, some cross-sections of buildings and data on water supply and fire-fighting equipment. However, he concentrated on the commercial areas of larger towns, and on smaller towns where there was a greater fire risk. Thus there is comprehensive coverage of the dock areas of ports such as Grimsby (21229) and Hartlepool (21231) where large quantities of timber were imported. In the West Riding of Yorkshire, insurance mapping was almost entirely confined to areas with textile warehouses. What was at first sight Goad's most puzzling subject, Campbeltown on the Kintyre peninsula (1898: 21218), can be explained by its predominant industry. At this time there were some twenty whisky distilleries in the town [Fig. 159].[119]

BRITISH TOWN MAPS

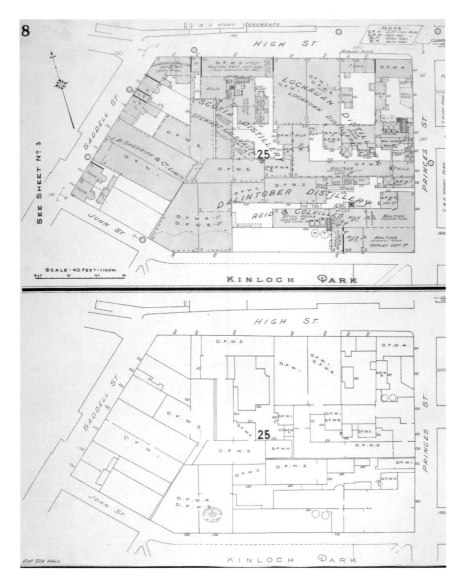

[Fig. 159] Insurance mapping was only conducted where there was a significant risk of fire. Generally this was not the case with food and drink, but an exception was whisky distilling, because of the flammability of the spirit product. Around 1900 Campbeltown in Argyllshire was host to about twenty distilleries, and so it was one of seven places in Scotland that were mapped by the Goad Company. (CBTM 21218) [British Library, Maps 145.b.6(3)]

Goad did not sell its maps; they remained the property of the company and were in effect hired. This meant that the company kept control of valuable data, and in effect anticipated the contemporary method of licensing data, rather than selling it outright.

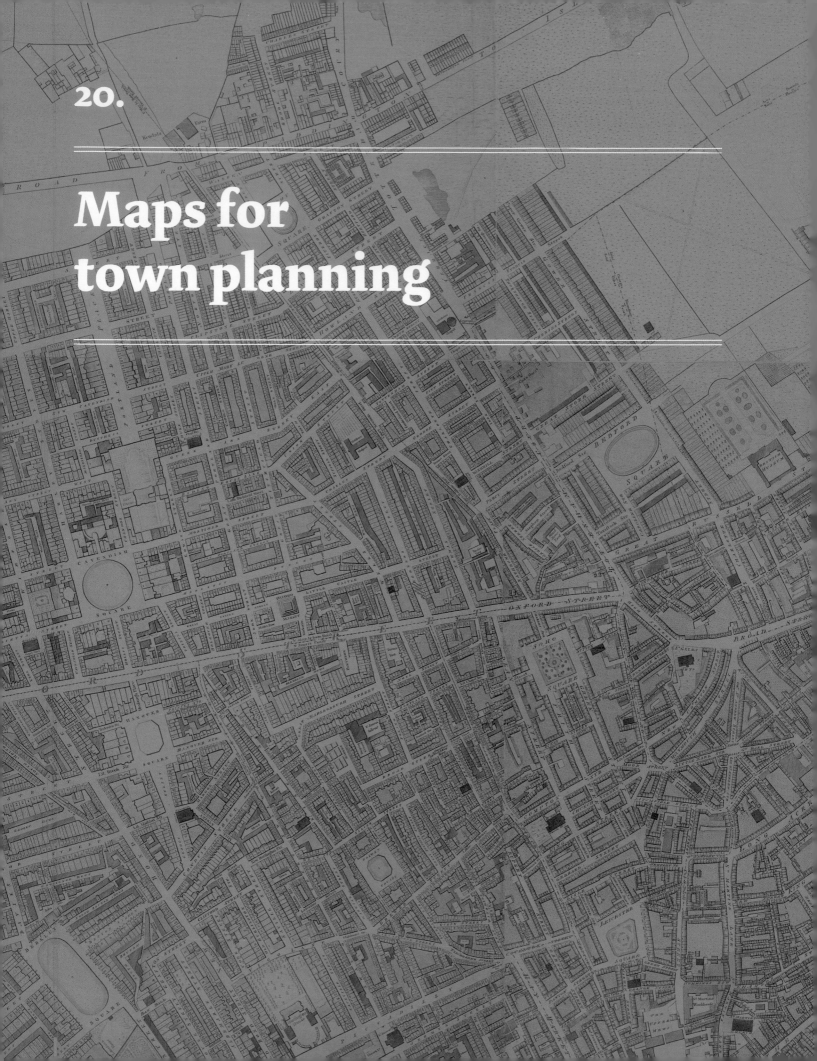

Maps for town planning

THERE ARE MANY EXAMPLES of regularly planned medieval townscapes to be found in Britain, not least among those towns founded as new settlements in the Middle Ages with regular grid street patterns. We have no evidence, however, that maps were used in the physical construction of these settlements. Renaissance town planning concepts, by contrast, focused attention on the drawn plan. Italian designers set out arrangements for 'ideal cities' on paper. Maps were an ideal medium to communicate these new ideas about space articulated around concepts of symmetry, perspective and regularity.[120] The well-known, but in the event abortive, schemes for rebuilding London after the Great Fire of 1666 show how these ideas diffused into British town planning [Fig. 160, *overleaf*].[121] An opportunity for modernising London after the Great Fire in the new classical idiom was lost, but classical Renaissance concepts were taken up in fast-developing spa towns such as Bath in the following century – the neo-classical elegance of street layout was very much in tune with the city's fashion-conscious spa visitors [Fig. 161, *p. 233*].[122] Similar concepts were applied in the construction of post-medieval new towns; there were a few of these in England and Wales, but they were more numerous in Scotland, especially in the north-east. Some were either completely new foundations, for example, Buckie, Golspie, Keith, Macduff, Portsoy and Rothes, or came about due to the removal and

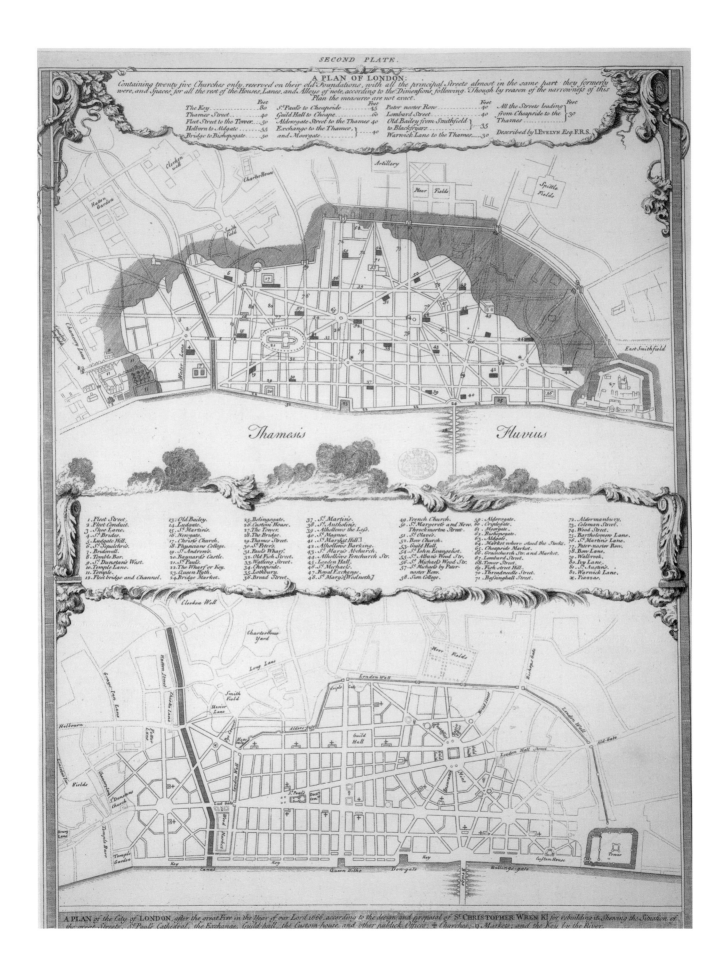

SECOND PLATE.

A PLAN OF LONDON:

Containing twenty five Churches only, reserved on their old Foundations, with all the principal Streets almost in the same part they formerly were, and Spaces, for all the rest of the Houses, Lanes, and Alleys of note, according to the Dimensions following. Though by reason of the narrowness of this Plan the measures are not exact.

	Feet		Feet		Feet		
The Key	80	St Pauls to Cheapside	45	Pater noster Row	40	All the Streets leading	
Thames Street	40	Guild Hall to Cheape	60	Lombard Street	40	from Cheapside to the	30
Fleet Street to the Tower	50	Aldersgate Street to the Thames	40	Old Bailey from Smithfield		Thames	
Holborn to Aldgate	55	Exchange to the Thames	40	to Blackfryars	35		
Bridge to Bishopsgate	50	and Moorgate	40	Warwick Lane to the Thames	30	Described by I.Evelyn Esq. F.R.S.	

Thamesis   *Fluvius*

1. Fleet Street.	13. Old Bailey.	25. Belingsgate.	37. St Martins.	49. French Church.	60. Aldersgate.	72. Aldermanbury.
2. Fleet Conduit.	14. Ludgate.	26. Custom House.	38. St Antholins.	50. St Margerets and New.	61. Criplegate.	73. Coleman Street.
3. Shoe Lane.	15. St Martins.	27. The Tower.	39. Alhollows the Less.	Throckmorton Street.	62. Moorgate.	74. Wood Street.
4. St Brides.	16. Newgate.	28. The Bridge.	40. St Magnus.	51. St Olaves.	63. Bishopsgate.	75. Bartholomew Lane.
5. Ludgate Hill.	17. Christ Church.	29. Thames Street.	41. St Mary Hill.	52. Bow Church.	64. Aldgate.	76. St Martins Lane.
6. St Sepulchres.	18. Physicians College.	30. St Peters.	42. Alhollows Barking.	53. Guild Hall.	65. Market where stood the Stocks.	77. Pater-noster Row.
7. Bridewell.	19. St Andrews.	31. Pauls Wharf.	43. St Marys Archurch.	54. St John Evangelist.	66. Cheapside Market.	78. Bow Lane.
8. Temple Bar.	20. St Pauls.	32. Old Fish Street.	44. Alhollows Fenchurch Str.	55. St Albans Wood Str.	67. Gracechurch Str. and Market.	79. Wallbrook.
9. St Dunstans West.	21. St Pauls.	33. Watling Street.	45. Leaden Hall.	56. St Michaels Wood Str.	68. Lombard Street.	80. Ivy Lane.
10. Temple Lane.	22. The Wharf or Key.	34. Cheapside.	46. St Michaels.	57. St Michaels by Pater-	69. Tower Street.	81. St Austins.
11. Temple.	23. Queen Hyth.	35. Lothbury.	47. Royal Exchange.	noster Row.	70. Threadneedle Street.	82. Warwick Lane.
12. Fleet bridge and Channel.	24. Bridge Market.	36. Bread Street.	48. St Marys Woolnoth.	58. Sion College.	71. Basinghall Street.	*. Piazzas.

A PLAN of the City of LONDON, after the great Fire in the Year of our Lord 1666 according to the design and proposal of Sir CHRISTOPHER WREN Kt for rebuilding it, shewing the Situation of the most Streets, St Pauls Cathedral, the Exchange, Guild Hall, the Custom-house, and other publick Offices. ✠ Churches. ✡ Markets. and the Key by the River.

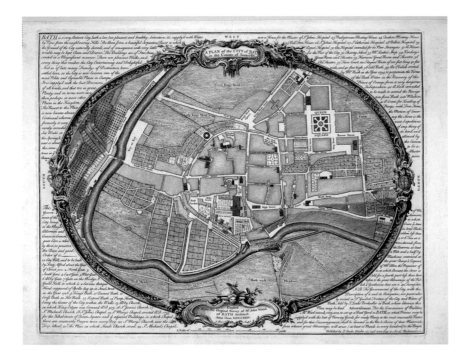

relocation of a settlement judged to be in inconvenient proximity to a landowner's residence, as at Cullen (1760s) and Fochabers (1770s). These planned towns are often characterised by relatively intensive mapping. There were six maps of Cullen produced between 1762 and 1860 (plus two more later in the nineteenth century), eight for Fochabers between *c.* 1770 and 1825, and six for Rothes between 1769 and 1868. For other towns output was more modest, but all have a cartographic record of the planning process [**Fig. 162**, *overleaf*].[123]

Comprehensive new town planning was only possible where there was either a single landowner or a closely associated group of landowners in control. Fleetwood in Lancashire was laid out by landowner Sir Peter Hesketh in 1836 on a greenfield site (actually a rabbit warren). Maps of 1838 and 1841 (20064, 20063)

[**Fig. 160,** *opposite*] The Great Fire of London in 1666 was an opportunity for radical rebuilding of the City, and for a rebuilding on the most advanced, up-to-date and fashionable lines then imaginable. Here are two of the plans submitted, by Christopher Wren and John Evelyn. Such a radical replanning, based as it was on a wholly new street pattern and division of property, was defeated by the complexities of existing ownerships and interests, and so the City was rebuilt to the same plan as before the Fire, though the structure and materials of buildings were regulated. [British Library, Maps K. Top.20.19.2]

[**Fig. 161,** *above*] By 1735 Bath had come a long way from its origins as a provincial medicinal spring, and was entering the age of its greatest fashion. The new, regularly laid out streets and terraces that extended the original settlement are shown in John Wood the Elder's *Plan of the City of Bath*, 1735. (CBTM 22593). [British Library, Maps K. Top. 37.14]

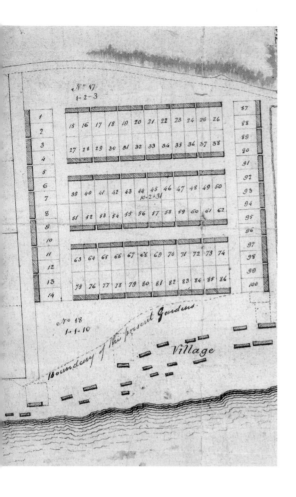

[Fig. 162] The process of planning new towns in Scotland is illustrated by Golspie, founded by the Duke of Sutherland early in the nineteenth century. This rather rough plan of 1830 shows that scattered plots had been taken up: further plots are shown behind the village, as yet unoccupied. (CBTM 21708) [National Library of Scotland, Dep 313/3591/14]

show a mixture of the projected but unrealised and the actual. At Middlesbrough development was by a consortium, the Owners of the Middlesbrough Estate, and there is a long sequence of maps through which the development of the town can be traced from its origins in 1830 into the 1860s [Fig. 163].[124] The same body was also interested in developing a resort along the coast at Saltburn, and again a sequence of maps resulted following the advent of the railway in 1861.[125]

At Edinburgh the town council provided a similar political drive to achieve planned extensions to the city in a classical manner. The best known of the schemes is for the so-called Edinburgh New Town, of the 1760s [Fig. 164, *overleaf*].

New streets were cut through the existing fabric of many larger cities in the Victorian period. Examples in London include Charing Cross Road, Shaftesbury Avenue and Victoria Street in Westminster. These affected limited areas and were as much about improving communications as for improving living conditions.

The Garden City movement of the early twentieth century was governed by spatial concepts ideologically opposite to those of earlier classicists. Ebenezer Howard mapped out ideas for strictly planned settlements to combine his ideas of the best elements of rural life with the beneficial features of urban living: a controlled, 'garden' environment with buildings at a low density set out along and around

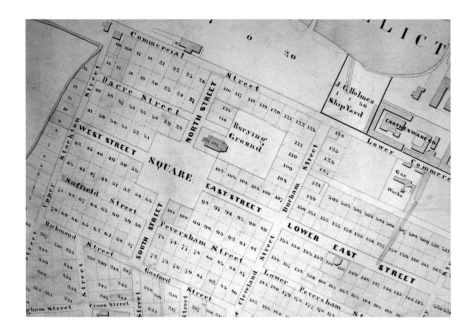

[Fig. 163] The town of Middlesbrough began to grow after an extension to the Stockton and Darlington Railway was opened in 1830. The growth of the town is recorded on a long series of plans made for the Owners of the Middlesbrough Estate: this one, 'Plan of the Middlesbro' estate in the North Riding of the county of York', was made by J. Richmond in 1848. The emphasis is on mapping plots rather than on mapping buildings. This extract shows the area around the original town square, which was very close to the original railway terminus. The centre of the town subsequently migrated southwards, and little remains of the original town. (CBTM 20158) [Teesside Archives, U/OME 8/13]

informally arranged streets and spaces. Letchworth and Welwyn Garden Cities were constructed in Hertfordshire, and Hampstead Garden Suburb was built in north London [Fig. 165, *overleaf*].

The first British town planning act was passed in 1909. It was voluntary, but was symptomatic of a flurry of interest in the topic and was followed by some comprehensive plans for towns. These invariably used Ordnance Survey mapping as a base updated by borough engineers. It was the effect of outdated Ordnance Survey mapping on town-planning schemes that was a major stimulus for the reform of the Ordnance Survey in the late 1930s. An emphasis on reconstruction from 1941 onwards, following bombing damage in World War II, led to a number of comprehensive planning schemes, of which Sir Patrick Abercrombie's for London is perhaps the best known, and that for Plymouth perhaps the

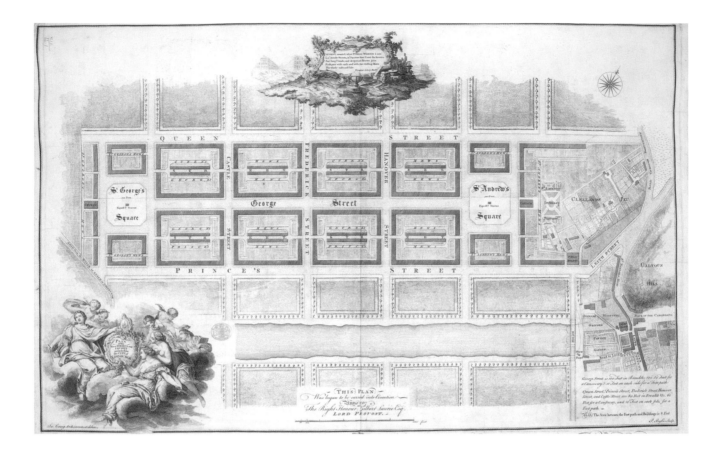

[Fig. 164, *above*] The possibility of a 'new town' to the north of Edinburgh was discussed from 1752 onwards: James Craig's winning design was approved in 1767. [James Craig, *Plan of the New Streets and Squares intended for the City of Edinburgh (1767–8)*: British Library, Maps K.Top.49.66.1]

[Fig. 165, *right*] One of the first fruits of the Garden City Movement was the scheme for Hampstead Garden Suburb by Raymond Unwin and Barry Parker of 1907. ['Hampstead Tenants Limited. Preliminary sketch Plan, shewing proposed development of land at Hampstead Garden Suburb. Barry Parker, and Raymond Unwin, Architects': British Library, Maps 3479. (106.)]

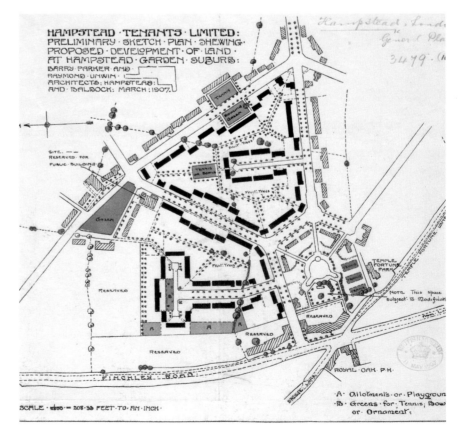

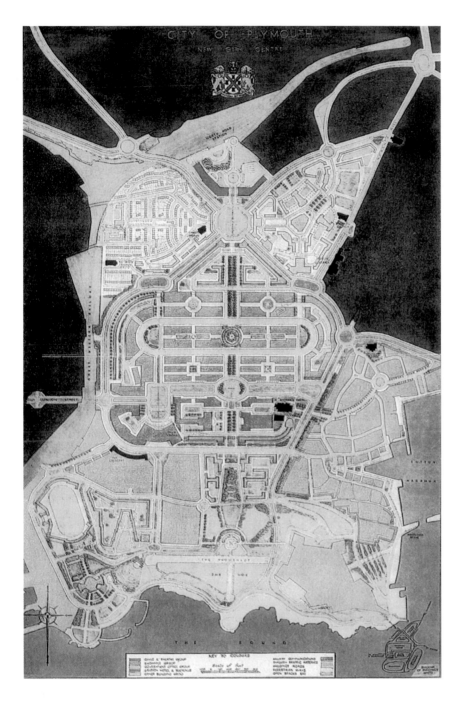

[Fig. 166] Proportionate to its population, Plymouth suffered the highest rate of casualties of any British city during World War II. There was correspondingly heavy bomb damage to buildings, and the opportunity was taken to replan the centre of the city completely. This is Sir Patrick Abercrombie's scheme. [Abercrombie's Plan for Plymouth as per Historical Atlas of South-West England]

most radical [Fig. 166]. All these schemes depended on Ordnance Survey mapping for layout and illustration; many were publicised in books with high production values. A comprehensive Town and Country Planning Act was passed in 1947, with maps as an integral part of the development control process, then as now.

Notes and references

1. Roger J. P. Kain and Richard Oliver, *The Tithe Maps of England and Wales: A cartographic analysis and county-by-county catalogue* (Cambridge: Cambridge University Press, 1995, reprinted 2010); Roger J. P. Kain, John Chapman and Richard R. Oliver, *The Enclosure Maps of England and Wales 1595–1918* (Cambridge: Cambridge University Press, 2004, reprinted 2010).

2. On John Hooker's map as a source for reconstructing the topography of Exeter *c.* 1600 see, C. G. Henderson, 'The City of Exeter from AD 50 to the early nineteenth century', in Roger Kain and William Ravenhill, eds, *Historical Atlas of South-West England* (University of Exeter Press, 1999 and reprinted 2000), pp. 482–98; W. L. D. Ravenhill and Margery Rowe, 'A decorated screen map of Exeter based on John Hooker's map of 1587', in Todd Gray, Margery M. Rowe and Audrey M. Erskine, *Tudor and Stuart Devon: The common estate and government* (Exeter, University of Exeter Press, 1992), pp. 1–12.

3. Maurice Beresford, *New Towns of the Middle Ages* (London: Lutterworth, 1967). The only post-1348 foundation was Queenborough in Kent in the 1360s, where the motive was at least as much defensive as economic.

4. Alan Everitt, 'The market town' in Joan Thirsk, ed., *The Agrarian History of England and Wales*, IV (Cambridge: Cambridge University Press, 1967), pp. 467–506.

5. *Instructions to draughtsmen and plan examiners*, 1906, p. 91: Ordnance Survey, unpublished.

6. For example, the 1:63,360 maps revised in 1897 and 1905 treat Kirton Lindsey in Lincolnshire as a 'town', whereas the 1:2500 map revised in 1905 treats it as a 'village'.

7. Many towns were mapped from 1670 onwards at scales around one inch to 1 mile (1:63,360): some were first mapped at this scale for Ogilby's *Britannia*, others were mapped from 1699 onwards as part of county surveys. As these depictions are invariably at an order of detail lower than that possible at 1:25,344 we have omitted them from the *Catalogue*. For a list of the post-1699 county surveys, with an indication of libraries holding them, see Elizabeth M. Rodger, *The Large Scale County Maps of the British Isles*

1596–1850: A union list, second edition (Oxford: Bodleian Library, 1972).

8. Maps of townships, parishes and wards: Leeds: 16782–3; London: 13794–13827, 13879–85, 18361–18385, 19386–19397, 22246–22273, 23181–23215, 23313–23315; Manchester: 19216, 19239.

9. H. S. L. Winterbotham, *A key to maps*, second edition (London & Glasgow: Blackie, 1939), p.28. Eighteenth-century illustrations of engraving appear in Laurence Worms and Ashley Baynton-Williams, *British map engravers* (London: Rare Book Society, 2011), pp. x–xiv. There is a detailed account of Ordnance Survey practice in Sir Henry James (ed.), *Account of the methods and processes... of the Ordnance Survey...* (London: HMSO, 1875), p. 165 ff.

10. This section is considerably indebted to Ian Mumford, 'Milestones in lithographed cartography from 1800', unpublished PhD thesis, University of Reading, 1999.

11. The decline of cartographic printing from stone has not been studied in detail. A stone last printed from in 1942 used to be exhibited in the museum area of the Ordnance Survey when its office was at Maybush, Southampton; this was for a geological map rather than a standard Ordnance Survey product. Still less is known about commercial practice; perhaps the Bartholomew archive at National Library of Scotland will shed some light.

12. The Laurie & Outhett map of London of 1837 (19449) had a reference system of close red squares added by hand, in addition to more conventional enhancement-colouring: this surely labour-intensive example remains unusual, if not unique.

13. Mumford, 'Milestones...', p. 43 ff.

14. See British Library copies of Land Registry revision of London 1:1056 sheets 141.10, 15.15 and 15.19.

15. The decline of hand-colouring was a gradual process: some limited-demand Geological Survey mapping was still being hand-coloured in the mid-twentieth century – at a premium price.

16. The following paragraphs are indebted to Mumford, 'Milestones...', pp. 153–266.

17. Alfred Hinde's directory map of Wolverhampton, published from 1894 onwards (copies in Wolverhampton Archives [Searchroom Map Cabinet]), was such a flagrant copy that it does not qualify as an independent cartographic production and so is not included in our database, but it is nationally significant in that it contributed materially to the defining of Crown Copyright in 1909–11: see papers in file 17304 in The National Archives [TNA] T1/11459.

18. This is the impression that we have gained from indexes in county record offices: we would be delighted to be proved unduly pessimistic.

19. These comments should be taken as applying more particularly to the main period of our study, up to 1900: we have not explored what may survive for more recently established publishers such as the Automobile Association or A–Z. It needs to be borne in mind that, by and large, the internal records of commercial companies do not enjoy the statutory protection of public records, and that survivals may be the result of either benevolence or serendipity.

20. There is a lively, if not necessarily academically very rigorous, introduction in Phyllis Pearsall, *A-Z Maps: the Personal Story, from Bedsitter to Household Name* (Sevenoaks: Geographers' A-Z Map Company, 1990).

21. Notable are *Report of the Departmental Committee appointed by the Board of Agriculture to inquire into the present condition of the Ordnance Survey...*, BPP (HC) 1893–4 [C.6895], LXXII, 305 [the 'Dorington Committee'], *Report of the Departmental Committee appointed by the Board of Agriculture to consider the arrangements to be made for the sale of Ordnance Survey maps*, BPP (HC) 1896 [C.8147], LXVIII, 361 and *Report of the Departmental Committee... to inquire into the pay and classification of the Ordnance Survey staff*, BPP (HC) 1911 [Cd.5825], XXXVII, 625: evidence [Cd.5826]. The last is especially valuable for Johnston and Philip.

22. We have only included in our database maps which are accessible in some form in a public collection, even if it is only via an indifferent photograph or transcript.

23. The example quoted is from a copy in a private collection.

24. We thank Peter Barber for drawing our attention to Royal MS 14.C.VII f.9.

25. We are grateful to Peter Barber for drawing this map to our attention.

26. Peter Barber, 'Mapmaking in England, ca. 1470–1650', in David Woodward, ed., *The history of cartography*, *Volume Three: Cartography in the European Renaissance* (Chicago and London: University of Chicago Press, 2007), pp. 1589–669, especially 1591–3.

27. P. D. A. Harvey, 'The Portsmouth map of 1545 and the introduction of scale maps into England', in John Webb, Nigel Yates and Sarah Peacock, eds, *Hampshire Studies* (Portsmouth: Portsmouth City Records Office, 1981), pp. 32–49.

28. See Sarah Tyacke, ed., *English Map-Making 1500–1650* (London: The British Library, 1983), p. 16; Peter Barber pointed out the parallel between sanctuary mapping and coastal mapping to us.

29. P. D. A. Harvey, *Maps in Tudor England* (London: Public Record Office and British Library, 1993), pp. 12–13.

30. BL Maps *30415 (6). We owe this reference to Peter Barber.

31. Matthew Champion, 'The cosmographical Glasse and 16th century English urban cartography', unpublished paper given at Warburg Maps and Society seminar, 27 November 2003.

32. Peter Barber, 'The Copperplate Map in context', in Ann Saunders and John Schofield, eds, *Tudor London: A map and a view*, London Topographical Society Publication 159 (London, 2001), pp. 16–32.

33. The map was first attributed to Ralph Agas by George Virtue in the early eighteenth century: James Howgego, *Printed Maps of London circa 1553–1850* (Folkestone: Dawson, 1978), p. 10.

34. Champion, 'The cosmographical Glasse…'

35. The totals given here exclude inset views of Buxton, Launceston and Nonesuch Palace. For more on Speed's own mapping see Sarah Bendall, 'Draft town maps for John Speed's *Theatre of the Empire of Great Britaine*', *Imago Mundi* 54 (2002), pp. 30–45. There are reproductions of the maps in Jeffery John Speed, *Tudor Townscapes: The town plans from John Speed's Theatre of the Empire of Great Britaine 1610* (Waddesdon, Buckinghamshire: Map Collector Publications, 2000).

36. Catherine Delano-Smith and Roger J. P. Kain, *English Maps: A history*, (London: British Library, 1999) p. 66 ff.

37. David Marsh, 'Maps, myths and gardens: Faithorne and Newcourt's map of London (1658)': unpublished paper given at Warburg Institute Maps and Society seminar, 25 January 2007.

38. E. G. R. Taylor, 'Robert Hooke and the cartographical projects of the late seventeenth century (1666–1696)', *Geographical Journal* 90 (1937), pp. 529–40. Ogilby may also have surveyed Maldon in Essex; Ralph Hyde, 'London actually survey'd by William Morgan, 1682', pp 5–15 of *The A to Z of Charles II's London 1682. London &c. Actually survey'd by William Morgan*', London Topographical Society Publication 174 (London, 2013).

39. J. B. Harley, 'The bankruptcy of Thomas Jeffreys: an episode in the economic history of eighteenth century map-making', *Imago Mundi* 20 (1966), pp. 27–48.

40. J. B. Harley, 'The re-mapping of England, 1750–1800', *Imago Mundi* 19 (1965), pp. 56–67, p. 67, citing W. Faden, *Catalogue of the geographical works, maps, plans, &c published by W. Faden…* (1822).

41. A. H. W. Robinson, *Marine Cartography in Britain: A history of the sea chart to 1855* (Leicester: Leicester University Press, 1962), pp. 71–2.

42. Paul Laxton, 'Introduction' in *The A to Z of Regency London* (Lympne: Harry Margary, 1985), p. vii.

43. Margaret E. Jones and H. L. Honeyman, 'Thomas Oliver and his plans for central Newcastle', *Archaeologia Aeliana*, Publications of the Society of Antiquaries of Newcastle upon Tyne, 4th Series, 29 (1951), pp. 239–52.

44. D. R. Mills and R. C. Wheeler, eds, *Historic Town Plans of Lincoln 1610–1920* (Lincoln: Lincoln Record Society, etc, 2004) [this includes a reproduction of Padley's map, in several versions]; we are indebted to Dr Wheeler for further discussion on Padley.

45. Brian Robson, 'John Wood 1: the undervalued cartographer' and 'John Wood 2: planning and paying for his town plans', *The Cartographic Journal*, 51 (2014), pp. 257–73 and 274–86. Our total differs from Robson's as we exclude the plan of Grantham, the existence of which is uncertain (Robson, 261).

46. We have excluded the mapping of Aberdeen, Dundee, Edinburgh, Glasgow and Leith from the total, as it is evident that they were derivatives by Wood designed to make up a plausible atlas. The make-up of the surviving copies of the atlas varies (Robson, 275). The map of Inveraray (21853) is an oddity, as it is at a relatively small scale (1:15,840) and includes a substantial unbuilt area around the town.

47. References to map-use of any sort in nineteenth-century fiction are exiguous, but for two examples of travellers consulting maps displayed in inns see R. S. Surtees, *Hawbuck Grange* (1847), chapter VI and Wilkie Collins, *The Dead Secret* (1857) in R. S. Surtees, *Mr Sponge's Sporting Tour* (1852) Chapter XIX, a visitor to a country house consults 'an old county map' to find the meeting place of a hunt.

48. Nick Millea, *Street Mapping: An A to Z of urban cartography*, (Oxford: Bodleian Library, 2003), especially pp. 24–27 on Geographers' A to Z Company; Pearsall, *A–Z Maps: The personal story*, 22 ff. An edition of c. 1938 was issued in facsimile in 2008.

49. There is an indication of Ordnance Survey progress in chapters 6 and 7 of Richard Oliver, *Ordnance Survey Maps: A concise guide for historians*, third edition (London: Charles Close Society, 2013).

50. For introductions see P. D. A. Harvey, *Maps in Tudor England* (London: The Public Record Office and The British Library, 1993), pp. 78–93, and P. D. A. Harvey, 'English estate maps: their early history and their use as historical evidence', in David Buisseret, ed., *Rural Images: Estate maps in the old and new worlds* (Chicago: Chicago University Press, 1996), pp. 27–61.

51. A. Sarah Bendall, *Maps, Land and Society: A history with a carto-bibliography of Cambridgeshire estate maps c. 1600–1836* (Cambridge: Cambridge University Press, 1992).

52. Examples are: Abbots Bromley (Staffordshire), 1826 (two: 20795, 20797); Bedale (Yorkshire, North Riding), c. 1772, 1786, c.1815 (20111, 20125, 20126); Bishops Castle (Shropshire), 1809, c.1825 (18754, 18753: there are at least eight others of fragments, which we have not recorded in our database); Market Lavington (Wiltshire), 1810, 1816 (two) (22976–22978); Methwold (Norfolk), 1772 (two), 1796 (18626–18628; enclosed in 1806, 18065); Moffat (Dumfriesshire), 1758, 1770, c. 1780 (21846, 21848, 21684); Newark (Nottinghamshire), 1788, 1790, 1804, 1820, 1827 (20544, 20548, 18646, 20546, 20547); Rockingham (Northamptonshire), 1615, 1806, 1815, 1822 (20854, 20857, 20858, 20855); Spilsby (Lincolnshire), c. 1780, 1821 (19511, 19510).

53. Downton (Wiltshire): c. 1740, 1745, 1784, 1819, 1854, 1865 (23172–23177); Huddersfield (Yorkshire, West Riding): 1716, 1778 (two), 1797, 1818, 1825, 1826, 1838, 1848, 1850 (20248, 19754, 20275, 19755, 20292, 19757, 20290, 20289, 20274 respectively); Woburn (Bedfordshire): 1661, 1738, 1821, c. 1840, 1850, 1868 (20667–20669, 20657, 20677, 20676).

54. Roger J. P. Kain, John Chapman, and Richard R. Oliver, *The Enclosure Maps of England and Wales 1595–1918* (Cambridge: Cambridge University Press, 2004).

55. For enclosure maps see Kain, Chapman and Oliver, *The Enclosure Maps of England and Wales*. For cadastral mapping more generally see Roger J. P. Kain and Elizabeth Baigent, *The Cadastral Map in the Service of the State: A history of property mapping* (Chicago and London: University of Chicago Press, 1992).

56. Richard R. Oliver and Roger J. P. Kain, 'Maps and the assessment of parish rates in nineteenth-century England and Wales', *Imago Mundi* 50 (1998), pp. 156–73.

57. Ralph Hyde, 'The "Act to Regulate Parochial Assessments", 1836, and its contribution to the mapping of London', *Guildhall Studies in London History*, 11 (1976), pp. 54–68. Accessible rating and other 'parish' maps are listed in Oliver and Kain, 'Maps and the assessment of parish rates…', and in the CBTM database: 13787–13798, 13801–13821, 13827, 13879–13883, 13885.

58. Tithes in Scotland had been commuted by an Act of 1617. For detailed studies of tithe surveys see Kain and Oliver, *The Tithe Maps of England and Wales*, and Roger J. P. Kain and Hugh C. Prince, *The Tithe Surveys of England and Wales* (Cambridge: Cambridge University Press, 1985 and reprinted 2006); *Tithe Surveys for Historians* (Chichester: Phillimore, 2000).

59. Examples of these are illustrated in Ralph Hyde, *Ward Maps of the City of London*, London Topographical Society Publication 54 (1999).
60. Letter of 20 March 1805 in British Library

Add MS 9409, f. 131, quoted in David Smith, 'The preparation of the town maps for Lysons' *Magna Britannia*', *Cartographic Journal*, 32 (1995), pp. 11–17.

61. Nicholas Alfrey, 'Landscape and the Ordnance Survey, 1795–1820', in Nicholas Alfrey and Stephen Daniels, eds, *Mapping the Landscape: Essays on art and cartography* (Nottingham: University Art Gallery and Castle Museum, 1990), pp. 23–27: quote on p. 25.

62. Gareth Shaw and Allison Tipper, *British Directories: A bibliography and guide to directories published in England Wales, 1850–1950, Scotland, 1773–1950*, second edition (London: Mansell Publishing, 1997).

63. Yorkshire: Kingston-upon-Hull (19766), Leeds (19760), Sheffield (19759), York (19758); Lancashire: Ashton-under-Lyne (19278), Blackburn (19282), Bolton (19283), Lancaster (19284), Liverpool (18762), Manchester (19630), Oldham (19220), Preston (19287), Rochdale (19288), Stockport (19300). (Stockport was geographically and administratively in Cheshire, but was sometimes treated as in Lancashire for topographical purposes, e.g. by the Ordnance Survey.)

64. Since the mid-1960s the Ordnance Survey has pursued a policy of increased cost-recovery, thus sharply increasing the relative cost of its products, and since the mid-1990s much of its mapping has been supplied as digital data: together these have reinforced the 'limited direct audience'.

65. The sole surviving example of the first edition of 1623 is in the Royal Library. The sole example of the 1653 edition is in the British Library (Maps Crace I.33). Peter Barber drew our attention to these references.

66. 18481, 19515, 19516, 22182, 22194, 22297, 23235.

67. 19841–19847, 21130, 21132, 22663.

68. Ralph Hyde, 'Maps that made cabmen honest', *The Map Collector*, 9 (Dec 1979), pp. 14–17.

69. *Guide to England and Wales*, Edinburgh: Black, 1864, pp. 220–1 (Liverpool, Birkenhead: 23387), 224–5 (Manchester, Salford: 23388), pp388–9 (Newcastle upon Tyne, Gateshead: 23389).
70. For more see Ralph Hyde, *Printed Maps*

of Victorian London, 1851–1900 (Folkestone: Dawson, 1975), pp. 19–21.

71. Copy in private collection.

72. www.barnettmaps.com: accessed 28 January 2015.

73. For more on the *Ordnance Atlas* see Ralph Hyde's introduction in Harry Margary, *The A–Z of Victorian London* (Lympne: Harry Margary, 1987).

74. Bacon's Atlas of London, second edition (Edinburgh and London: W. & A. K. Johnston & G. W. Bacon Ltd, 1963): copies in BL Maps 47.a.50 and London Metropolitan Archives [open access].

75. Bartholomew Printing Record [in National Library of Scotland, Map Library]. It should be noted that such printing records, whilst invaluable for dates and quantities, will not necessarily indicate whether the mapping was for sale in the ordinary way, or was a special commision for a customer.

76. Information from unpublished data held by the authors.

77. Pearsall, *A-Z Maps: The personal story*, 22 ff. An edition of the London A–Z of c. 1938 was issued in facsimile in 2008.

78. Little has been published on the development of grids: for the Ordnance Survey experience see Richard Oliver, 'The evolution of the Ordnance Survey National Grid', *Sheetlines* 43 (1995), pp. 25–46.

79. Copy of 1923 version in British Library Maps 3480 (349); copy of 1924 printing in private collection.

80. There is no coherent or comprehensive account published of the history of military mapping in Britain, or by the British military overseas: such a history would cover much ground on which, for example, histories of the British Ordnance Survey are practically silent. David Smith has made a study of the military mapping of British and Irish towns from c. 1519 to 1815, which is unpublished: an 'Archive' of his manuscript drafts and notes is deposited in the British Library (Maps 235.b.83). His general conclusions are published as David Smith, 'The military mapping of British towns c. 1519–c. 1815', *Bulletin of the Society of Cartographers*, 44 (2010), pp. 53–9. The 'Archive' includes more general background material and some valuable analyses of changes between successive manuscript maps of some towns.

81. In this we differ from the conclusions in Smith, 'The military mapping of British towns *c.* 1519–*c.* 1815', though our emphasis here is *urban* rather than *military* history.

82. The change from 'siege' to 'battle' warfare is noted in Sven Widmalm, 'Accuracy, rhetoric, and technology: the Paris-Greenwich triangulation, 1784–88', in Tore Frängsmyr, J. L. Heilbron and Robin E. Rider, *The Quantifying Spirit in the 18th Century* (Berkeley: University of California Press, 1990), pp. 179–206, esp. 201, and cited in M. H. Edney, 'British military education, mapmaking and military "map-mindedness" in the later Enlightenment', *Cartographic Journal*, 31 (1994), pp. 14–20, esp. 14.

83. P. D. A. Harvey, *Maps in Tudor England* (London: Public Record Office and British Library, 1993), pp. 27–30.

84. David Smith, 'Archive', section 'The English Civil Wars 1642–48'.

85. A useful and lively introduction, which sets fortification schemes in the overall context of defence policy and practice, are the two volumes by Norman Longmate: *Defending the Island: From Caesar to the Armada* (London: Hutchinson, 1989), and *Island Fortress: The defence of Great Britain 1603–1945* (London: Hutchinson, 1991). See also A. D. Saunders, *Fortress Britain* (Liphook: Beaufort, 1989). A more specialised study of the Tudor period is in H. M. Colvin *et al.*, eds, *The History of the King's Works*, IV (London: HMSO, 1982), pp. 367–606 passim. There are numerous more local studies of varying degrees of merit: here we draw attention to R. A. Erskine, 'The military coast defences of Devon, 1500–1956', in Michael Duffy *et al.*, *The New Maritime History of Devon*, I (London: Conway Maritime Press and University of Exeter, 1992), pp. 119–29, and Michael Duffy, 'Coastal defences and garrisons, 1480–1914', in Roger Kain and William Ravenhill, eds, *Historical Atlas of South-West England* (Exeter: University of Exeter Press, 1999), pp. 158–65. For fiscal and other non-military functions see Hilary L. Turner, *Town Defences in England and Wales* (London: John Baker, 1971), pp. 15–16, 71, 87–95 (esp. 89–90), 130; for the more detailed workings in one English city see Maryanne Kowaleski, *Local Markets and Regional Trade in Medieval Exeter* (Cambridge: Cambridge University Press, 1995), pp. 192–202, esp. 195, 200.

86. Donald Hodson, *Maps of Portsmouth before 1801*, City of Portsmouth Record Series no. 4 (1978). The 1691 mapping is discussed on pp. 43–5.

87. An introduction is Mark Brayshay and others, 'Plymouth', in Kain and Ravenhill, eds, *Historical Atlas…*, esp. pp. 524–9, and F. W. Woodward, *Forts or Follies?* (Tiverton: Devon Books, 1998). For maps to 1800 see Elisabeth Stuart, *Lost Landscapes of Plymouth: Maps, charts and plans to 1800* (Stroud: Alan Sutton, 1991).

88. Widmalm, 'Accuracy, rhetoric, and technology …', p. 202.

89. Jeffrey E. Dorman, *Guardians of the Humber* (Hull: Humberside Leisure Services, 1990).

90. Untitled volume of 116 manuscript town plans of Europe, n.d., ?*c.* 1650, BL Add. MS. 11564. The maps of British towns are: Bath (22825), Bristol (22829), Canterbury (22844), Cardiff (22820), Cardigan (22823), Carlisle (22840), Chichester (22824), Colchester (22838), Coventry (22826), Durham (22834), Edinburgh (22843), Exeter (22835), Gloucester (22821), Hereford (22837), Lincoln (22836), Newcastle upon Tyne, Gateshead (22831), Northampton (22841), Norwich (22822), Oxford (22839), Pembroke (22830), Rochester (22842), Shrewsbury (22832), Southampton (22833), Stamford (22827), Winchester (22819), Worcester (22818), York (22828).

91. See John Walter Hawkins, 'The Duc de Chaulnes Atlas; a seventeenth-century French atlas of manuscript military maps of British and Continental towns and cities in the British Library', *Imago Mundi* 67(2) (2015), 215–28.

92. Plans accompanying reports of 8–9 September 1768, in TNA MF 1/54: Rochester and Chatham (23497), Dover (23496), Exmouth (23498), Littlehampton (23501), Lyme Regis (23499), Maldon (23500), Newhaven (23502), Plymouth (20588), Southampton (23500).

93. Longmate, *Island Fortress*, especially pp. 173, 183–4, 200–9, 231, 246–8; Erskine, 'The military coast defences of Devon…', pp. 123–6, for some examples of raids and defences.

94. We are indebted to Peter Barber for drawing our attention to this point.

95. Of course, this involves arguing from negative evidence, but it can also be argued that there may have been losses both for Edinburgh and for other centres, such as Stirling, for which more mapping is known, and that what is important is the relative proportions rather than absolute numbers.

96. The account of the Ordnance Survey here is based on Richard Oliver: *The Ordnance Survey in the Nineteenth Century: Maps, money and the growth of government* (London: Charles Close Society, 2014): this differs in several respects from earlier accounts such as that in W. A. Seymour, ed., *A History of the Ordnance Survey* (Folkestone: Dawson, 1980).

97. J. H. Andrews, *A Paper Landscape: The Ordnance Survey in nineteenth century Ireland* (Oxford: Clarendon Press, 1975), pp. 185, 229.

98. By 'castle' we mean substantial structures with outer earthworks, rather than smaller structures such as the numerous concrete blockhouses built in World War II. For the Palmerston defences see Longmate, *Island Fortress*, pp. 334–44.

99. The earliest that we have found is for St Anne Black Friars, of 1772 (13799). We have records of thirty maps of City of London parishes produced between 1771 and 1854, but of these later ones only St Leonard Eastcheap of 1838 (13800) and St Gabriel Fenchurch Street (first half of nineteenth century; 13826) can readily be categorised as 'boundary maps'. Examples elsewhere of other pre-1850 boundary maps that we know of: Marylebone, 1768 (22853); Lincoln St Mark, 1774 (19504); Lewes, 1799 (21302); Glasgow, Gorbals, 1803 (22774); St Botolph in the East, 1827 (23476); St Leonard, Shoreditch, 1829 (23464); Norwich, St Peter Mancroft, *c.* 1840 (22552); Eccleshall, Staffordshire, 1849 (20801: not detailed). We have records of another twenty-two maps of City parishes produced between 1858 and 1914, some of which probably had an important 'boundary function': this includes fragmentary mapping of the boundaries of some City of London parishes of *c.* 1862. The map of Canterbury St Margaret of 1855 (21522) is an unusually late example of a parish boundary map.

100. Hyde, *Ward Maps of the City of London*.

101. The ward maps are 18360–18385, 19386–19397, 22201, 22246–22272, 23181–23221, 23250, 23251, 23290, 23294, 23313–23315.

102. Most of the compilation materials survive, and are in TNA T 72/8 to /11; the published maps are in *Report of the Commissioners appointed to report and advise upon the boundaries and wards of certain boroughs and corporate towns (England and Wales.)*, Part I, BPP (HC) 1837 (238) XXVI.1, Part

II, BPP (HC) 1837 (238) XXVII.1, Part III, BPP (HC) 1837 (238) XXVII.1.

103. Inverness, 1841 (22925); Oban, 1846 (21850); Aberdeen, 1862 (22963); Arbroath, 1863 (21921); Dumbarton, 1869 (21928).

104. The published maps are in *Report of the Boundary Commissioners for England and Wales. 1868*, BPP (HC) 1867–8, XX [3972], 1. Commissioners' reports are in TNA T 96; there are few maps, and the only ones which we have included in our database are of part of Nottingham (19327), Macclesfield (19328), and Jarrow (19329). The Jarrow map is a clear derivative from the OS 1:2500.

105. *Report… on an inquiry into the sanitary condition of the labouring population of Great Britain*, BPP (HC) 1842 (6), XXVI, 1, pp 330–34, republished in Edwin Chadwick, ed. M. W. Flynn, *Report on the sanitary condition of the labouring population of Great Britain* [1842] (Edinburgh: Edinburgh University Press, 1965), pp. 386–90. For a reaction to Chadwick's criticisms see *The Builder*, I, 1843, pp. 207–9.

106. For the introduction of the 1:1056 scale to Ireland see Andrews, *A Paper Landscape*, pp. 82–3; for the introduction of the scale to Britain see Oliver, *the Ordnance Survey in the Nineteenth Century*, pp. 183–90.

107. The original of the Windsor survey has not been traced, but an extract from it (20952) was published in the Second Report of the Health of Towns Commission.

108. Ida Darlington, 'Edwin Chadwick and the first large-scale Ordnance Survey of London', *Transactions of the London and Middlesex Archaeological Society XXII* (1969), pp. 58–63.

109. For more on the Board of Health surveys see Oliver, *The Ordnance Survey in the Nineteenth Century*, pp. 190–3. The surveys prepared by the OS were: Alnwick (published by OS); Ashby-de-la-Zouch; Barnard Castle (published by OS); Berwick upon Tweed (published by OS); Braintree; Burslem (16742, 16743); Cardiff (14884, 14885); Chelmsford (14094); Coventry (16740, 16741); Dartford (original deposited in Centre for Kentish Studies, Maidstone after CBTM was compiled); Derby (17001); Gloucester (15055); Hitchin (14173); Kingston upon Hull (17128); Knighton; Margate (21528); Merthyr Tydfil (14883); Nantwich (15323); Newcastle under Lyme; Ormskirk; Plymouth (published by OS); Sandgate; Sheerness; Stratford-upon-Avon (11882); Tormoham

[Torquay]; Uxbridge; Ware (14174); Warwick (17007); Woolwich (23490); Worthing (14307). Apart from Dartford, only those published by the Ordnance Survey or with numbers are known to be extant, and some of these are known only as transcripts (e.g. Burslem and Chelmsford) or lithographed versions (e.g. Hitchin, Woolwich and Worthing). While the making of most of the Ordnance Survey surveys is documented, notably in the various town files in TNA MH 13, we do not know of any reliable indication of which other towns were surveyed at this time by private surveyors. If the pattern of survival of non-Ordnance Survey plans is similar to that of Ordnance Survey ones, then it suggests that the Ordnance Survey may have been responsible for around 30 to 40 per cent of the towns mapped in the 1850s.

110. For detailed studies of this episode see J. B. Harley, 'Cartography and politics in nineteenth-century England: the case of the Ordnance Survey and the General Board of Health, 1848–1856', unpublished paper presented at the VIIIth International Conference on the History of Cartography, Berlin, 1979, and J. B. Harley, 'The Ordnance Survey 1:528 Board of Health town plans in Warwickshire 1848–1854', in T. R. Slater and P. J. Jarvis, *Field and Forest: An historical geography of Warwickshire and Worcestershire* (Norwich: Geo Books, 1982), pp. 347–84.

111. Oliver, *The Ordnance Survey in the Nineteenth Century*, pp. 229–31, 267–9.

112. For a detailed list by town 1:1056, 1:528 and 1:500 surveys and re-surveys see Oliver, *Ordnance Survey Maps: A concise guide*, chapter 6.

113. For the background to the demise of the Ordnance Survey 'town scales' as a state-funded series and their use by the Land Registry see Oliver, *The Ordnance Survey in the Nineteenth Century*, pp. 357–87, more especially 378–81, 384–5, also 456–62.

114. This has been inferred from legal deposit holdings: both the inception and the demise of the 1:1250 enlargements are exiguously documented. For Land Valuation mapping see: Oliver, *The Ordnance Survey in the Nineteenth Century*, pp. 463–4, Brian Short, *The Geography of England and Wales in 1910: An evaluation of Lloyd George's 'Domesday' of land ownership*, Historical Geography Research Series 22, (London: Royal Geographical Society, 1989); Brian Short, *Land and Society in Edwardian Britain* (Cambridge: Cambridge University Press, 1997); Geraldine Beech and Rose Mitchell, *Maps for Family and Local*

History (Kew: The National Archives, 2004), pp. 36–68; Kain and Baigent, *The Cadastral Map*, pp. 261–2.

115. *Final report of the Departmental Committee on the Ordnance Survey*, London: HMSO, 1938, pp. 13–15; H. St J. L. Winterbotham, 'The town plans', *Empire Survey Review IV* (1938), pp. 425–30.

116. Oliver, *Ordnance Survey Maps: A concise guide*, especially chapters 1, 6.

117. W. Ristow, *American Maps and Mapmakers: Commercial cartography in the nineteenth century* (Detroit: Wayne State University Press, 1985), pp. 244–7. An example of the map is BL Maps K.Top.122.68.

118. There is an introduction to the Goad plans, together with a summary listing, in Glyn Rowley, *British Fire Insurance Plans* (Old Hatfield: Chas E. Goad, 1984).

119. Notes by Gilbert T. Bell on *Campbeltown 1898* (Argyllshire 257.8) (Leadgate: Alan Godfrey Maps, 2006).

120. Delano-Smith and Kain, *English Maps: A history*, pp. 207–11.

121. As these post-Great Fire schemes are speculative, we have not included them in our database.

122. Elizabeth Baigent, 'Revealing the city in maps: Bath seen, built, and imagined', *Journal of Historical Geography*, 37 (2011), pp. 385–9.

123. Buckie (Banff): 1780, 1786, c. 1824 (21824–21826); Cullen (Banff): 1762, 1764, 1797, 1817, 1825, 1860, also 1873, 1894 (21764, 21860, 21818–21820, 21614, 21821, 21822, 21861); Fochabers (Elgin/Moray): c. 1770 (two), 1773, 1774, c. 1780, 1783, 1808, 1825 (21879, 21939, 21880, 21882, 21881, 21938, 21883, 21940, 21941); Golspie (Sutherland): 1811, 1830 (two) (21706–21708); Keith (Banff), 1764, c. 1768, c. 1780 (21887–21889); Macduff (Banff): 1826, 1832, c. 1845, c. 1860 (21921, 21929, 21927, 21925); Portsoy (Banff): c. 1770, 1802, 1817 (21718, 21891, 21890); Rothes (Elgin/Moray): 1769, 1790 (two maps), 1817, 1859, 1868 (21950–21955).

124. 20014, 20153, 20155, 20156, 20158–20160, 20163-20166, 20172.

125. 20175, 20164, 20176–20178.

Index to Online Catalogue of British Town Maps

This index provides a physical linkage to the electronic *Catalogue of British Town Maps* (CBTM). A full Guide to Users can be downloaded from: http://townmaps.data.history.ac.uk

Each entry in the Catalogue has a unique identifying number and the numerical ranges of these numbers relate to the date of primary library and archive searches.

(1) CBTM numbers in the range 18217–23525 are a majority of the maps catalogued and this work was done funded by the AHRC, between 1999 and 2006.

(2) CBTM numbers in the range 00001–11830 derive from an investigation of tithe maps of the mid-nineteenth century, funded by the Leverhulme Trust, between 1987 and 1991.

(3) CBTM numbers in the range 11831–18216 relate to maps of towns discovered during research on enclosure, rating, sanitary and other unpublished 'parish' maps funded by the Economic & Social Research Council, mainly between 1993 and 1997.

(4) CBTM numbers in the range 200003 to 200146 relate to 144 entries, largely from Scotland, for which there are no extant town maps other than an Ordnance Survey Map. The CBTM entries for these places have limited information listing only the town, county, year, and scale of the relevant Ordnance Survey map(s).

The contents of CBTM have been static since April 2008. For this reason it does not take account of some more recent work, notably at the Post Office Archive.

Archives and Libraries searched:
CBTM was compiled from searches in the following archives and libraries. In all cases where a town or city library is listed, it is the central library of that place unless specified otherwise. It should be noted that these titles are liable to change.

Aberdeen City Archives
Accrington Library Local Studies
Anglesey Archives, Llangefni
Ashmolean Museum
Ayrshire Archives
Bath City Archives
Bath Library
Bedford Central Library Local Studies
Bedfordshire Archives
Berkshire Record Office
Berwick-upon-Tweed Archives
Birkenhead Library
Birmingham Central Library, Archives
Birmingham Central Library, Local Studies
Bishopsgate Institute, London Collection
Bodleian Library
Bolton Archives and Local Studies, Central Library, Bolton
Borthwick Institute, York
Bournemouth Library, Local Studies Section
Bradford Central Library, Local Studies
Bridgend Library
Brighton History Centre
Bristol City Archives
British Library
Buckinghamshire Record Office
Bury Archives
Cambridge City Library, Cambridgeshire Collection
Cambridgeshire Record Office
Cambridgeshire Record Office, Huntingdon Branch
Cambridge University Library
Camden Local Studies

Canterbury Cathedral Archives
Canterbury City Library, Local Studies
Cardiff City Library, Local Studies Section
Carlisle Public Library, Local Studies
Carmarthen Record Office
Carnarvon Record Office
Centre for Kentish Studies
Cheltenham Library
Cheshire Record Office
Chesterfield Library, Local Studies
City of London Record Office
Clwyd [Denbighshire] Record Office, Denbigh
Clwyd [Flint] County Record Office, Hawarden
Colchester Library, Local Studies
Colne Library
Cornish Studies Centre, Redruth
Cornwall Record Office
Coventry City Archives
Crosby Library
Cumbria Archives, Kendal
Cumbria Archives, Carlisle
Cumbria Record Office, Barrow-in-Furness
Darlington Library, Local Studies Library
Derby Town Local Studies Library
Derbyshire Local Studies Library, Matlock
Derbyshire Archives, Matlock
Devon & Exeter Institution, Exeter
Devon Record Office, Sowton, Exeter
Doncaster Archives
Doncaster Library, Local Studies
Dorset Record Office
Dover Library Local Studies Section
Dudley Archives

Dumfries, Ewart Library
Dundee Central Library, Local History Section
Durham County Record Office, Durham
Durham University Library (Manuscripts)
East Kent Archives, Whitfield, Dover
East Suffolk Record Office, Ipswich
East Sussex Record Office, Lewes
East Yorkshire Archives, Beverley
Edinburgh Central Library, Edinburgh Room
Edinburgh City Archives
East Suffolk Record Office
East Sussex Record Office, Lewes
Essex Record Office, Chelmsford
Essex Record Office, Colchester Branch
Essex Record Office, Southend on Sea Branch
Falkirk, History Research Centre
Gateshead Library, Local Studies
Guildhall Library, London
Glamorgan Record Office, Cardiff
Glasgow City Archives
Glasgow, Mitchell Library, Local Studies
Gloucester Library, Local Studies
Gloucestershire Record Office
Greater Manchester Record Office
Greenwich Heritage Centre, Woolwich
Grimsby Central Library
Guildhall Library
Gwent Record Office, Cwmbran
Glasgow University Library
Hackney Archives
Halifax Library, Reference Section
Hamilton Reference Library
Hammersmith & Fulham Archives & Local History Centre

Hampshire Record Office
Harrogate Library, Local Studies
    Section
Hastings Public Library,
    Local Studies Section
Hereford City Library, Reference Section
Herefordshire Record Office, Hereford
Hertfordshire Record Office
Highland Council Archive, Inverness
Horsham Museum
Hull University Library
Isle of Wight Record Office
Islington Central Library,
    Local Studies and Archives
Keighley Central Library
Kensington Library, Local Studies
Centre for Kentish Studies, Maidstone
Kidderminster Library Local Studies
Kings Lynn Borough Archives
Kingston upon Hull City Archives
Kingston upon Hull City Library, Local
    Studies
Kirkcaldy Public Library
Knowsley Archives
Lancashire Record Office, Preston
Lancaster Library
Leamington Library
Leeds Central Library, Family History
    & Local Studies
Leeds Central Library, Local Studies Section
Leicester Municipal Library
Lichfield Joint Record Office
Lincoln City Library
Lincolnshire Archives
Lincolnshire Archives Office
Liverpool Record Office
London Metropolitan Archives
Lord Louis Library, Newport, Isle of Wight,
    Local History Room
Lowestoft Library: Archives
Luton Library
Maidenhead Library, Local Studies
Manchester Central Library Archives
Margate Library, Heritage Room
Medway Archives
Merionydd Archives
Middleton Library Local Studies
Minet Library, Lambeth
Morley Public Library, Local History
    Collection
Morpeth Records Centre
National Archives of Scotland
National Library of Scotland
National Library of Wales
Newcastle Central Library, Local Studies
Newport [Gwent] Public Library, Reference
    Section
Norfolk Record Office
North-East Lincolnshire Archives, Grimsby
North-east Scotland Library Headquarters,
    Oldmeldrum
Northampton Public Library
Northamptonshire Record Office

North Ayrshire Local History Library,
    Ardrossan
Northumberland Record Office, Gosforth
North Yorkshire Record Office, Northallerton
Norwich Library, Norfolk Heritage Centre
Nottingham Central Library, Local Studies
Nottinghamshire Archives
Oldham Archives
Oxford Library, Oxfordshire Studies
Oxfordshire Archives
Perth & Kinross Archives
Perth, A. K. Bell Library, Local Studies
Peterborough Central Library
Plymouth Central Library, Local Studies
Poole Local History Centre
Portsmouth Central Library
Portsmouth City Record Office
Post Office Archive, London
Powys Archives, Llandrindod Wells
Preston, Harris Library
Reading Central Library Local Studies
Royal Geographical Society with the Institute
    of British Geographers
Rochdale Local Studies Library
Rotherham Library, Archives
Royal Scottish Geographical Society
Rugby Library, Local Studies Section
St Helens Library, Archives & Local Studies
St John's College, Cambridge, Archives
Salford Archives
Salford Museum – Local History Library
Sandwell Archives
Scarborough Library
Shakespeare Birthplace Trust, Stratford-
    upon-Avon
Sheffield Archives
Sheffield Library
Shropshire Records and History Centre,
    Shrewsbury
Somerset Record Office
Southampton City Archives
Southampton Library, Local Studies
    Section
Southport Library, Reference and Local
    Studies
South Shields Library, Local Studies
Southwark Local Studies Library
Staffordshire Record Office
Stockport Archives
Stockport Central Library
Stoke-on-Trent Museum, Archaeology
    Section
Stornoway Public Library
Sunderland Library Local Studies
Surrey History Centre, Woking
Swansea City Archives
Swansea Library, Reference Section
Tameside Archives
Teeside Archives
The National Archives [formerly Public
    Record Office]
Tower Hamlets Library, Local Studies
    Section

Trafford Local Studies Library, Sale
Tyne & Wear Archives
University of Exeter Geography Department
    Map Collection
Wakefield Library, Local Studies
Walsall Local History Centre
Waltham Forest Archives, Walthamstow
Warrington Library, Archives
Warwickshire Record Office
West Country Studies Library, Exeter
West Devon Record Office, Plymouth
West Glamorgan Record Office
West Lothian Local History Library
Westminster Archives
West Suffolk Record Office, Bury St Edmunds
West Sussex Record Office, Chichester
West Yorkshire Archives Service, Bradford
    Office
West Yorkshire Archives Service, Halifax
    Office
West Yorkshire Archives Service,
    Huddersfield Office
West Yorkshire Archives Service, Leeds
    [Sheepscar] Office
West Yorkshire Archives Service, Wakefield
    Office
Wigan Archives
Wiltshire Record Office
Wirral Archive Service
Wisbech Museum
Wolverhampton Archives
Worcestershire Record Office
York City Library
York Minster Archives
Yorkshire Archaeological Society, Leeds

CBTM Online Catalogue

This page shows the CBTM entry for record 19290 with the accompanying index map.

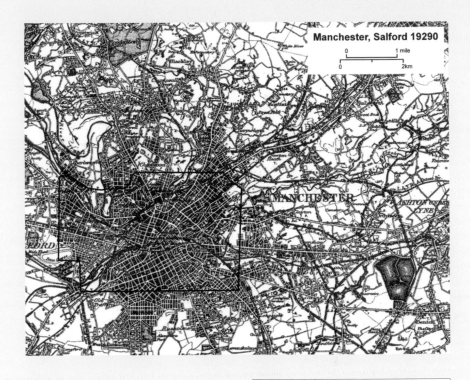

Manchester, Salford 19290

Area covered by the Map [View]	The base-maps are mostly derived from Ordnance Survey 1:63,360 mapping published 1874-1914. Base-maps at 1:10,560, 1:126,720 and 1:243,440 are derived from Ordnance Survey material of similar date, except for limited 1:126,720 mapping in northern Scotland which is derived from Bartholomew mapping of the early 1900s.
Year	2.1.1832
Type	General Purpose
Place	Manchester, Salford
County	Lancashire
Extent of cover	whole built-up area.
National grid reference	SJ840980
Exter coverage diagram reference	SJ 8691
Map title	'Bancks & Co.'s plan of Manchester and Salford, with their environs, showing the division of property & the length of each street, from an actual survey by Richard Thornton, commenced under the auspices of his late Majesty and now dedicated by permission to his most gracious majesty, William the fourth.: The survey completed in the year 1831.'
Dedicee of map	King William IV.
Comments on map	Detailed, including privvies or sheds in back yards
Scale	1:3168
Map-maker	Richard Thornton [sv], J. & A. Walker, London, & 33 Pool Lane, Liverpool [eng], Bancks & Co., Exchange St, Manchester [pb].
Production mode	engraved.
Dimensions [in centimetres]	187 x 122 [mounted as one].
Number of parts	4
Legends	boundaries, other: Street lengths.
Stated measurements	other: Street lengths of more important streets.
Road names	generally.
Building names	outside built-up area only.
Buildings	shown, stables/coach houses, public buildings emphasised [One or two namd stables].
Tenement boundaries	apparently fairly complete.
Turnpikes	shown
Canals	shown, wharf.
Railways	routes, named, rails, passenger stations, misc: Railway Off. in Market St.
Miscellaneous transport-related	A few dotted lines for presumably intended streets but not many.

Post and telegraphs	post-offices
Industry	chemicals, food/drink, paper/print, rope walk, textiles, misc: [Print Works]; Coal Yards.
Sanitary and utility information	gas works, reservoirs.
Places of Worship	shown comprehensively: Quaker M.H. is simply 'Meeting House'.
Cemeteries	shown.
Public Buildings	town hall/administrative, olice, misc: Manor Office.
Penal	jails/reformatories: 'Internal walls shown at New Bailey Prison].
Defence and military	barracks: [Cook House, Guard House, &c at Barracks are identified].
Welfare and charitable	deaf & dumb, dispensaries, infirmaries, workhousees: [Deaf & Dumb School].
Education and academic	schools: Includes Chetham's College; the school by St Thomas in Salford has a 'pole' to the east. Suspicious lack of schools in the more built-up part.
Markets and exchanges	exchanges, markets: [A variety of fish, pig, etc, markets, with divisions in Shambles].
Service and professional	insurances offices: [Assurance Off.].
Inns, hospitality and refreshment	shown.
Leisure and entertainment	baths/spa, theatres, etc.

Clubs and societies	mechanics institutes, learned socleties
Waterbodies	shown.
Recreation and sports venues	sports grounds.
Woodland	shown.
Parkland	public parks: [Vauxhall Gardens].
Gardens	shown, nurseries: [Some 'marginal' comment may include orchards rather than gardens].
Public / administrative boundaries	ecclesiastical districts, township.
Landowners and occupiers	industrial owners.
Borders	decorative.
Known copies of map	Lee.47: BLML Maps 3215(15), BOL C17:70 Manchester d.2, Manchester RO AA/43 [DX 6/1/2], Manchester Central Library f912.4273 T1, f912.4273 T3, TNA [PRO] RAIL 1033/169-172, Stockport M/1547, Tameside L.912 Sq 1729160 [1828/31]; CUL Maps.68.83.3,1-2 [1832]; Cheshire RO PM/4; Tameside Q.Box 676304 [1831/1983 repro]; Manchester RO K/5 [repro]; Trafford map 34 ['1834': reproduction]; BLML Maps 3215(8) [?1840].

Ordnance Survey/s	1844-9	1:1056
		1:10,560
	1888-9	1:500
		1:2500
		1:10,560

Abbots Bromley: 6; 1826–1900
Abbotsbury: 3; 1814–86
Aberaeron: 3; 1843–87
Aberavon: 3; 1843–97
Abercirder: 2; 1797–1865
Aberdare: 3; 1846–98
Aberdeen: 28; 1745–1900
Aberdovey: 5; 1841–1900
Aberfeldy: 4; 1820–99
Aberford: 6; 1818–90
Aberfraw: 3; 1845–99
Abergavenny: 9; 1740–1899
Abergele: 5; 1839–98
Abernethy: 2; 1859–99
Abersychan: 3; 1841–99
Abertillery: 3; 1841–99
Aberystwyth: 6; 1809–85
Abingdon: 7; 1550–1898
Accrington: 8; 1835–91
Acle: 3; 1799–1884
Acton: 4; 1842–91 [see also London]
Airdrie: 5; 1825–97
Albrighton: 3; 1846–81
Alcester: 1; 1886
Aldborough: 4; 1709–1892
Aldbourne: 3; 1837–99
Aldeburgh: 5; 1600–1881
Alderley Edge: 3; 1842–97
Aldermaston: 3; 1841–98
Aldershot: 7; 1841–95
Alexandria: 2; 1859–97 [OS only]
Alford: 2; 1839–87
Alfreton: 4; 1816–98
Allendale Town: 4; 1847–95
Alloa: 5; 1790–1899
Alnwick: 6; 1769–1897
Alston: 2; 1859–98 [OS only]
Alton: 5; 1666–1895
Altrincham: 4; 1835–97
Alva: 2; 1861–99 [OS only]
Alwinton: 3; 1863–96 [OS only]
Alyth: 2; 1862–98 [OS only]
Ambleside: 2; 1858–97 [OS only]
Amersham: 5; 1742–1897
Amesbury: 5; 1726–1899
Amlwch: 6; 1831–1900
Ammanford: 2; 1841–76
Ampthill: 4; 1808–1900
Andover: 4; 1836–94
Annan: 5; 1759–1898
Anstruther: 5; 1737–1893
Appleby: 6; 1754–1897
Appledore (Devon): 2; 1839–85
Appledore (Kent): 3; 1841–96
Arbroath: 6; 1822–91
Ardrossan: 5; 1813–95
Arundel: 5; 1785–1896
Ashbourne: 5; 1547–1898
Ashburton: 3; 1831–85

Ashby de la Zouch: 4; 1735–1881
Ashford: 6; 1818–96
Ashover: 5; 1816–97
Ashton in Makerfield: 2; 1844–92 [OS only]
Ashton-under-Lyne: 5; 1824–92
Ashwell: 4; 1841–97
Askrigg: 3; 1840–92
Aston: 13; 1758–1900
Atherstone: 1; 1888 [OS only]
Atherton [formerly Chowbent]: 3; 1839–88
Attleborough: 3; 1815–81
Auchterarder: 4; 1755–1900
Auchtermuchty: 3; 1823–93
Audlem: 3; 1842–97
Aveley: 4; 1593–1895
Axbridge: 3; 1839–83
Axminster: 2; 1842–87
Aylesbury: 3; 1802–98
Aylsham: 3; 1838–84
Aynho: 3; 1812–98
Ayr: 8; 1654–1895
Bacup: 3; 1848–91
Bagillt: 5; 1824–98
Bagshot: 3; 1823–95
Baildon: 6; 1846–91
Bakewell: 4; 1799–1897
Bala: 3; 1841–99
Baldock: 3; 1851–97
Ballater: 4; 1808–66
Bampton (Devon): 2; 1842–87
Bampton (Oxon): 6; 1789–1898
Banbury: 6; 1836–99
Banchory: 1; 1863 [OS only]
Banff: 4; 1800–67
Bangor: 7; 1610–1899
Barking: 6; 1652–1895
Barkway: 3; 1804–96
Barmouth: 3; 1841–1900
Barnard Castle: 4; 1827–96
Barnet: 4; 1818–95
Barnoldswick: 2; 1849–93
Barnsley: 6; 1779–1900
Barnstaple: 8; 1650–1895
Barrhead: 2; 1857–96
Barrow-in-Furness: 8; 1842–90
Barry: 4; 1622–1898
Barton upon Humber: 3; 1796–1886
Basingstoke: 7; 1762–1894
Bath: 77; 1588–1902
Bathgate: 3; 1767–1896
Batley: 5; 1822–93
Battersea: 7; 1760–1897 [see also London]
Battle: 4; 1724–1897
Bawtry: 3; 1840–91
Beaconsfield: 4; 1795–1897
Beaminster: 2; 1842–86

Beaumaris: 6; 1610–1900
Beccles: 3; 1836–82
Beckenham: 3; 1840–95
Beckingham: 2; 1770–1886
Bedale: 7; 1772–1891
Bedford: 16; 1610–1900
Bedworth: 3; 1840–86
Beeston: 2; 1880–99
Beith: 3; 1790–1895
Belford: 4; 1820–97
Bellingham: 3; 1845–95
Belper: 4; 1791–1898
Bere Alston: 2; 1844–82
Bere Regis: 4; 1775–1900
Berkeley: 4; 1839–79
Berkhamstead: 5; 1840–97
Bermondsey: 6; 1720–1894 [see also London]
Berwick-upon-Tweed: 28; 1572–189
Bethseda: 3; 1839–99
Betley: 3; 1842–98
Beverley: 8; 1747–1891
Bewdley: 5; 1831–83
Bexhill: 5; 1839–99
Bicester: 3; 1753–1899
Bideford: 3; 1836–85
Bidford on Avon: 1; 1885 [OS only]
Biggar: 2; 1858–96 [OS only]
Biggleswade: 3; 1838–1900
Bildeston: 2; 1839–83
Billericay: 6; 1593–1895
Billesdon: 2; 1850–85
Bilston: 9; 1832–92
Binbrook: 1; 1886 [OS only]
Bingham: 3; 1840–99
Bingley: 9; 1817–90
Birkenhead: 30; 1823–1900
Birmingham: 60; 1731–1900
Birstall: 4; 1822–89
Bishop Auckland: 3; 1839–96
Bishop's Castle: 3; 1809–82
Bishop's Lydeard: 2; 1838–87
Bishop's Stortford: 4; 1823–96
Bishop's Waltham: 4; 1831–95
Bisley: 2; 1842–82
Blackburn: 4; 1822–92
Blackpool: 6; 1838–97
Blaenavon: 3; 1840–99
Blairgowrie: 2; 1863–99 [OS only]
Blakeney (Gloucestershire): 2; 1840–79
Blakeney (Norfolk): 2; 1769–1885
Blandford: 6; 1731–1900
Blennerhasset: 2; 1863–99
Bletchingley: 4; 1835–95
Blockley: 4; 1773–1900
Blyth (Northumberland): 4; 1840–96
Blyth (Nottinghamshire): 3;

1843–97
Blythburgh: 2; 1841–82
Bodmin: 3; 1836–80
Bognor: 6; 1825–96
Bolingbroke: 3; 1719–1887
Bollington: 2; 1870–97 [OS only]
Bolsover: 3; 1637–1897
Bolton: 9; 1792–1890
Bo'ness: 3; 1766–1895
Bonhill: 2; 1859–97 [OS only]
Bootle (Cumberland): 3; 1837–97
Bootle (Lancashire): 7; 1839–95
Boroughbridge: 4; 1846–92:
Boscastle: 2; 1842–82
Bossiney: 2; 1842–82
Boston: 8; 1742–1887
Botesdale: 3; 1817–85
Botley: 3; 1839–95
Bourne: 2; 1770–1886
Bournemouth: 18; 1805–98
Bovey Tracey: 3; 1640–1887
Bow (Devon): 2; 1841–86
Bow (Middlesex): 7; 1768–1893 [see also London]
Bowdon: 3; 1839–97
Bowes: 4; 1850–92
Bowmore: 4; 1825–98
Bowness: 2; 1858–97 [OS only]
Brackley: 6; 1760–1898
Bradford: 47; 1722–1900
Bradford on Avon: 5; 1837–99
Brading: 3; 1840–96
Bradninch: 2; 1839–87
Braintree: 5; 1814–96
Bramber: 2; 1872–96 [OS only]
Bramley: 4; 1822–90
Brampton: 3; 1850–99
Brandon: 3; 1809–80
Brechin: 3; 1823–62
Brecon: 9; 1610–1887
Brentford: 10; 1635–1894
Brentwood: 5; 1789–1895
Brewood: 5; 1808–1900
Bridgend: 4; 1841–97
Bridge of Allan: 4; 1832–96
Bridgnorth: 8; 1625–1882
Bridgwater: 6; 1730–1886
Bridlington: 4; 1850–99
Bridport: 6; 1774–1887
Brierfield: 3; 1843–91
Brierley Hill: 5; 1820–82
Brigg: 2; 1805–86
Brighouse: 7; 1788–1893
Brightlingsea: 3; 1840–96
Brighton: 58; 1545–1899
Bristol: 69; 1479–1900
Briton Ferry: 2; 1875–97 [OS only]
Brixham: 5; 1781–1868
Brixton: 4; 1843–94 [see also London]

Broadstairs: 4; 1824–96
Bromley (Kent): 7; 1763–1895
Bromley (Middlesex): 6; 1812–94
[see also London]
Brompton: 3; 1838–96
Bromsgrove: 2; 1840–85
Bromyard: 3; 1844–85
Broseley: 3; 1620–1882
Brough: 3; 1841–97
Broughton in Furness: 4; 1846–89
Broughty Ferry: 3; 1861–99
Bruton: 4; 1838–85
Brynmawr: 2; 1841–78
Buckfastleigh: 2; 1843–85
Buckie: 4; 1780–1866
Buckingham: 10; 1610–1899
Buckley: 5; 1839–98
Bude: 2; 1840–93
Budleigh Salterton: 2; 1845–88
Builth: 2; 1842–87
Bulwell: 6; 1841–99
Bungay: 3; 1845–84
Buntingford: 3; 1838–96
Burford: 3; 1823–98
Burgess Hill: 3; 1845–97
Burghead: 3; 1808–70
Burgh le Marsh: 2; 1842–88
Burnham Market: 5; 1825–85
Burnham on Crouch: 4; 1836–95
Burnham on Sea: 5; 1806–83
Burnley: 6; 1841–96
Burntisland: 5; 1743–1894
Burry Port: 2; 1841–78
Burslem: 6; 1832–98
Burton in Kendal: 4; 1822–97
Burton upon Stather: 4; 1806–85
Burton upon Trent: 9; 1857–1900
Bury: 8; 1840–99
Bury St Edmunds: 15; 1740–1883
Buxton: 9; 1631–1897
Caergwrle: 3; 1850–98
Caerleon: 4; 1801–1900
Caerphilly: 2; 1873–1900 [OS only]
Caerwys: 5; 1742–1898
Caistor: 1796–1887
Callander: 5; 1739–1899
Callington: 5; 1793–1881
Calne: 12; 1750–1899
Camberwell: 7; 1834–97
Camborne: 6; 1819–77
Cambridge: 75; 1574–1900
Camelford: 2; 1841–81
Campbeltown: 8; 1769–1898
Cannock: 3; 1841–1900
Canterbury: 40; 1588–1896
Cardiff: 44; 1610–1899
Cardigan: 7; 1610–1888
Carlisle: 29; 1610–1899
Carluke: 3; 1808–96
Carmarthen: 8; 1610–1885
Carnarvon: 12; 1610–1897
Carnforth: 4; 1836–90
Carnoustie: 1; 1857 [OS only]
Carnwath: 2; 1858–96 [OS only]
Cartmel: 3; 1807–90

Castle Acre: 4; 1779–1883
Castle Cary: 5; 1670–1884
Castle Combe: 3; 1841–99
Castle Donington: 2; 1779–1882
Castle Douglas: 4; 1793–1894
Castleford: 5; 1812–88
Castle Hedingham: 6; 1592–1896
Castle Rising: 4; 1588–1883
Cawood: 3; 1780–1890
Cawston: 2; 1840–84
Caxton: 4; 1750–1900
Cerne Abbas: 5; 1768–1901
Chadderton: 3; 1840–91
Chagford: 2; 1840–84
Chapel-en-le-Frith: 2; 1877–97 [OS only]
Chard: 9; 1799–1885
Charing: 3; 1840–96
Charlbury: 4; 1761–1898
Chatham: 16; 1688–1896
Chatteris: 6; 1819–1900
Cheadle (Cheshire): 5; 1840–97
Cheadle (Staffordshire): 3; 1843–98
Cheddar: 4; 1801–84
Chelmsford: 6; 1591–1895
Chelsea: 14; 1664–1900 [see also London]
Cheltenham: 34; 1804–1901
Chepstow: 7; 1686–1900
Chertsey: 5; 1814–94
Chesham: 3; 1843–97
Cheshunt: 7; 1785–1896
Chester: 45; 1550–1898
Chesterfield: 13; 1637–1898
Chesterton: 3; 1841–98
Chester le Street: 4; 1846–95
Chewton Mendip: 4; 1740–1883
Chichester: 25; 1595–1900
Chilham: 3; 1839–96
Chippenham: 8; 1800–99
Chipping Campden: 2; 1883–1900
Chipping Norton: 4; 1770–1898
Chipping Ongar: 1760–1895
Chipping Sodbury: 3; 1770–1881
Chiswick: 5; 1847–99
Chorley: 3; 1839–99
Christchurch: 4; 1840–96
Chudleigh: 3; 1754–1886
Chulmleigh: 2; 1841–86
Church: 5; 1785–1891
Church Stretton: 2; 1839–82
Cilgerran: 2; 1844–88
Cinderford: 2; 1856–78
Cirencester: 7; 1795–1887
Clacton on Sea: 4; 1839–96
Clapham: 6; 1838–94
Clare: 2; 1846–84
Clayton: 4; 1848–91
Clayton le Moors: 5; 1785–1891
Cleator Moor: 4; 1825–98
Cleckheaton: 8; 1797–1889
Cleethorpes: 3; 1843–87
Cleobury Mortimer: 2; 1846–83
Clerkenwell: 11; 1720–1898 [see also London]

Clevedon: 3; 1839–83
Cley next the Sea: 3; 1812–85
Clifton: see Bristol
Clitheroe: 7; 1781–1884
Clovelly: 2; 1840–84
Clun: 2; 1847–83
Clydebank: 2; 1860–96 [OS only]
Coalbrookdale: 2; 1848–81
Coatbridge: 2; 1858–97 [OS only]
Cockermouth: 6; 1770–1898
Coggeshall: 4; 1758–1896
Colchester: 36; 1610–1896
Coldstream: 3; 1818–97
Coleford: 3; 1842–1900
Coleshill: 3; 1783–1886
Colinsburgh: 2; 1852–93 [OS only]
Colnbrook: 4; 1815–98
Colne: 4; 1805–91
Colwyn, Colwyn Bay: 4; 1839–98
Colyton: 2; 1843–87
Combe Martin: 2; 1843–86
Congleton: 5; 1818–97
Connahs Quay: 3; 1839–98
Consett: 4; 1781–1895
Conwy: 6; 1819–99
Corbridge: 5; 1778–1895
Corby: 2; 1841–86
Corfe Castle: 4; 1586–1900
Corsham: 5; 1830–99
Corwen: 3; 1840–99
Coseley: 7; 1816–84
Cottingham: 4; 1839–88
Coventry: 25; 1610–1900
Coupar Angus: 3; 1862–98
Cowbridge: 3; 1843–97
Cowdenbeath: 2; 1853–94
Crail: 3; 1832–93
Cranborne: 3; 1844–1900
Cranbrook: 4; 1811–96
Crediton: 2; 1839–86
Crewe: 4; 1840–97
Crewkerne: 6; 1772–1885
Criccieth: 3; 1839–99
Crickhowell: 2; 1844–85
Cricklade: 3; 1775–1898
Crieff: 3; 1822–99
Cromarty: 3; 1825–73
Cromer: 6; 1747–1896
Cromford: 3; 1840–98
Crook: 3; 1839–96
Crowland: 3; 1869–1900
Crowle: 2; 1862–85
Croydon: 9; 1800–95
Cuckfield: 4; 1818–96
Cullen: 10; 1762–1894
Cullompton: 3; 1633–1887
Culross: 3; 1832–95
Cumnock: 2; 1856–95 [OS only]
Cupar: 7; 1642–1894
Dalbeattie: 2; 1848–94
Dalderby: 1; 1887 [OS only]
Dalkeith: 4; 1822–93
Dalry: 2; 1855–95 [OS only]
Dalton in Furness: 4; 1825–90
Darlaston: 4; 1837–86

Darlington: 12; 1826–96
Dartford: 3; 1838–95
Dartmouth: 5; 1619–1885
Darvel: 2; 1856–95 [OS only]
Darwen: 3; 1844–91
Daventry: 6; 1788–1899
Dawlish: 3; 1840–90
Deal: 8; 1819–97
Debenham: 2; 1837–84
Deddington: 3; 1808–98
Dedham: 4; 1803–96
Denbigh: 8; 1610–1898
Denny: 2; 1860–96 [OS only]
Denton: 3; 1844–95
Deptford: 8; 1623–1894
Derby: 21; 1610–1899
Devizes: 10; 1759–1899
Devonport: 66; 1584–1899
Dewsbury: 8; 1600–1893
Dinas Mawddwy: 3; 1841–1900
Dingwall: 5; 1789–1874
Diss: 3; 1820–85
Ditchling: 3; 1839–96
Dodbrooke: 2; 1843–84
Dolgelly: 3; 1842–1900
Dollar: 2; 1861–99 [OS only]
Doncaster: 16; 1778–1894
Donington: 1; 1887 [OS only]
Dorchester (Dorset): 14; 1610–1886
Dorchester (Oxfordshire): 3; 1845–97
Dorking: 6; 1649–1895
Dornoch: 2; 1832–73
Doune: 3; 1782–1899
Dover: 37; 1530–1905
Dowlais: 4; 1850–97
Downham Market: 4; 1818–85
Downton: 10; 1740–1899
Driffield: 4; 1742–1892
Droitwich: 7; 1690–1884
Dronfield: 4; 1850–97
Droylesden: 3; 1844–91
Dudley: 19; 1787–1883
Dufftown: 3; 1832–84
Dukinfield: 6; 1692–1898
Dulverton: 4; 1790–1887
Dumbarton: 9; 1777–1897
Dumfries: 8; 1819–99
Dunbar: 3; 1830–93
Dunblane: 2; 1862–99 [OS only]
Dundee: 23; 1777–1901
Dunfermline: 5; 1771–1896
Dunkeld: 3; 1823–99
Dunoon: 2; 1863–98 [OS only]
Duns: 4; 1824–98
Dunstable: 3; 1840–1900
Dunster: 4; 1775–1886
Dunwich: 4; 1753–1882
Durham: 24; 1595–1895
Dursley: 3; 1844–81
Dysart: 3; 1832–95
Ealing: 7; 1777–1891
Earith: 5; 1812–1901
Earlestown: 3; 1838–91
Earls Colne: 4; 1598–1896

Earlsferry: 2; 1852–93 [OS only]
Easingwold: 5; 1812–89
Eastbourne: 13; 1841–1900
East Coatham: 5; 1848–93
East Cowes: 3; 1845–96
East Dereham: 4; 1757–1882
East Grinstead: 4; 1831–97
East Ham: 6; 1800–94
East Harling: 3; 1804–83
East Ilsley: 5; 1812–98
Eastleigh: 4; 1840–95
East Looe: 4; 1839–81
Eastney: 3; 1838–96
East Retford: 4; 1836–98
Ebbw Vale: 4; 1840–99
Ecclefechan: 2; 1857–98
Eccles: 4; 1845–92
Eccleshall: 4; 1839–1900
Eckington: 4; 1804–97
Edenbridge: 3; 1844–96
Edinburgh: 108; 1544–1900
Edgware: 3; 1845–95
Egremont: 3; 1842–98
Egton: 3; 1842–92
Elgin: 6; 1822–68
Elham: 3; 1844–96
Elland: 7; 1750–1888
Ellesmere: 5; 1835–1900
Ellesmere Port: 3; 1839–97
Ellon: 3; 1868–99
Elsdon: 4; 1731–1896
Eltringham: 3; 1841–60
Ely: 10; 1610–1885
Emsworth: 7; 1665–1896
Enfield: 3; 1803–95
Epping: 4; 1751–1895
Epsom: 6; 1838–95
Epworth: 2; 1803–85
Erdington: 1; 1884 [OS only]
Erith: 3; 1843–95
Eston: 3; 1839–93
Eton: 8; 1742–1897
Evershot: 2; 1838–86
Evesham: 6; 1820–85
Ewell: 4; 1802–94
Exeter: 51; 1587–1900
Exmouth: 4; 1768–1888
Eye: 3; 1836–84
Eyemouth: 5; 1842–98
Failsworth: 3; 1843–91
Fairford: 4; 1834–80
Fakenham: 4; 1650–1885
Falfield: 2; 1841–78
Falkirk: 5; 1812–96
Falkland: 2; 1853–94 [OS only]
Falmouth: 10; 1567–1895
Fareham: 6; 1665–1895
Faringdon: 2; 1876–98 [OS only]
Farnborough: 4; 1841–95
Farnham: 5; 1800–95
Farnworth: 2; 1844–95 [OS only]
Farsley: 5; 1758–1889
Faversham: 4; 1770–1896
Felixstowe: 4; 1741–1899
Fenny Stratford: 5; 1813–98

Ferrybridge: 3; 1840–91
Ferry Port on Craig: 2; 1853–93 [OS only]
Ffestiniog: 2; 1842–88
Filey: 3; 1791–1890
Finchley: 4; 1814–95
Findochty: 4; 1833–92
Finsbury: 9; 1720–1894 [see also London]
Fishguard: 6; 1814–88
Fleetwood: 5; 1838–90
Flint: 6; 1610–1898
Fochabers: 10; 1760–1869
Folkestone: 14; 1782–1898
Folkingham: 2; 1841–87
Fordingbridge: 5; 1832–95
Fordwich: 3; 1839–96
Forfar: 3; 1823–60
Forres: 3; 1828–69
Fortrose: 5; 1788–1871
Fort William: 12; 1696–1899
Foulsham: 3; 1813–84
Fowey: 4; 1779–1880
Framlingham: 3; 1842–82
Frampton: 2; 1839–86
Frampton on Severn: 1; 1880 [OS only]
Fraserburgh: 1; 1868 [OS only]
Frodsham: 4; 1838–97
Frome: 6; 1813–84
Fulham: 8; 1813–97
Fulwood: 3; 1843–92
Gainsborough: 5; 1748–1898
Galashiels: 5; 1795–1897
Galston: 4; 1770–1895
Garstang: 4; 1740–1891
Garston: 6; 1840–88
Gatehouse of Fleet: 2; 1849–94 [OS only]
Gateshead: 43; 1590–1896
Gillingham [Dorset]: 3; 1841–1900
Gillingham [Kent]: 3; 1838–96
Girvan: 4; 1833–94
Gisburn: 3; 1847–93
Glasgow: 75; 1765–1899
Glastonbury: 6; 1778–1884
Glossop: 2; 1878–97 [OS only]
Gloucester: 26; 1610–1900
Godalming: 5; 1808–95
Godmanchester: 4; 1803–84
Golspie: 4; 1811–72
Gomersal: 4; 1839–92
Goole: 9; 1825–96
Gorleston: 11; 1734–1890
Gosport: 34; 1665–1897
Goudhurst: 3; 1840–96
Gourock: 4; 1832–99
Govan: 3; 1857–94
Grampound: 2; 1841–78
Grange [over Sands]: 3; 1847–1900
Grangemouth: 10; 1814–96
Grangetown: 3; 1839–93
Grantham: 5; 1836–86
Grantown on Spey: 3; 1768–1868
Grassington: 3; 1846–90

Gravesend: 9; 1835–95
Great Bardfield: 4; 1755–1896
Great Bedwin: 4; 1751–1899
Great Chesterford: 4; 1802–96
Great Dunmow: 4; 1806–96
Great Harwood: 2; 1844–90 [OS only]
Great Limber: 2; 1815–86
Great Malvern: 6; 1843–98
Great Torrington: 4; 1836–85
Great Witcombe: 2; 1838–82
Great Yarmouth: 38; 1588–1890
Greenlaw: 4; 1771–1898
Greenock: 9; 1818–96
Greenwich: 10; 1695–1894 [see also London]
Greetland,: 3; 1831–90
Greta Bridge: 4; 1839–92
Greys Thurrock: 3; 1840–95
Grimsby: 23; 1600–1898
Grosmont: 3; 1841–99
Guildford: 12; 1739–1895
Guisborough: 4; 1773–1893
Guiseley: 6; 1796–1891
Hackney: 10; 1823–94 [see also London]
Haddington: 6; 1773–1893
Hadleigh: 3; 1668–1884
Haggerston: 3; 1848–94 [OS only; see also London]
Hailsham: 3; 1842–98
Halesowen: 3; 1840–82
Halesworth: 2; 1840–82
Halifax: 17; 1775–1900
Hallaton: 2; 1770–1885
Halstead: 4; 1840–96
Halton: 3; 1845–97
Haltwhistle: 4; 1844–95
Hamilton: 8; 1781–1897
Hammersmith: 9; 1830–97 [see also London]
Hampstead: 18; 1762–1900 [see also London]
Handsworth: 6; 1794–1900 see also Birmingham]
Hanley: 6; 1832–75
Harewood: 3; 1822–88
Harleston: 3; 1839–83
Harlow: 4; 1849–96
Harrington: 3; 1844–98
Harrogate: 11; 1778–1893
Harrold: 3; 1799–1900
Harrow on the Hill: 5; 1763–1895
Hartington: 3; 1804–97
Hartland: 2; 1843–84
Hartlepool: 11; 1585–1896
Harwich: 19; 1600–1896
Haslemere: 5; 1735–1895
Haslingden: 2; 1846–91 [OS only]
Hastings (including St Leonards): 27; 1764–1899
Hatfield: 4; 1838–96
Hatfield Broadoak: 3; 1838–95
Hatherleigh: 2; 1839–94

Haughley: 3; 1844–84
Havant: 8; 1665–1895
Haverfordwest: 7; 1689–1887
Haverhill: 3; 1737–1884
Hawarden: 4; 1815–98
Hawes: 3; 1840–93
Hawick: 3; 1824–97
Hawkshead: 2; 1848–89 [OS only]
Haworth: 4; 1847–92
Hay: 2; 1847–87
Hayfield: 3; 1851–96
Hayle: 3; 1842–76
Haywards Heath: 4; 1843–96
Hazel Grove: 4; 1842–97
Heacham: 5; 1592–1886
Heanor: 3; 1792–1899
Hebden Bridge: 3; 1835–88
Heckmondwike: 3; 1847–89
Hedon: 6; 1804–89
Helensburgh: 5; 1838–97
Helmsdale: 2; 1820–71
Helmsley: 4; 1792–1891
Helston: 4; 1836–76
Hemel Hempstead: 3; 1841–97
Hendon: 3; 1840–95
Henley in Arden: 1; 1885 [OS only]
Henley on Thames: 4; 1842–97
Heptonstall: 3; 1833–90
Hereford: 27; 1610–1900
Herne Bay: 5; 1839–96
Hertford: 9; 1610–1897
Hesket Newmarket: 3; 1852–99
Hexham: 4; 1826–95
Heytesbury: 4; 1785–1899
Heywood: 3; 1848–91
Hickling: 3; 1808–84
Higham: 4; 1762–1898
Higham Ferrers: 4; 1591–1899
High Bentham: 3; 1839–93
Highbridge: 3; 1806–83
Highworth: 2; 1873–98 [OS only]
High Wycombe: 6; 1821–97
Hilborough: 2; 1843–83
Hinckley: 4; 1782–1899
Hindley: 3; 1840–88
Hindon: 3; 1844–1900
Hingham: 3; 1776–1881
Hitchin: 10; 1700–1897
Hoddesdon: 5; 1573–1896
Hodnet: 4; 1815–1900
Holbeach: 3; 1840–86
Holborn: 10; 1720–1900 [see also London]
Holcombe Rogus: 2; 1840–87
Hollingworth: 3; 1846–96
Holme Cultram: 3; 1849–99
Holmfirth: 3; 1834–88
Holsworthy: 2; 1843–83
Holt (Denbighshire): 4; 1831–98
Holt (Norfolk): 3; 1810–85
Holyhead: 6; 1820–1900
Holywell: 5; 1800–98
Honiton: 4; 1780–1888
Hook Norton: 3; 1774–1898
Hope: 3; 1850–98

Hornby: 3; 1844–90
Horncastle: 4; 1722–1888
Horndon on the Hill: 3; 1839–95
Hornsea: 5; 1786–1890
Hornsey: 3; 1865–94
Horsforth: 6; 1822–90
Horsham: 6; 1770–1896
Horton: 2; 1839–81
Horwich: 4; 1620–1892
Houghton le Spring: 3; 1838–95
Hounslow: 5; 1635–1894
Hove: see Brighton
Hovingham: 2; 1853–90 [OS only]
Howden: 4; 1832–89
Hoylake: 5; 1813–97
Hoxton: 4; 1720–1849
   [see also London]
Hucknall Torkard: 4; 1771–1899
Huddersfield: 17; 1716–1888
Hugh Town: 4; 1791–1887
Hungerford: 3; 1819–99
Hunmanby: 3; 1801–88
Hunstanton: 5; 1760–1885
Huntingdon: 13; 1610–1900
Huntly: 3; 1770–1870
Huntspill: 4; 1776–1883
Hurstpierpoint: 4; 1841–96
Huyton: 4; 1844–91
Hyde: 3; 1841–97
Hythe: 6; 1684–1897
Idle: 8; 1838–94
Ilchester: 5; 1723–1885
Ilford: 5; 1653–1895
Ilfracombe: 8; 1839–95
Ilkeston: 4; 1798–1899
Ilkley: 6; 1847–93
Ilminster: 4; 1768–1886
Ingatestone: 6; 1601–1895
Inveraray: 4; 1825–98
Inverbervie: 2; 1832–63
Inverkeithing: 3; 1832–95
Inverness: 13; 1718–1899
Inverurie: 3; 1832–98
Ipswich: 34; 1610–1900
Ireby: 3; 1844–99
Ironbridge: 2; 1848–81
Irvine: 6; 1819–95
Isleworth: 7; 1635–1894
Islington: 12; 1580–1897
   [see also London]
Itchen: 4; 1852–96
Ivinghoe: 7; 1800–98
Ivybridge: 4; 1836–85
Ixworth: 3; 1807–82
Jarrow: 5; 1817–95
Jedburgh: 7; 1770–1897
Johnstone: 5; 1782–1896
Kegworth: 2; 1780–1883
Keighley: 5; 1612–1890
Keith: 4; 1764–1868
Kelso; 6; 1820–97
Kelvedon: 3; 1839–95
Kemsing: 3; 1839–95
Kendal: 12; 1610–1897
Kenfig: 4; 1600–1897

Kenilworth: 2; 1877–86
Kenninghall: 4; 1795–1883
Kennington: 7; 1681–1894
   [see also London]
Kensington: 18; 1717–1898
   [see also London]
Keswick: 7; 1787–1898
Ketsby: 2; 1840–88
Kettering: 8; 1587–1899
Kettlewell: 3; 1847–93
Keynsham: 3; 1841–82
Kidderminster: 13; 1753–1900
Kidsgrove: 3; 1841–98
Kidwelly: 2; 1840–78
Kilham: 3; 1772–1888
Kilmarnock: 9; 1790–1895
Kilrenny: 3; 1832–93
Kilsyth: 2; 1859–96 [OS only]
Kilwinning: 4; 1789–1895
Kimbolton: 3; 1764–1900
Kincardine: 2; 1860–95 [OS only]
Kineton: 1; 1885 [OS only]
Kinghorn: 3; 1832–94
Kingsbridge: 2; 1843–84
Kingsclere: 5; 1725–1894
King's Cliffe: 4; 1800–1900
Kings Lynn: 19; 1588–1892
Kings Norton: 2; 1840–82
Kingston upon Hull: 54; 1560–1900
Kingston upon Thames: 11;
   1763–1895
Kingswinford: 3, 1822–82
Kington: 3; 1822–85
Kingussie: 2; 1870–99 [OS only]
Kinross: 4; 1807–95
Kintore: 2; 1832–65
Kinver: 3; 1851–81
Kirkby Lonsdale: 2; 1857–97 [OS
   only]
Kirkby Malzeard: 4; 1820–90
Kirkby Moorside: 6; 1780–1891
Kirkby Stephen: 3; 1839–97
Kirkcaldy: 7; 1809–94
Kirkcudbright: 7; 1684–1894
Kirkham: 3; 1837–92
Kirkintilloch: 2; 1859–96 [OS only]
Kirkoswald: 3; 1844–98
Kirkwall: 4; 1832–1900
Kirriemuir: 3; 1829–1900
Kirton [in Holland]: 2; 1873–87
Kirton Lindsey: 2; 1801–85
Knaresborough: 7; 1830–89
Knighton: 3; 1831–87
Knottingley: 4; 1800–91
Knutsford: 3; 11848–97
Lambeth: 15; 1720–1894
   [see also London]
Lambourn: 4; 1805–99
Lampeter: 2; 1843–86
Lanark: 4; 1825–96
Lancaster: 17; 1610–1891
Landport: 13; 1716–1896
   [see also Portsmouth]
Langholm: 2; 1857–98 [OS only]
Langport: 2; 1838–85

Largs: 3; 1811–95
Larling[ford]: 3; 1817–82
Lauder: 5; 1803–97
Laugharne: 2; 1846–87
Launceston: 4; 1831–83
Laurencekirk: 1; 1863 [OS only]
Lavenham: 2; 1841–83
Leamington: 17; 1818–99
Learmouth: 3; 1842–96
Leatherhead: 5; 1629–1894
Lechlade: 3; 1838–80
Ledbury: 6; 1788–1886
Leeds: 39; 1727–1894
Leek: 4; 1838–98
Lees: 2; 1843–91 [OS only]
Leicester: 35; (SK 584044)
Leigh: 3; 1845–88
Leigh [on Sea]: 4; 1839–95
Leighton Buzzard: 5; 1819–1900
Leiston: 2; 1841–81
Leith: 13; 1693–1892
   [see also Edinburgh]
Lenham: 3; 1838–96
Leominster: 3; 1836–85
Leonard Stanley: 1; 1881 [OS only]
Lerwick: 2; 1877–1900 [OS only]
Leslie: 2; 1854–94 [OS only]
Leven: 2; 1854–94 [OS only]
Lewes: 19; 1724–1900
Leyburn: 7; 1804–91
Leyton: 11; 1839–94
Lichfield: 12; 1610–1900
Lifton: 2; 1840–82
Lincoln: 24; 1610–1902
Linktown: 3; 1832–95
Linlithgow: 8; 1773–1895
Linslade: 2; 1878–98 [OS only]
Linton: 7; 1600–1885
Liskeard: 5; 1836–81
Litcham: 2; 1841–82
Littleborough (Lancashire): 2;
   1847–90 [OS only]
Littleborough (Nottinghamshire);
   5; 1722–1898
Little Brickhill: 2; 1880–98
   [OS only]
Littlehampton: 7; 1760–1896
Littleport: 4; 1839–85
Little Walsingham: 2; 1812–85
Liverpool: 101; 1539–1898
Liversedge: 7; 1804–92
Llandaff: see Cardiff
Llandilo/Llandeilo Fawr: 3; 1841–84
Llandovery: 3; 1836–86
Llandrindod Wells: 2; 1868–87
Llandudno: 8; 1845–1900
Llandyssul: 2; 1846–87
Llanelly: 4; 1829–77
Llanerchymedd: 3; 1844–99
Llanfair Caereinion: 2; 1842–84
Llanfechell: 3; 1843–99
Llanfyllin: 4; 1850–1900
Llangadog: 2; 1839–84
Llangefni: 5; 1831–99
Llangollen: 3; 1843–98

Llanidloes: 8; 1831–85
Llanrhaiadr-ym-Mochnant: 3;
   1841–98
Llantrissant: 3; 1843–98
Llantwitfarde: 3; 1840–97
Llanwrst: 3; 1839–99
Lochgelly: 4; 1774–1894
Lochgilphead: 2; 1864–98 [OS only]
Lochmaben: 4; 1786–1898
Lockerbie: 3; 1857–98
Loddon: 2; 1837–84
Loftus: 5; 1813–93
London: 404; 1300–1900 [includes
   Westminster, Southwark; see also
   suburbs by name]
London [divisions of City]: 163;
   1720–1914
Long Eaton: 4; 1766–1899
Long Melford: 3; 1820–85
Longnor: 3; 1849–97
Longridge: 4; 1837–92
Long Stratton: 2; 1839–83
Long Sutton: 2; 1845–86
Longton: 7; 1777–1898
Longtown: 3; 1849–1900
Lossiemouth: 3; 1780–1870
Lostwithiel: 4; 1831–80
Loughborough: 3; 1837–83
Loughor: 3; 1841–97
Louth: 10; 1779–1888
Lower Darwen: 2; 1844–92 [OS only]
Lowestoft: 11; 1830–90
Ludgershall: 3; 1841–99
Ludlow: 7; 1831–83
Luton: 9; 1839–1900
Lutterworth: 2; 1853–86
Lydd: 3; 1838–97
Lydney: 3; 1840–1901
Lye: 3; 1828–82
Lyme Regis: 7; 1768–1887
Lymington: 7; 1831–97
Lynton 3; 1840–87
Lytham: 7; 1700–1897
Macclesfield: 9; 1804–97
Macduff: 7; 1826–68
Machynlleth: 4; 1832–1900
Madeley: 2; 1848–81
Maenclochog: 2; 1841–88
Maesteg: 3; 1841–97
Maiden Bradley: 3; 1840–1900
Maidenhead: 12; 1817–97
Maiden Newton: 3; 1835–86
Maidstone: 13; 1821–96
Maldon: 9; 1768–1897
Malmesbury: 8; 1805–99
Malpas: 3; 1840–97
Malton: 8; 1770–1890
Manchester: 81; 1650–1897
Manningtree: 3; 1843–1896
Mansfield: 6; 1845–98
Marazion: 2; 1840–76
March: 5; 1620–1900
Margate: 13; 1821–1900
Market Bosworth: 3; 1850–85
Market Deeping: 3; 1815–99

Market Drayton: 5; 1780–1900
Market Harborough: 5; 1776–1899
Market Lavington: 7; 1778–1899
Market Rasen: 3; 1780–1886
Market Stainton: 1; 1887 [OS only]
Market Weighton: 5; 1776–1889
Markinch: 2; 1854–94 [OS only]
Markyate: 3; 1877–97
Marlborough: 10; 1831–99
Marlow: 5; 1831–97
Marshfield: 4; 1744–1880
Martock: 5; 1811–85
Marylebone: 25; 1768–1898
    [*see also* London]
Maryport: 4; 1834–1900
Masham: 4; 1799–1890
Matlock: 3; 1849–98
Matlock Bath: 3; 1848–98
Maxwelltown: 7; 1832–99
Maybole: 2; 1856–95 [OS only]
Melbourne: 4; 1791–1899
Melcombe Regis: *see* Weymouth
Melksham: 8; 1835–1899
Melrose: 3; 1826–97
Melton Mowbray: 6; 1787–1900
Membury: 2; 1843–87
Mendlesham: 2; 1839–84
Mere: 4; 1821–1900
Merthyr Tydfil: 5; 1836–98
Methwold: 6; 1772–1883
Mevagissey: 2; 1842–79
Mexborough: 4; 1695–1890
Middleham: 3; 1839–91
Middlesbrough: 30; 1618–1894,
    Yorkshire, North Riding (NZ
    496203)
Middleton: 5; 1760–1889
Middleton in Teesdale: 3; 1840–96
Middlewich: 4; 1771–1897
Midhurst: 4; 1841–96
Milborne Port: 4; 1781–1885
Mildenhall: 6; 1812–81
Milford: 1; 1861 [OS only]
Millbrook: 9; 1780–1892
Millom: 2; 1859–98 [OS only]
Millport: 4; 1772–1895
Milnathort: 2; 1853–95 [OS only]
Milngavie: 2; 1820–96
Milnrow: 3; 1843–91
Milnthorpe: 2; 1857–97 [OS only]
Milton Abbas: 3; 1769–1900
Milton Regis: 3; 1838–96
Milverton: 2; 1842–87
Minchinhampton: 4; 1803–82
Minehead: 8; 1792–1886
Mirfield: 4; 1819–88
Mitcheldean: 2; 1839–78
Mitchell: 2; 1840–79
Modbury: 2; 1841–85
Moffat: 7; 1758–1900
Mold: 4; 1839–98
Moniavie: 2; 1856–99 [OS only]
Monifieth: 1; 1857 [OS only]
Monk Wearmouth: 3; 1839–95
Monmouth: 8; 1610–1900

Montgomery: 4; 1610–1884
Montrose: 5; 1746–1862
Morecambe: 5; 1833–91
Moreleigh: 2; 1843–86
Moretonhampstead: 2; 1840–84
Moreton in Marsh: 3; 1821–1900
Morley: 6; 1706–1889
Morpeth: 6; 1604–1896
Mossley: 2; 1844–90 [OS only]
Motherwell: 2; 1858–97 [OS only]
Mountain Ash: 3; 1846–98
Mountsorrel: 1; 1883 [OS only]
Much Wenlock: 3; 1840–82
Muker: 3; 1841–92
Musselburgh: 5; 1778–1893
Nailsworth: 3; 1820–82
Nairn: 4; 1821–90
Nantwich: 6; 1691–1897
Narberth: 5; 1831–97
Navenby: 1; 1886 [OS only]
Nayland: 2; 1837–84
Neath: 8; 1601–1897
Needham Market: 3; 1772–1884
Nefyn: 3; 1839–99
Nelson: 3; 1844–90
Neston: 3; 1847–98
Nether Stowey: 3; 1750–1885
Nevern: 2; 1843–88
Newark [Newark upon Trent]: 13;
    1646–1899
New Alresford: 4; 1807–95
New Bolingbroke: 1; 1887 [OS only]
Newborough: 3; 1846–99
Newbridge: 3; 1842–98
New Buckenham: 4; 1597–1882
Newburgh: 2; 1853–94 [OS only]
Newbury: 8; 1757–1898
Newcastle Emlyn: 3; 1839–87
Newcastle under Lyme: 12;
    1691–1898
Newcastle upon Tyne: 58;
    1580–1896
Newent: 3; 1840–82
New Galloway: 3; 1832–94
Newhaven: 5; 1760–1898
Newmarket (Flintshire): 3; 1844–98
Newmarket (Suffolk): 3; 1770–1884
New Mills: 3; 1841–96
New Milns: 2; 1856–95 [OS only]
Newnham2; 1839–78
Newport (Essex): 4; 1840–96
Newport (Isle of Wight): 17;
    1610–1896
Newport (Monmouthshire): 22;
    1750–1900
Newport (Pembrokeshire): 2;
    1845–88
Newport (Shropshire): 3;
    1840–1900
Newport on Tay: 2; 1853–93
    [OS only]
Newport Pagnell: 2; 1880–99
    [OS only]
Newquay (Cardiganshire): 2;
    1847–87

Newquay (Cornwall): 2; 1839–79
New Radnor: 4; 1610–1887
New Romney: 3; 1841–97
Newton Abbot: 4; 1842–87
Newton in Makerfield: 5; 1745–1891
Newtown (Isle of Wight): 5;
    1768–1896
Newtown (Montgomeryshire): 2;
    1843–83
Newtown Stewart: 4; 1829–1900
Neyland: 2; 1838–61
Norham: 3; 1842–97
Northallerton,: 9; 1793–1893
Northampton: 25; 1610–1899
North Berwick: 4; 1804–93
North Bovey: 2; 1841–84
North Curry: 3; 1787–1886
Northfleet: 3; 1838–95
North Frodingham: 3; 1808–90
Northleach: 3; 1825–1900
North Molton: 2; 1842–87
North Ormesby: 5; 1839–93
North Petherton: 4; 1816–86
North Shields: 10; 1805–95
North Tawton: 2; 1847–86
North Walsham: 3; 1814–84
Northwich: 4; 1650–1897
Norton St Philip: 2; 1839–93
Norwich: 75; 1541–1899
Nottingham: 44; 1610–1899
Nuneaton: 1; 1887 [OS only]
Oakengates: 2; 1847–81
Oakham: 6; 1610–1884
Oban: 7; 1791–1898
Odiham: 3; 1842–94
Okehampton: 3; 1841–89
Oldbury: 4; 1845–85
Oldham: 11; 1817–98
Old Meldrum: 1; 1866 [OS only]
Ollerton: 5; 1779–1897
Olney: 2; 1880–99 [OS only]
Orford: 3; 1600–1880
Ormskirk: 5; 1609–1891
Orpington: 3; 1841–95
Orton: 2; 1858–97 [OS only]
Ossett: 4; 1822–90
Oswaldtwistle: 4; 1835–91
Oswestry: 6; 1833–1900
Otford: 3; 1841–95
Otley: 5; 1783–1889
Ottery St Mary: 4; 1774–1888
Oundle: 4; 1810–99
Over: 3; 1846–97
Overton (Flintshire): 3; 1838–98
Overton (Hampshire): 4; 1795–1894
Oxford: 92; 1588–1900
Oystermouth: 4; 1845–97
Paddington: 15; 1828–98
    [*see also* London]
Padiham: 3; 1839–90
Padstow: 2; 1841–80
Paignton: 3; 1566–1861
Painswick: 3; 1820–82
Paisley: 8; 1781–1896
Parkgate: 3; 1847–98

Partick: 4; 1842–94
Pateley Bridge: 5; 1838–90
Pathhead: 3; 1832–95
Patrington: 4; 1769–1889
Peebles: 6; 1775–1897
Pembridge: 2; 1841–85
Pembroke: 8; 1610–1863
Pembroke Dock: 3; 1836–63
Penarth: *see* Cardiff
Pendlebury: 3; 1843–91
Penistone: 2; 1850–91 [OS only]
Penkridge: 3; 1827–1900
Penmaenmawr: 3; 1839–99
Penrice: 3; 1846–96
Penrith: 6; 1787–1898
Penryn: 5; 1567–1878
Pensford: 5; 1776–1883
Penzance: 6; 1836–98
Pershore: 1; 1884 [OS only]
Perth: 27; 1716–1900
Peterborough: 12; 1610–1900
Peterhead: 7; 1739–1900
Petersfield: 3; 1840–95
Petworth: 6; 1610–1896
Pevensey: 3; 1842–99
Pickering: 3; 1839–91
Pitlochry: 2; 1862–99 [OS only]
Pittenweem: 3; 1832–95
Plumstead: 4; 1842–94
Plymouth [includes Devonport,
    Stonehouse]: 77; 1584–1899
Plympton Earls: 7; 1780–1862
Plympton St Mary: 3; 1780–1862
Pocklington: 4; 1844–91
Polesworth: 2; 1850–85
Pollockshaw: 3; 1857–96
Pontefract: 8; 1648–1889
Pontypool: 4; 1836–99
Pontypridd: 6; 1840–98
Poole: 11; 1580–1900
Poplar: 4; 1848–98 [see also London]
Porlock: 2; 1841–88
Porthcawl: 3; 1843–97
Port Glasgow: 8; 1770–1899
Portmadoc: 4; 1843–99
Portobello: 6; 1824–96
Portpatrick: 3; 1840–93
Portree: 1; 1877 [OS only]
Portsmouth: 49; 1552–1900
Portsoy: 5; 1770–1890
Potton: 4; 1754–1900
Poulton-le-Fylde: 3; 1839–91
Prees: 6; 1788–1900
Prescot: 3; 1847–91
Prestatyn: 4; 1839–98
Presteigne: 3; 1845–84
Preston: 20; 1684–1891
Prestonpan: 2; 1852–92 [OS only]
Prestwich: 4; 1839–91
Prestwick: 3; 1780–1895
Princes Risborough: 4; 1823–97
Probus: 2; 1840–78
Puckeridge: 3; 1778–1896
Pucklechurch: 2; 1843–80
Puddletown: 3; 1842–85

Pudsey: 6; 1817–89

Pulham St Mary Magdalene: 3; 1838–83

Pwllheli: 5; 1834–99

Quarry Bank: 3; 1822–82

Queenborough: 10; 1688–1896

Queen Camel: 5; 1795–1885

Queensbury: 6; 1779–1891

Queensferry: 4; 1820–95

Radcliffe: 4; 1841–96

Radstock: 6; 1759–1883

Raglan: 3; 1841–1900

Ramsbottom: 4; 1842–91

Ramsey: 3; 1839–1900

Ramsgate: 10; 1736–1896

Rastrick: 5; 1806–92

Rattray: 2; 1863–99 [OS only]

Ravenglass: 3; 1843–97

Ravensthorpe: 4; 1819–88

Ravenstonedale: 2; 1857–97 [OS only]

Rawmarsh: 3; 1848–90

Rawtenstall: 2; 1844–91 [OS only]

Rayleigh: 2; 1839–95

Reach: 3; 1814–86

Reading: 30; 1610–1898

Redcar: 7; 1815–93

Redditch: 2; 1870–94

Redhill: 6; 1774–1895

Redruth: 5; 1819–77

Reepham: 3; 1844–84

Reeth: 3; 1839–91

Reigate: 10; 1774–1895

Renfrew: 3; 1832–95

Repton: 3; 1829–99

Rhayader: 5; 1829–88

Rhuddlan: 5; 1756–1898

Rhyl: 8; 1836–98

Rhymney: 3; 1846–99

Richmond (Surrey): 14; 1635–1894

Richmond (Yorkshire, North Riding): 12; 1610–1892

Rickmansworth: 4; 1828–97

Riddings: 2; 1877–98 [OS only]

Ringwood: 5; 1811–96

Ringwould: 3; 1840–96

Ripley (Derbyshire): 6; 1821–98

Ripley (Yorkshire, West Riding): 3; 1838–89

Ripon: 10; 1733–1900

Rishton: 3; 1844–91

Rochdale: 5; 1824–91

Rochester: 30; 1588–1896

Rochford: 3; 1840–95

Rockingham: 7; 1615–1899

Romford: 3; 1849–95

Romsey: 5; 1818–95

Rosehearty: 1; 1870 [OS only]

Ross on Wye: 2; 1840–87

Rothbury: 3; 1848–96

Rotherham: 7; 1764–1886

Rotherhithe: 13; 1720–899 [see also London]

Rothes: 7; 1769–1870

Rothesay: 5; 1759–1896

Rothwell: 4; 1813–99

Rowley Regis: 2; 1883

Royston: 3; 1870–97

Royton: 5; 1847–98

Rugby: 5; 1833–88

Rugeley: 5; 1823–1900

Runcorn: 4; 1844–97

Rushden: 2; 1883–99 [OS only]

Rutherglen: 4; 1832–93

Ruthin: 6; 1823–99

Ryde: 10; 1783–1896

Rye: 11; 1591–1897

Saffron Walden: 9; 1758–1896

St Agnes: 3; 1841–78

St Albans: 18; 1634–1900

St Andrews: 13; 1580–1894

St Annes on the Sea: 4; 1700–1891

St Asaph: 5; 1610–1898

St Austell: 2; 1842–79

St Blazey: 2; 1840–81

St Clears: 2; 1841–87

St Colomb Major: 2; 1840–79

St Davids: 3; 1610–1887

St Day: 6; 1819–77

St Germans: 4; 1793–1883

St Helens: 9; 1841–92

St Ives (Cornwall): 5; 1800–76

St Ives (Huntingdonshire): 5; 1728–1900

St Johns Chapel: 3; 1842–96

St Leonards: see Hastings

St Mary Cray: 3; 1841–95

St Mawes: 4; 1597–1898

St Michael Church: 2; 1840–86

St Monace: 2; 1852–93 [OS only]

St Neots: 4; 1770–1900

St Pancras: 15; 1804–97 [see also London]

St Stephens by Launceston: 3; 1768–1882

Salcombe: 3; 1841–85

Sale: 6; 1807–97

Salen: 2; 1877–98 [OS only]

Salford: 3; 1740–72 [see also Manchester]

Salisbury: 18; 1610–1900

Saltash: 8; 1584–1892

Saltburn: 12; 1815–93

Saltcoats: 5; 1789–1895

Saltfleet: 3; 1838–88

Sandbach: 4; 1831–97

Sandgate: 5; 1831–97

Sandown: 3; 1840–96

Sandwich: 11; 1757–1896

Sanquhar: 7; 1808–99

Sawbridgeworth: 3; 1839–96

Sawley: 3; 1879–99

Saxmundham: 2; 1840–81

Scarborough: 20; 1586–1899

Scotter: 1; 1885 [OS only]

Scunthorpe: 5; 1828–85

Seaford: 5; 1760–1898

Seamer: 2; 1850–89 [OS only]

Seaton: 2; 1840–88

Sedbergh: 3; 1838–93

Sedgefield: 3; 1838–96

Sedgeley: 8; 1816–84

Selby: 4; 1800–91

Selkirk: 4; 1823–97

Setchey: 2; 1839–84

Settle: 3; 1843–94

Sevenoaks: 3; 1839–95

Shaftesbury: 12; 1615–1900

Shanklin: 4; 1842–96

Shap: 3; 1820–97

Shaw: 5; 1843–98

Sheepwash: 2; 1839–84

Sheerness: 16; 1688–1896

Sheffield: 30; 1736–1894

Shefford: 3; 1799–1900

Shepshed: 2; 1823–83

Shepton Mallet: 3; 1841–84

Sherborne: 9; 1570–1886

Sherburn in Elmet: 3; 1824–90

Sheringham: 4; 1811–95

Shifnal: 2; 1840–81

Shipley: 8; 1800–90

Shipston on Stour: 5; 1793–1900

Shipton: 2; 1848–82

Shoeburyness: 6; 1687–1896

Shoreditch: 8; 1720–1900 [see also London]

Shoreham: 4; 1789–1896

Shrewsbury: 26; 1580–1901

Shrivenham: 3; 1844–98

Sidbury: 3; 1833–88

Sidmouth: 3; 1835–00

Silloth: 3; 1849–99

Silverton: 2; 1842–87

Sittingbourne: 3; 1838–96

Skegness: 3; 1831–88

Skelton: 3; 1846–93

Skipton: 6; 1832–90

Sleaford: 3; 1780–1887

Slough: 6; 1773–1897

Smarden: 3; 1838–96

Smeeth: 3; 1840–96

Smethwick: 6; 1857–1900

Snaith: 4; 1840–88

Snettisham: 4; 1750–1885

Soham: 3; 1841–86

Solihull: 2; 1840–86

Solva: 2; 1839–87

Somerton: 2; 1842–85

Southam: 1; 1885 [OS only]

Southampton: 30; 1560–1900

South Bank: 4; 1838–93

Southborough: 3; 1838–95

South Brent: 2; 1841–85

South Cave: 5; 1759–1888

Southend: 3; 1840–96

South Molton: 3; 1836–87

South Petherton: 4; 1828–85

Southport: 19; 1824–92

Southsea: 14; 1716–1896

South Shields: 6; 1768–1895

South Tawton: 2; 1847–83

Southwark: 23; 1541–1899 [see also London]

Southwell: 3; 1840–99

Southwick: 5; 1839–95

Southwold: 5; 1588–1882

Sowerby Bridge: 7; 1804–88

Spalding: 7; 1732–1887

Spennymoor: 5; 1839–96

Spilsby: 3; 1780–1887

Spofforth: 3; 1845–88

Stafford: 15; 1600–1900

Staindrop: 4; 1805–96

Staines: 4; 1724–1895

Stalbridge: 3; 1839–1900

Stalham: 2; 1841–84

Stallingborough: 2; 1844–86

Stalybridge: 7; 1692–1894

Stamford: 12; 1610–1899

Stamfordham: 3; 1839–95

Standon: 5; 1835–96

Stanhope: 3; 1842–96

Staveley: 2; 1858–97 [OS only]

Stepney: 15; 1683–1900 [see also London]

Stevenage: 4; 1839–97

Stewarton: 2; 1856–95 [OS only]

Steyning: 6; 1792–1896

Stilton: 3; 1805–1900

Stirling: 13; 1725–1896

Stockbridge: 3; 1842–94

Stockport: 17; 1680–1899

Stockton on Tees: 15; 1722–1898

Stogumber: 2; 1842–86

Stoke Ferry: 4; 1817–83

Stoke Newington: 8; 1820–98

Stoke on Trent: 6; 1832–98

Stokesley: 2; 1853–93 [OS only]

Stone: 2; 1879–99 [OS only]

Stonehaven: 2; 1823–65

Stonehouse (Devon): 5; 1683–1893 [see also Plymouth]

Stonehouse (Gloucestershire): 5; 1803–81

Stonehouse: 2; 1858–96

Stony Stratford: 2; 1880–98 [OS only]

Stornoway: 9; 1762–1896

Storrington: 3; 1841–96

Stourbridge: 6; 1781–1884

Stourport: 5; 1834–83

Stowmarket: 2; 1839–84

Stow on the Wold: 2; 1882–1900 [OS only]

Stranraer: 6; 1832–1900

Stratford upon Avon: 10; 1769–1899

Strathavon: 2; 1858–96 [OS only]

Strathmiglo: 2; 1853–94 [OS only]

Stratton: 2; 1840–83

Streatham: 5; 1840–98

Stretford: 4; 1838–92

Stretham: 3; 1605–1886

Stromness: 1; 1879 [OS only]

Stroud: 3; 1825–82

Sturminster Marshall: 3; 1844–1900

Sturminster Newton: 4; 1840–1900

Sudbury: 10; 1714–1881

Sunderland: 18; 1723–1896

Surbiton: 3; 1868–95
Sutton: 5; 1840–1900
Sutton: 6; 1785–1895
Sutton Coldfield: 4; 1851–95
Sutton in Ashfield: 5; 1610–1898
Swaffham: 5; 1797–1883
Swanage: 3; 1840–1900
Swansea: 17; 1803–1900
Swindon: 6; 1804–99
Swineshead: 1; 1887 [OS only]
Swinton: 3; 1844–89
Tadcaster: 4; 1841–91
Tain: 3; 1750–1873
Talgarth: 2; 1841–86
Tamworth: 5; 1831–1900
Tarporley: 3; 1837–97
Tarvin: 3; 1838–97
Tattershall: 3; 1798–1887
Taunton: 9; 1791–1886
Tavistock: 6; 1790–1883
Teddington: 2; 1863–95 [OS only]
Teignmouth: 5; 1759–1890
Tenbury: 3; 1843–83
Tenby: 3; 1836–88
Tenterden: 5; 1822–97
Tetbury: 3; 1838–98
Tewkesbury: 9; 1798–1901
Thame: 3; 1826–97
Thaxted: 3; 1844–96
Thetford: 10; 1806–90
Thirsk: 5; 1796–1892
Thornaby: 7; 1850–98
Thornbury: 3; 1841–79
Thorncombe: 2; 1840–86
Thorne: 4; 1825–91
Thorney: 3; 1728–1900
Thornhill (Dumfriesshire): 7; 1772–1899
Thornhill (Yorkshire, West Riding): 4; 1602–1892
Thorpe le Soken: 3; 1841–96
Thrapston: 3; 1781–1899
Thurso: 3; 1801–72
Tickhill: 3; 1848–91
Tideswell: 4; 1821–97
Tilbury: 3; 1840–95
Tillicoutry: 2; 1861–99 [OS only]
Timperley: 4; 1838–97
Tintagel: 2; 1842–82
Tipton: 5; 1837–84
Titchfield: 9; 1753–1895
Tiverton: 5; 1792–1887
Tobermory: 2; 1876–97 [OS only]
Toddington: 5; 1581–1900
Todmorden: 6; 1823–89
Tonbridge: 3; 1838–95
Tong: 2; 1838–81
Topcliffe: 4; 1838–90
Topsham: 5; 1836–88
Torpoint: 23; 1694–1893
Torquay: 11; 1848–95
Totnes: 6; 1830–86
Tottenham: 5; 1818–94
Towcester: 3; 1855–99

Tower Hamlets: 9; 1797–1894
[see also London]
Tow Law: 5; 1774–1895
Towyn: 4; 1841–1900
Tredegar: 3; 1840–99
Tregaron: 2; 1842–87
Tregoney: 4; 1597–1878
Treknow: 2; 1842–82
Tremadoc: 3; 1843–99
Trevena: 2; 1842–82
Tring: 3; 1799–1896
Troon: 6; 1806–95
Trowbridge: 7; 1802–99
Truro: 6; 1597–1878
Tunbridge Wells: 14; 1738–1895
Tunstall: 7; 1822–98
Turriff: 2; 1819–70
Turton: 2; 1843–90 [OS only]
Tutbury: 6; 1810–1900
Tuxford: 4; 1776–1898
Twickenham: 9; 1635–1895
Tyldesley: 3; 1845–90
Tynemouth: 13; 1725–1895
Uckfield: 3; 1843–98
Uffculme: 3; 1840–87
Ulgham: 4; 1843–96
Ulverston: 5; 1832–1900
Upholland: 3; 1845–92
Uppingham: 5; 1804–84
Upton or Overchurch: 3; 1839–98
Upton on Severn: 3; 1850–84
Usk: 4; 1800–99
Uttoxeter: 5; 1658–1900
Uxbridge: 3; 1825–95
Ventnor: 9; 1729–1896
Wadebridge: 2; 1842–79
Wainfleet: 3; 1838–88
Wakefield: 13; 1728–1890
Wallasey: 11; 1656–1898
Wallingford: 8; 1831–97
Wallsend: 3; 1841–96
Walmer: 4; 1835–97
Walsall: 17; 1679–1889
Waltham Abbey: 5; 1590–1895
Waltham on the Wolds: 1; 1884 [OS only]
Walthamstow: 10; 1699–1894
Walton-le-Dale: 3; 1839–92
Walton on the Naze: 3; 1841–96
Wandsworth: 4; 1848–98
Wantage: 4; 1803–98
Ware: 5; 1820–97
Wareham: 10; 1746–1900
Warkworth: 4; 1842–96
Warminster: 9; 1780–1899
Warrington: 14; 1772–1896
Warsop: 2; 1883–98 [OS only]
Warwick: 26; 1610–1900
Watchet: 6; 1801–86
Watford: 3; 1842–96
Wath upon Dearne: 4; 1842–90
Watlington: 3; 1815–97
Watton: 3; 1803–82
Wednesbury: 4; 1846–88
Weldon: 2; 1883–99

Wellingborough: 5; 1838–99
Wellington: 4; 1806–81
Wellington: 2; 1841–87
Wells: 9; 1735–1885
Wells next the Sea: 8; 1780–1885
Welshpool: 3; 1836–84
Wem: 6; 1631–1900
Wendover: 8; 1620–1898
Weobley: 3; 1838–85
West Bromwich: 8; 1804–1900
Westbury: 7; 1808–1900
West Cowes: 7; 1795–1896
Westerham: 3; 1843–95
Westgate on Sea: 3; 1872–96
West Ham: 19; 1821–1900
West Hartlepool: 5; 1839–96
West Kirby: 4; 1844–97
West Looe: 3; 1840–81
West Malling: 3; 1840–95
Westminster: 48; 1593–1898
[see also London]
Weston super Mare: 10; 1815–91
Weston Zoyland: 3; 1840–84
West Tarring: 3; 1838–96
West Wickham: 3; 1840–95
Wetherby: 5; 1811–92
Weybridge: 6; 1801–95
Weymouth: 14; 1773–1901
Whalley: 2; 1843–92 [OS only]
Whaplode: 2; 1843–86
Whitby: 12; 1740–1899
Whitchurch (Hampshire): 6; 1730–1894
Whitchurch (Shropshire): 6; 1761–1899
Whitechapel: 8; 1720–1894
[see also London]
Whitefield: 3; 1843–91
Whitehaven: 10; 1690–1898
Whithorn: 3; 1832–94
Whitley: 6; 1805–95
Whitstable: 3; 1842–96
Whittlesey: 4; 1800–1901
Whitwick: 2; 1807–82
Whitworth: 2; 1843–91 [OS only]
Wick: 6; 1802–72
Wickham Market: 2; 1842–81
Wicklewood: 2; 1843–81
Wickwar: 2; 1838–79
Widnes: 4; 1842–88
Wigan: 11; 1827–93
Wigmore: 2; 1841–84
Wigton: 3; 1832–99
Wigtown: 4; 1832–1900
Willenhall: 5; 1800–84
Willesden: 4; 1823–91
Williton: 5; 1801–86
Wilmslow: 6; 1840–97
Wilton: 9; 1567–1900
Wimbledon: 7; 1776–1894
Wimborne Minster: 6; 1775–1900
Wincanton: 3; 1838–85
Winchcombe: 2; 1882–1901 [OS only]
Winchelsea: 9; 1595–1897

Winchester: 17; 1610–1900
Windermere: 2; 1858–97 [OS only]
Windsor: 15; 1607–1898
Wingham: 3; 1840–96
Winkleigh: 2; 1843–86
Winsford: 3; 1841–97
Winslow: 2; 1878–98 [OS only]
Winster: 2; 1876–97 [OS only]
Winterton (Lincolnshire): 1; 1885 [OS only]
Winterton (Norfolk): 2; 1845–83
Wirksworth: 3; 1849–98
Wisbech: 7; 1836–1900
Wishaw: 2; 1858–96, [OS only]
Wiston: 3; 1843–87
Witham: 4; 1839–95
Witheridge: 2; 1839–87, Devon (SS 803144)
Withernsea: 4; 1794–1889
Withington: 6; 1845–92
Witney: 3; 1840–98
Wiveliscombe: 3; 1816–87
Wivenhoe: 4; 1781–1896
Woburn: 10; 1661–1900
Woking: 4; 1719–1895
Wokingham: 5; 1823–98
Wolsingham: 4; 1767–1895
Wolverhampton: 22; 1751–1901
Wolverton: 4; 1804–98
Woodbridge: 4; 1650–1881
Woodbury: 2; 1841–88
Woodstock: 5; 1760–1898
Wooler: 3; 1843–97
Woolpit: 3; 1845–93
Woolwich: 12; 1749–1894
Wootton Bassett: 4; 1831–99
Worcester: 29; 1610–1894
Workington: 6; 1569–1898
Worksop: 11; 1763–1898
Worstead: 3; 1827–84
Worthen: 2; 1845–82
Worthing: 12; 1810–1900
Wotton under Edge: 3; 1847–81
Wragby: 1; 1886 [OS only]
Wrexham: 5; 1833–98
Wrington: 2; 1839–83
Wrotham: 3; 1839–95
Wye: 4; 1746–1896
Wymondham: 5; 1808–81
Yalding: 3; 1840–95
Yarm: 4; 1840–93
Yarmouth (Isle of Wight): 3; 1840–96
Yate: 2; 1839–81
Yaxley: 3; 1821–1900
Yeadon: 4; 1822–91
Yeovil: 4; 1831–85
Yetminster: 2; 1840–85
York: 51; 1540–1895

List of figures

1. John Hooker's Map of Exeter, *c.* 1587

2. Ordnance Survey 1:500 of part of Manchester

3. John Speed's map of Warwick, 1610

4. The Old and New Towns o f Edinburgh in *c.* 1820

5. The Steyne at Brighton, 1778

6. The High Street, Oxford, in 1803

7. Cambridge marketplace, 1803

8. Tuesday Market Place, King's Lynn, Norfolk, 1797

9. Beckenham, Kent in 1908

10. Beckenham, Kent in 1930

11. Clacton, Essex 1896

12. Automobile Association Map of Lichfield, 1925.

13. Automobile Association Map of Northampton, 1925.

14. John Geddy's map of St Andrews, *c.* 1580

15. Bakewell, Derbyshire, 1934

16. The 'Copperplate Map' of London, late 1550s

17. John Ogilby's map of London, *c.* 1676

18. John Rocque's map of London, 1746

19. Richard Horwood's map of London, 1792–9

20. The Ordnance Survey 5 feet to 1 mile map of London, early 1870s

21. Stanford's Library map of London, 1862

22. School Board map of London, 1879

23. Edward Salmon's map of Nottingham, 1862

24. The 'District Railway' Map of London, *c.* 1879

25. Ordnance Survey 1:2500 map of Cheltenham, 1884

26. Ordnance Survey 'Town Map' of Southampton, *c.* 1921

27. E. Monson's map of Cambridge, 1859

28. Ordnance Survey six-inch map of Llandeilo, Carmarthenshire, late 1880s

29. Business Street Map of Croydon, Surrey, *c.* 1895

30. Business Street Map of Croydon, Surrey, *c.* 1895: detail

31. Henry C. Roper's mapping of Widnes, Lancashire, 1879

32. Harwich, 1729

33. Braun and Hogenberg's map of London, 1572

34. London in the Chronicles of Geoffrey of Monmouth, *c.* 1300

35. Robert Ricart's map of Bristol, late 1470s

36. Portsmouth, *c.* 1552

37. Ashbourne, Derbyshire, 1547

38. William Cuningham's map of Norwich, 1559

39. Braun and Hogenberg's map of London, 1572

40. Richard Lyne's map of Cambridge, 1574

41. Ralph Agas' map of Oxford, 1588

42. Ralph Agas' map of Toddington, Bedfordshire, 1581

43. John Speed's map of Oxford, 1611

44. Rutger Hermannides' map of Oxford, 1661

45. Philip Lea's map of Oxford, *c.* 1689

46. Oxford, by Matthias Merian, *c.* 1650, or by J. C. Beer, *c.* 1690

47. Richard Newcourt and William Faithorne's map of London, 1658

48. Ogilby and Morgan's map of Queenhithe and Vintry wards, City of London, *c.* 1676

49. Queenhithe and Vintry wards as depicted in Stow's *Survey of London*, 1720

50. William Fairbank and Thomas Jeffreys' map of Sheffield, 1771

51. Louth, Lincolnshire, as mapped by Andrew Armstrong in 1778

52. Grimsby, Lincolnshire, by W. Smith and G. Parker, *c.* 1812

53. Isaac Taylor's map of Wolverhampton, 1751

54. Brecon, mapped by Meredith Jones in 1744

55. A 'Sand Bank' on Darton & Harvey's map of London, 1804

56. A 'Sand Bank' on Horwood's map of London, 1790s

57. Beilby, Knott & Beilby's map of Birmingham, 1828

58. Thomas Oliver's map of Newcastle upon Tyne, 1831

59. Thomas Oliver's reduced map of Newcastle upon Tyne, 1832

60. The dedication on Salmon's map of Nottingham, 1862

61. Decoration on Beilby's map of Birmingham, 1828

62. John Wood's map of Ayr, 1818

63. John Wood's map of Berwick-upon-Tweed, 1822

64. Dewhirst & Nichols' map of Cambridge, 1840

65. Blackpool as mapped by the Ordnance Survey in 1844

66. Blackpool as mapped by John Bartholomew in 1869

67. John Bartholomew's map of Dundee, 1899

68. Bolingbroke, Lincolnshire, mapped by Jarred Hill in 1719

69. Methwold, Norfolk, mapped by Thomas Bainbridge in 1796

70. Enclosure map of Bampton, Oxfordshire, 1821

71. Poor-rating map of Lenham, Kent, by Thomas Thurston, 1838

72. Tithe map of Brighton, 1851

73. Tithe map of Swansea, *c.* 1842

74. John Speed's map of Berwick-upon-Tweed, 1611

75. Rutger Hermannides' map of Berwick-upon-Tweed, 1661

76. Philip Lea's map of Berwick-upon-Tweed, *c.* 1689

77. Berwick-upon-Tweed, by Matthias Merian or J. C. Beer

78. Bridport, Dorset, mapped for Thomas Hutchins, 1774–5

79. Fulham, Middlesex, to illustrate Thomas Faulkner's history, 1813

80. Hampstead, north London, to illustrate John James Park's history, 1814

81. Tottenham, north London, to illustrate William Robinson's history, 1818

82. Kensington, west London, to illustrate Thomas Faulkner's history, 1820

83. Kings Lynn, Norfolk, to illustrate William Richards' history, 1812

84. Malmesbury, Wiltshire, to illustrate J. M. Moffatt's history, 1805

85. Chester, to illustrate John Britton's *The Beauties of England and Wales*, 1805

86. Leeds, by Charles Fowler for Edward Baines, 1821–2

87. Map for Pigot's directory of Manchester, 1836

88. John Bartholomew's six-inch map of Edinburgh, 1897

89. Llandudno, Carnarvonshire, by T. T. Marks, 1900

90. Ordnance Survey six-inch 'Town Map' of South Shields, County Durham, 1923

91. Curtiss & Sons' Map of Portsmouth, *c.* 1881

92. London Pulloutmap by Compass Maps, 2011

93. Drink Map of Oxford, 1883

94. John Overton's map of London, *c.* 1676

95. Thomas Bowles' Pocket Map of London, 1727

96. Henry Overton's map of London, 1720

97. Distance circles on Pigot's plan of London, *c.* 1824

98. J. Friedrichs, The Circuiteer, or distance map of London, *c.* 1847

99. Llewellyn Syers' cab-fare map of Liverpool, 1868

100. Sheffield by Bartholomew for A. & C. Black, 1864–84

101. Bartholomew's 15-inch map of Edinburgh, 1891

102. Richard Collinson's map of Stretford, Lancashire, *c.* 1887

103. E. J. Burrow's map of Southport, Lancashire, 1931

104. G. & I. Barnett's map of Wokingham, Berkshire, *c.* 1965

105. G. W. Bacon's four-inch map of London, 1870s

106. Bacon's Atlas of London, 1963

107. H. G. Collins' street atlas of London, 1854

108. *The A to Z Atlas of London*, 1948

109. Cribb & Co.'s map of central London, 1923

110. Cardiff, as shown in a Philip street atlas of 2004

111. Richard Baker's map of Cambridge, 1830, illustrating a guidebook

112. Edinburgh for Murray's Handbook, 1867

113. Edinburgh for Murray's Handbook, 1873

114. Edinburgh for Murray's Handbook, 1894

115. Redcar, Yorkshire, by Bartholomew for a guidebook, 1868

116. Forster's plan of Bridlington, Yorkshire, *c.* 1891

117. Hastings, Sussex, by Bartholomew for Abel Heywood, *c.* 1869

118. Weymouth, Dorset, for a railway company guide, 1897

119. Barmouth, Merionethshire, in a Ward Lock guide of 1929

120. Harrogate, Yorkshire, by Bartholomew for a guidebook, 1909

121. Dover, 1532

122. Dover by P. Symans, 1577

123. Wenceslaus Hollar's Plymouth siege map, 1643

124. Great Yarmouth by Sir Bernard de Gomme, 1668

125. Schematic diagram of Vauban's town defence methodology

126. Portsmouth by Talbot Edwards, 1716

127. Plymouth Dock, mapped by Benjamin Donn, 1765

128. Defences at Hull, 1840

129. Coast erosion at Harwich, Essex, 1729

130. Coast erosion at Harwich, Essex, 1752

131. Coast erosion at Harwich, Essex, 1808

132. River Medway, Kent, 1750

133. Mile Town, Sheerness, Kent, 1815

134. Blue Town, Sheerness, Kent, 1811

135. French map of Dover, 1768

136. Fortification at Liverpool, 1759: before and after

137. Inverness, *c.* 1802

138. Fortification of Gosport, Hampshire, 1757

139. Ordnance Survey 1:500 map of Portsmouth, 1879

140. A battery at Portsmouth, 1879

141. The Liberties of Ipswich, 1812

142. Bassishaw Ward, City of London, 1858

143. Boundary map of Aberdeen, 1832

144. Boundary map of Bideford, Devon, 1837

145. Ordnance Survey five-foot map of Wigan, Lancashire, 1848

146. Ordnance Survey five-foot 'skeleton' map of London, 1850

147. Ordnance Survey 10-foot map of Barnard Castle, County Durham, 1852

148. Ordnance Survey 1:500 map of Gateshead, County Durham, 1857

149. Ordnance Survey 1:500 map of Guildford, Surrey, 1870

150. Ordnance Survey 1:500 map of Walsall, Staffordshire, 1884-5

151. Ordnance Survey 1:500 map of Stockton-on-Tees, County Durham, 1893

152. Ordnance Survey 1:2500 map of Aberystwyth, 1885

153. Ordnance Survey 1:2500 map of Aberystwyth, 1904

154. Ordnance Survey 1:2500 map of Aberystwyth, 1938

155. Ordnance Survey 1:1250 map of Exeter, late 1940s

156. Ordnance Survey 1:1250 map of Exeter, late 1950s

157. Loveday's insurance map of London waterside, 1857

158. Charles E. Goad's insurance mapping of Liverpool docks, 1888

159. Goad insurance map of Campbeltown, Argyllshire, 1898

160. Plans for rebuilding London after the Great Fire, 1666

161. John Wood's plan of Bath, 1735

162. Golspie, Sutherland, 1830

163. J. Richmond's map of plots at Middlesbrough, 1848

164. James Craig's plan for Edinburgh New Town, 1767

165. Raymond Unwin and Barry Parker's plan for Hampstead Garden Suburb, north London, 1907

166. Sir Patrick Abercrombie's scheme for rebuilding Plymouth, 1943

Index

Figures in *italic* refer to illustrations.

Abercrombie, Sir Patrick 235
Aberdeen 172, 207, 209
Aberystwyth 220, 221
Adams, John 25
advertising maps 54, 55, 60–1, 153–5
Agas, Ralph 72, 73, 74–5, 105
'Agas' map 70
Airdrie 97–8
Albert, Prince 212
Aldershot 203
Alfrey, Nicholas 125
Anderson, James W. 191
Angell, Samuel 206
Antiquities of Warwickshire, The (Dugdale) 118
Arbroath 209
Armstrong, Andrew 85
Ashbourne 66, 67
Atlas of London 159, 160, 161
Atlas of Scotland 173
atlases 75, 96, 159, 161–2, 167, 173; and A–Z 102, 157, 162, 163, 165
Authentic Atlas (Geographia) 161
Automobile Association (AA) 30
Ayr 97
A–Z Atlas 102, 157, 162, 163, 165

Bacon, G. W. 49, 54, 60, 134; and atlases 158, 159, 161–2
Baddeley, M. J. B. 177
Bainbridge, Thomas 107
Baines, Edward 132
Baker, Richard 91, 170, 171
Bakewell 33
Bampton 109
Barmouth 178
Barnard Castle 215
Bartholomew, John & Son 49, 53, 54, 59–60, 99, 101, 103, 135; and atlases 161; and guidebooks 172–3, 174–5, 178, 179; and street maps 150, 151, 152
Bath 18, 118, 144, 169, 171; and town planning 231, 233
Beauties of England and Wales, The 125, 127, 129
Beckenham 24, 25
Bedford Level 111
Bedfordshire 74–5, 107
Beer, Johann Christoph 2, 77, 118, 121
Beilby Knott & Beilby 92, 96
Bellin, J. N. 194
Bendall, Sarah 106
Berkshire 155
Berwick-upon-Tweed 98, 120, 183, 189
Bideford 208
bird's-eye views 11, 12, 13, 67, 68
Birkenhead 91, 150
Birmingham 87, 91, 92, 96, 162, 169; and directories 131, 132; and street maps 144, 153
Bishops Stortford 111
Black Death (1348–9) 17

Black of Edinburgh 150, 173, 176, 177
Blackpool 24, 99, 101
Board of Ordnance 189, 197–201; *see also* Ordnance Survey
Bolton 110
books 117, 118–19, 122, 125; *see also* atlases; guidebooks
Borough and County Advertising Company 34–5, 153
boroughs 24, 25, 206
Boston 86
boundaries, administrative 35, 37
boundary maps 205–7, 209
Bournemouth 24, 144, 223
Bowles, Thomas 143
Bradford 131, 162
Bradford, Samuel 87
Braun, Georg 61, 70, 71, 117
Brecon 88, 89
Bridlington 176
Bridport 119, 122
Brighton 20–1, 144, 161, 171; and tithes 114, 115
Bristol 63–4, 65, 79, 91, 117, 131
Britannia 79, 82
Britannia Magna 76
British Atlas, The 125, 127
British Library 60
Britton, John 125, 129
Bromley 19
buildings 11, 137, 150–1, 200, 207, 209
Buildings of England, The 179
Bureau d'Industrie 194
Burrows, E. J. 154, 155
Burton-upon-Trent 99
'business street maps' 55
Buxton 24

Caio, John 72
Cambridge 23, 52, 70, 72, 74, 75, 100; and books 117; and guidebooks 169, 170, 171; and 'prodigy' map 91; and street maps 145
Cambridgeshire 106
Campbeltown 228, 229
Canada 228
Cannock Chase 203
Cardiff 166
Carlisle 197
Cassell, Messrs 178
Catalogue of British Town Maps (CBTM) 8, 10, 29, 60
Chadwick, Edwin 14, 211, 212, 215
Chamberlain, Thomas 192
Chambers, W. 193
Charles II, King 79
charters 17, 18
Chatham 189, 191
Cheltenham 51, 131
Chester 125, 129
Chronicles (Geoffrey of Monmouth) 63
Circuiteer, or distance map of London, The (Friedrichs) 148, 149, 150
Civitates orbis terrarum 61, 70, 71, 117–18
Clacton 25, 27

Cleer, Thomas 118
Clifton 171
coastal defences 182, 185
Coats, Rev Charles 119, 122
Colchester 125, 184
Coldridge, John 211
Collins, H. G. 159, 160, 161
Collinson, Richard 55, 151
colour printing 48–50
copper, engraving on 45–6, 48
'Copperplate Map' 36, 37, 61, 68, 70, 117
Cornwall 171–2
Coronelli, Vincenzo 118
Cosmographical Glasse, The 66, 68
county histories 119, 122, 125
county mapping 75, 79, 82, 84–6, 165, 167
Coventry 87, 118, 153
Crewe 18
Cribb & Co. 164, 165
crime 64
Cromwell, Thomas 64
Croydon 19, 54, 55, 110
Cullen 233
Cuningham, William 66, 68, 75, 117, 118
Curtiss & Sons 139

Darton & Harvey 90
Dawson, Lt Robert Kearsley 206, 207
Delamotte, William 22
Derby 59
Devon 171–2
Devonport 18, 186–7, 188, 200
Dewhirst & Nichols 98–9, 100
digital mapping 223
directories, street 131–2, 134–5
disease 37
distance-circles 145, 148
District Railway Map of London 50
Dorchester 119
Dorset 119
Dover 64, 182, 183, 187, 195, 203
Downton 107
drainage maps 111
'drink maps' 141
Duchy estates 105
Dudley 131
Dugdale, William 118
Dumbarton 209
Dundee 99, 103, 172

Eastleigh 18
Ecclesiastical Commissioners 209
Edict of Nantes (1598) 185
Edinburgh 59, 66, 87, 91, 223; and directories 134, 135; and guidebooks 172, 173, 174; and military maps 198–9; and New Town 18, 19, 234, 236; and street maps 144, 152
Edwards, Talbot 188
education 9–10, 35
electoral districts 37, 40, 206
Elizabeth I, Queen 13
Ely 111, 127
enclosure maps 108–10
engineering 64, 99, 102, 181
England 32, 33, 96, 198
English Civil War 183–4

engraving 45–6, 54, 97
environmental conservation 9
estate maps 31, 35, 74–5, 105–7
Evans W. H. & Sons 137
Evelyn, John 232
Everitt, Alan 25
Exeter 11, 12, 13, 75, 96, 224–5; and guidebooks 171–2; and sanitation maps 211

Faden, William 85–6, 125
Fairbanks family 84, 85
Faithorne, William, and Newcourt, Richard 79, 80–1
Falmouth 18
Faulkner, Thomas 123, 127
fire insurance maps 227–9
Fleetwood 233–4
Fochabers 233
Forster, Messrs 176
Fort William 198
fortifications 181, 183, 185–6, 188, 197, 203
Fowler, Charles 132
Friedrichs, J. 148, 150
frontispieces 119, 122, 128

G. & I. Barnett 155
Gall & Inglis 49
Garden City movement 234–5
Gateshead 218
gazetteers 159
Geddy, John 32
General Board of Health 214–15
Geoffrey of Monmouth 63
Geographers A–Z Map Company 60
Geographia 161, 162
Glasgow 31, 134, 144, 162, 169, 172
Goad, Charles E. 228–9
Golspie 231, 234
Gomme, Bernard de 184–5
Google Maps 8
Gosport 186, 200, 203
Great Fire of London (1666) 79, 141, 142, 231
Great Yarmouth 185
Green, Robert 141
'greenfield' sites 19
grids, alpha-numeric 145, 146–7, 165
Grimsby 86, 87, 91, 228
Gross, Alexander 162
Guide for Cuntrey men in the famous Cittey of London (Norden) 141
Guide to All the Watering and Sea-bathing Places, A (Longman) 171
Guide to England and Wales (Black) 150–1
guidebooks 54, 144, 169, 171–3, 176–7, 179
Guildford 218

hackney carriage fares 88, 148, 149, 150
Hall, Robert 86
Handbooks for Travellers (John Murray) 171–2, 173, 174
Handy Reference Atlas of London and Suburbs 157

Hanseatic League 68
Harding, J. W. 154–5
Harrogate 24, 179
Hartlepool 228
Harwich 58, 200, 203; and military maps 183, 187, 189, 190, 191
Hastings 177
Health of Towns Commission 212
Heffers 145
Henry VIII, King 181–2, 186
Hereford 87
Hermannides, Rutgur 76, 118
Hesketh, Sir Peter 233
Hexham 97
Heywood, Abel 176–7
Higham Ferrers 105
Hill, Jarred 105
Hinderwell, Thomas 169
Historia Cantebrigensis academiae (Caio) 72
histories 117, 119, 122, 125
History and Antiquities of Reading, The (Coats) 119, 122
History of Lynn, The (Richards) 119, 128
Hodnet 111
Hogarth, William 84
Hogenberg, Remigius 70, 71, 117
Hollar, Wenceslaus 184
Hooker, John 11, 12, 13, 75
Horwich 18
Horwood, Richard 37, 40–1, 88, 90, 227
house buying 151, 153
Howard, Ebenezer 234–5
Huddersfield 107
Hutchins, Thomas 119
Hyde, Ralph 205

iconography 13
Ilfracombe 172
illustrations 63, 70, 117, 118
Index villaris (Adams) 25
industrialisation 18
Inverness 172, 198, 199, 200–201, 209
Ipswich 82, 205
Ireland 198, 201, 211
Isle of Wight 203

Jacobite uprisings 197, 198–9
Jeffreys, Thomas 84–5
Johnson, Thomas 118
Jones, Meredith 88

Kelly's Directories 131, 132, 134, 135
Kemp & Nichols 98–9, 100
Kettering 105
Kings Lynn 23, 86, 128
Kingston upon Hull 84, 187, 189, 200
Kirkcaldy 209

Lacelli, Federico 47
Lancashire 132
Lancaster 105
Land Registry maps 221–2
land rights 11, 17, 108
Lea, Philip 77, 121
Leeds 29, 84, 133, 144, 162, 212
legal profession 9, 66

Leicester 153
Lenham 112
Lenny & Croft 111
Letchworth Garden City 235
Lewis, Samuel 26
libraries 8, 10, 60
Lichfield 30
Lincoln 91, 127
Lincolnshire 85, 98
lithography 46–8, 49, 54, 97, 169, 171
Liverpool 88, 91, 125, 127, 134, 228; and atlases 162; and guidebooks 169; and military maps 197; and street maps 144, 150
Llandeilo 53
Llandudno 137
Local Boards of Health 58
Lock, Ward 177
London 29, 36, 37, 79, 80–1; and 'Agas' map 70; and atlases 157, 158, 159, 160, 161, 164, 165; and A–Z Atlas 102; and books 118–19; and boundary maps 205; and *Civitates orbis terrarum* 60, 70, 71, 117–18; and directories 132; 'District Railway' map 49, 50, 153; and fire insurance maps 227–8; and histories 117; and Horwood 88; and land registration 221–2; and military maps 194, 203; and Ogilby 82; and Ordnance Survey 42; and parish maps 40, 111, 113; and Rocque 82, 84; and sanitation maps 214; and street maps 140–4, 145, 146–7, 148–50; and town planning 231, 232, 234, 235; *see also* 'Copperplate Map'
London areas: Cheapside 38; City of London 29, 83, 110, 205, 206; Finsbury 43; Fulham 119, 123; Gin Lane 84; Hampstead 119, 124; Hampstead Garden Suburb 235, 236; High Holborn 39; Highgate 63; Kensington 119, 177; Lambeth 90, 113; Moorfields 36; Tottenham 119, 126; West End 40–1; Westminster 61
'London from the North' 63
lost maps 57–9
Louis XIV of France, King 79, 185
Loveday's London Waterside Surveys 227–8
Lyne, Richard 70, 72, 75, 117

Magna Britannia 125
Maire of Bristowe is Kalendar, The 64, 65
Maitland, William 119
Malmesbury 122, 129
Manchester 13–14, 15, 29, 54–5, 125, 127, 212; and atlases 162; and directories 132, 134; and 'prodigy' map 91; and street maps 144, 148, 150, 151, 152
manuscripts 45, 57–9
March 111
Market Harborough 96
markets 17, 18, 19, 23, 25
Marks, T. T. 137

Medway River 187, 191, 192, 203
Meisner, Daniel 118
Melton Mowbray 96
Meredith, Michael 206
Merian, Matthias 2, 77, 121
Methwold 106–7
Metropolitan Board of Works 43
Metropolitan Commissions of Sewers 212, 214
Middlesbrough 18, 234, 235
Milford Haven 203
military maps 33, 35, 64, 74, 181–94; and Board of Ordnance 197–200, 201; and Ordnance Survey 202, 203
Millerd, James 79
Moffatt, J. M. 129
Monson, E. 52
Morden, Robert 142
Morgan, William 82
Morpeth 97
Municipal Corporations Act (1835) 207
Murray, John 171, 176, 177

Nantwich 111
Napoleonic Wars 125, 203
National Library of Scotland 59
naval defences 186–7
New Business Map of Cardiganshire 60–1, 154
New Ordnance Atlas of London & Suburbs 158, 159
new towns 231, 233
Newark 184
Newcastle upon Tyne 91, 93, 94, 97
Newcourt, Richard 79, 80–1
Newhaven 203
Noorthouck, John 119
Norden, John 79, 105, 141
Norman conquest (1066) 17
Northampton 30
Norwich 64, 66, 68, 69, 75, 117, 118
Nottingham 48, 49, 91, 95, 110

Oban 172, 209
Official Guide to the Great Western Railway, The 178
Ogilby, John 38, 79, 82, 83, 118
Ogilby & Morgan 37
Oliver, Thomas 91, 93, 94
open spaces 137
Ordnance Survey 9, 24–5, 26, 27, 31, 35, 48, 101, 218–21, 224–5, 235; and atlases 165, 167; and boundary maps 206–7, 209; and derivatives 99, 101; and guidebooks 173; and hand-colouring 50, 51, 219, 220; and land registration 222; and London 37, 42; and Manchester 13–14, 15; and manuscripts 58–9; and military maps 33, 201, 202, 203; and photography 52–3, 54; and sanitation maps 212, 214, 215; and street maps 137, 138, 140, 144–5
orientation 161
Osbourne, John 52

Overton, Henry 145, 146–7
Overton, John 142
Oxford 22, 70, 72, 73, 74, 75, 76–7, 87; and guidebooks 169; and military maps 184; and street maps 140, 141

Padley, James Sandby 91
Paris, Matthew 63
Park, John James 4–5, 124
Parker, Barry 236
Parker, G. 86
Parliamentary Boundary Commissioners 47
Parliamentary enclosure 108
Parochial Assessment Act (1836) 111
Pearsall, Phyllis 102, 162
Perth 131, 172, 198
Peterborough 127
Petrie, Edmund 227
Pevsner Architectural Guides 179
Philip, George 53, 60, 161, 165, 167
Phoenix Fire Insurance Company 88, 227
photography 50, 52–5
Pigot & Co 132, 134, 148
Plymouth 171–2, 184, 187, 200, 203; and town planning 235, 237
Pocket Map of London, A (Bowles) 143
politics 13, 64, 66
Poole 119
Poor Law Amendment Act (1834) 111, 211
poor rates 110–11
Popinjay, Richard 183
'PopOut' maps 140
population figures 17, 18
port towns 18, 86–7, 194
portability, of maps 137, 143, 157
Portland 203
Portsmouth 64, 66, 110, 139; and military maps 183, 186, 187, 188, 202, 203
printing 10, 31, 48–50
'prodigy maps' 89, 91, 92–5
property 9, 11, 47
Public Health Act (1848) 214
public health reform 14, 19, 24

railways 18–19, 151
Raistrick, William 86
rating maps 110–13
Reading 119, 122, 131
Recueil des villes ports d'Angleterre (Bellin) 194
Red Guides (Lock) 177, 179
Redcar 173, 175, 176
reference maps 35–7
reference systems 145, 146–7
religious maps 40
resort towns 24–5
Ricart, Robert 64
Richards, William 119, 128
Richmond, J. 235
Ripon 84–5
Robinson, William 126
Rochester 205
Rocque, John 37, 39, 82, 84
Roper, Henry 48, 57
Rothes 231, 233

Rounthwaite, R. S. 37, 40
Rowlandson, Thomas 23

St Andrews 31, 32, 172
Salisbury 169
Salmon, Edward 48, 49, 95
'sanctuary maps' 40, 64
sanitary conditions 14, 24
sanitary planning 35, 37, 99, 211–12, 214–15, 220
Saxton, Christopher 25, 46, 75
scale 29, 31, 36–7, 64, 68, 89; and military maps 201, 203; and standardisation 217, 218, 220–1, 222–3; and surveying 211–12; and variable 157
Scarborough 85, 169, 183
School Board maps 40, 43
schools 9–10, 35
Scotland 18, 25, 31, 32–3, 66, 87–8; and boundary maps 207, 209; and guidebooks 172–3; and military maps 198–9; and new towns 231, 233; and Wood 96, 97–8
seaside towns 24–5
Sedley, J.S. 199
Seld, Jörg 68
Senefelder, Alois 46, 47
Seven Years War 194, 197
Sheerness 18, 187, 191, 193, 194, 198
Sheffield 84, 85, 151
Skegness 25
Smith, W. 86
Smith, William 79
South Shields 138
Southampton 51
Southport 154
Southwark 64
Speed, John 17, 18, 75, 76, 79, 117–18
Spooner, Thomas 99
Stanford, Edward & Co 43, 173
Stephens & Mackintosh 153
Stirling 172, 198
Stockton-on-Tees 219
Stow, John 118
street maps 137, 140–5, 148, 150–1, 153–5
street names 137, 150
Strype, John 118
subscriptions 88
suburbs 19, 29
Sunderland 40, 97
Surbiton 19
Surrey 119, 167
Survey of London (Stow) 118, 205–6
surveys 99, 132
Swansea 115
Swindon 18
Syers, Llewellyn 150
Symans, P. 183

Taunton 96
Tavistock 107
Taylor, Isaac 87
Taylor, Thomas 145
telephone directories 135
Theatre of the Empire of Great Britain, The (Speed) 75, 76
Thermae Bathonicae (Johnson) 118
Thompson's 135
Thornton, William 119
Thorough Guides (Baddeley) 177, 179

Thurston, Thomas 112
Times Atlas, The 59–60
Tithe Commutation Act (1836) 113
tithes 32–3, 35, 47, 58, 113–15
Tiverton 96
Toddington 74–5, 105
topography 13, 14, 15, 25–6, 125
Torquay 172
Town and Country Planning Act (1947) 237
town planning 9, 231, 233–5, 237
trade 17
transport 37, 137
Treasury 211, 212, 217, 220–1
Treswell, Ralph 105

United States of America 227, 228
Unwin, Raymond 236
Uppingham 96
urban districts 24, 25

'Vandyke process' 53
Vauban 185, 186
visualisations 63

W. H. Smith 165
Wales 32, 33, 88, 96
Walks in Oxford 169
wall maps 89, 91, 92–5, 96, 159
Walsall 219
War Office 47, 197, 203
Ward Lock, Messrs 178
ward maps 205–6
Wareham 119
warfare 181, 183–4, 185
Warwick 18
watermen's fares 148
wayfinding 35, 36, 55, 137, 140, 143–4
Weekly Dispatch Atlas 159
Weiditz, Hans 68
Weller, Edward 172
Welwyn Garden City 235
West Riding 228
Weymouth 169, 178
Whitehaven 115
Widnes 48, 57
Wigan 212, 213
William III, King 186
Windsor 212
Woburn 107
Woking 19
Wokingham 155
Wolverhampton 87
Wood, John 10, 31, 93, 96–8
Wood, John, the elder 233
Worcester 131
World War II 235
Worthing 19
Wren, Sir Christopher 232
Wyld, James 48, 214

York 64, 85, 99, 169
Yorkshire 84–5, 132, 133
Yorkshire (Black) 173, 175, 176

zincography 47–8, 52, 53, 217, 218